Images of the Arab Future

Images of the Arab Future

Ismail-Sabri Abdalla
Ibrahim S. E. Abdalla
Mahmoud Abdel-Fadil
Ali Nassar

Translated from Arabic by
Maissa Talaat

Frances Pinter (Publishers), London

THE UNITED NATIONS UNIVERSITY

First published in Great Britain in 1983 by
Frances Pinter (Publishers) Limited
5 Dryden Street, London WC2E 9NW

British Library Cataloguing in Publication Data

Abdalla, Ismail-Sabri
Images of Arab future.
1. Arab countries—Economic conditions
I. Title II. Abdalla, Ibrahim S. E.
III. Abdel-Fadil, Mahmoud IV. Nassar, Ali
330.917'4927 HC498

ISBN 0-86187-341-6

Typeset by Joshua Associates, Oxford
and printed by SRP Ltd., Exeter

CONTENTS

PREFACE

In line with its policy of encouraging research workers in their national and regional environments and building up networks of research institutions, the United Nations University decided to initiate major regional research projects in the Third World. Each project is to be tailored in close co-operation with social scientists from the region concerned so that it meets the real needs that differ from one region to another. The first of the regional projects undertaken within this framework covers the region which includes the member countries of the League of Arab States and is entitled *Arab Alternative Futures.* This project was co-ordinated by the Middle East Office of the Third World Forum.

Concerned mainly with futures studies, the project gives priority to the unexplored areas of research in order to avoid duplication and overlapping. It has focused on the social, economic and cultural dynamics which could lead to alternative paths to development and upon various images of Arab futures. One of the main aims of the project is to familiarize Arab researchers with the images of the Arab future as depicted by World futures studies and as perceived by those responsible for Arab strategic planning, with a view to raising awareness of the need for new Arab futures studies, identifying the nature of these studies and the manner in which they can be conducted and, in general, stimulating the interest of researchers and decision-makers in this type of study at the pan-Arab level.

The present book, *Images of the Arab Future*, consists of an Introduction and three parts. The introduction deals with the subject of futures studies, their importance and rationale, in a general manner. Part I presents images of the Arab future as depicted in the principal global models, examines the nature of the assumptions on which they are based and analyses how valid these assumptions are and, accordingly, how far global models can be relied on to give accurate representations of the Arab future. Part II makes a critical review of the principal Arab strategy documents drawn up by specialized Arab agencies, in an attempt to ascertain how far they could constitute a consistent overall strategic vision of the Arab future. Finally, Part III sets out to analyse some of the reasons why there is a pressing need for futures studies of a new kind, to indicate the appropriate methodological orientation of these studies and to emphasize how important it is for studies dealing with the Arab future to be undertaken by Arab researchers.

This book is a collective production, and the views it expresses are shared by all the authors, who worked closely together in planning, drafting and discussing the scientific material that went into the book during the period between January and June of 1981. In many cases, parts of the book were rewritten to conform to the collective viewpoint of the authors.

Among the many people to whom they are deeply indebted, the authors wish to single out Dr Nader Fargany (Arab Planning Institute, Kuwait), Dr Ibrahim El-Essawy and Dr Ahmed Shalaby (National Planning Institute, Cairo), who have given unstintingly of their time, views and suggestions. Not only did Dr Fargany contribute to the planning and writing of Part I with Dr Ali Nassar, but several of his other writings were sources on which Dr Nassar drew in preparing the first draft of that section. In addition, a number of Dr Fargany's detailed written suggestions were incorporated into the final text.

Dr Ibrahim El-Assawy joined the authors in the many sessions they held to discuss Part I, while Dr Ahmed Shalaby took part in discussions of all the sections of the book. Many revisions were made to the text in the light of their remarks. While acknowledging their debt of gratitude to these invaluable contributions, the authors assume full responsibility for the contents of this book.

Ismail-Sabri Abdalla
Co-ordinator
Arab Alternative Futures
UNU, Global and Regional Studies Division

1 INTRODUCTION

Past, present and future

The response which any talk of the future usually elicits from the Arab, as indeed it does from any Third-World citizen, is a negative one, in the sense that he feels such talk to be beyond his comprehension. He regards the future as an area over which he can have no control, for in his mind there is no continuity between past, present and future. For him, the future is a world far removed from the concerns of his daily life and from the hardships and challenges he is facing today. Nor is this true only of the ordinary citizen. Even the educated 'élite' are confused as they try to follow what is happening in the advanced industrial world. They remember the books on 'futurology' that they read back in the sixties, which made intuitive long-term visions of the world some half a century or more hence, where automation would have come to replace man in practically everything. This optimistic view was based on the then steady high pace of scientific progress and technological application. The message was repeated in a wave of books which were published in a decade of sustained economic growth accompanied by dramatic breakthroughs in science, notably in the field of electronics, which was described at the time as the 'scientific and technological revolution'. In the wake of that generation of writers came a school of political commentators, who were quick to play down the importance of social sciences, ideology and the social and political aspirations of fully one-third of humanity who were living on what has been called the 'poverty line'. Technology was deified as the new god which would unlock all secrets and make our planet a world run by machines. Although some sceptics believed such a world would be closer to hell than to heaven,[1] technology, like all gods, had its loyal priesthood which alone was privy to its secrets and guarded them jealously from the uninitiated, much as the priests of Ancient Egypt guarded the secret of how the pyramids were built. This left

Third-World citizens with no part to play in shaping the future and they were thus relegated to the role of onlookers, waiting passively for whatever it might have in store for them.

As economic growth slowed down in the seventies, and as it gradually became apparent that the industrial West—and with it the world economy—had entered a period of crisis with implications no one could forsee, and which governments were powerless to overcome despite all the science and technology at their disposal, a new school of thinkers emerged who focused their attention on a closer future. These claimed to shun the intuitive approach in favour of concrete facts supported by figures which they used to build up intricate mathematical models with the help of computers. For the most part, the new thinkers expressed reservations, not to say outright pessimism, about the future. A case in point is the earliest and most famous model put out by this school, whose conclusions were published by the Club of Rome under the title, 'Limits to Growth'.[2] All these efforts displayed such a marked degree of technical complexity that the most a layman could hope to grasp was the deductions reached by the models and not the reasoning on which they were based. Like the earlier works of futurology before them, these analyses of future prospects based on mathematical handling of quantifiable data alone deprived most people of access to knowledge, let alone of the chance to take part in the debate or of the ability to put these models to use in formulating or applying policies. In other words, people had no say in their future, no role in determining it and no awareness of its relationship with the present and with their actions in that present.

In actual fact, of course, nothing could be further from the truth. Time flows in an unbroken sequence. It is not a play of many acts, where the curtain falls at the end of each act to rise again at the beginning of the next. The history of mankind and the life of any society is made up, in the final analysis, of the interaction of events over the unfolding year, of the persistence of certain phenomena despite the changes undergone by a society and of the interpenetration and interaction of the sequels to certain events long after the events themselves have been played out. True, change is a feature of our universe. Again, it is an established fact that compared with natural change, social change is extremely rapid. Indeed, so abruptly do some social changes set in that they appear to be totally unrelated to what came before them. Others occur so smoothly as to pass unnoticed by the very people who wrought them. Still others are the product of conscious decisions taken by society or by whoever runs its affairs as logical steps or in response to legitimate aspirations. The fact that time flows in an unbroken sequence does not imply that events follow one another in an orderly fashion or that history repeats itself. On the other hand, continuous change in no way implies that the present is cut off from the past or from the present.

No real mental effort is required to realize that the Arab nations's present is a child of its past, albeit a child growing in a local and global environment very different from that of its parent. Taking the image one step further, one could liken a number of cultural factors to genes, in that both continue to exert an influence on each person from birth on. But then there is also what a child learns from the developed society in which it lives, what it gains in the way of knowledge and experience, what it acquires as values and what it later practises as a productive activity, all of which contribute to the formation of its personality. In developed societies these add up to what has come to be termed the 'generation gap'. For each moment in the life of any society is the product of interaction between its inherited economic, social, political and cultural structures on the one hand and what it acquires in any of these fields on the other.

It is clear then that the present flows into the future without interruption. The future is not a new chapter in the book of history, a blank page on which we shall start writing but, rather the cumulative product of unfolding events, whether emanating from within a society or from without. Thus before setting out to make any predictions on the future of the Arab nation at the end of this century or the beginning of the next, we must first be aware that this future will be the product of what the Arabs do or do not do from now until then. If they aspire to comprehensive development, to education, to pan-Arab unity, to social equality, to a strong position in the field of international relations or to other such goals, they must be aware that none of these goals can be reached unless they set themselves on the right track now. For the decisions we take today will determine the direction our future will take. But, side by side with these conscious decisions, processes of change are taking place in the very fabric of Arab society—in behaviour, social values, aims—which have a cumulative effect in shaping the future without our being aware of all the long-term implications of these processes. There is the fact too that we do not live in isolation from the rest of the world. Quite the reverse, as the many ties between the Arabs and others are multiplying in countless ways. These links also have a cumulative effect in shaping the Arab future. Thus future studies are more than just mental exercises indulged in by a few intellectuals or attempts to escape from a harsh reality to a better future. They have a practical and immediate use in that they enable us to know the long-term effects of what is happening in our countries today: the decisions being taken, the changes now occurring in habits, the ties we are building or consolidating with the outside world.

Alternative images of the future

Given that the future is not subject to inevitable predetermination, it follows that its shape is not foreordained. In other words, at any given moment in its history, each society is faced with many alternatives for its future. These should be identified and an attempt made to trace the main features of each. This would entail studying such potentials of the society in question as are known and open to investigation, the patterns according to which it puts them to use, how aware it is of the far-reaching effects these patterns will have and the degree to which it is free to change them. As the study of the future was linked to mathematical models in the last decade, and with mathematics becoming a common language in every field of science, we shall avail ourselves of some mathematical terms here. The 'freedom' of any society today is not absolute in the sense that when the decision-maker makes his decision, the opinion-former forms his opinion or when the ordinary person acts in his everyday life in one way or another, they are not exercising a conscious and voluntary option that they can change at will. Social will is hemmed in at all levels by numerous 'constraints'. Some of these constraints are natural, such as the volume of material resources available to a society; others are social, such as the economic, social, political and cultural structures governing that society. Then, too, some of these constraints are self-imposed, as it were, chosen consciously and deliberately, while others apply without conscious thought or deliberation, but are accepted by society as being in the natural order of things. Yet a third classification of constraints is to divide them into those which are endogenous and others which are exogenous, deriving from a society's multiple relations with other societies. Constraints can also be divided into *real* ones which cannot be overcome in any foreseeable future and others which can be overcome or circumscribed through study and research. Thus any society has a choice of futures, subject only to the degree of freedom it can achieve in its attempt to chart the shape of its future itself.

What is certain, and particularly for Third-World countries, is that the worst possible scenario of the future is the one which will result from a passive attitude that relinquishes the freedom of human will and lets events shape the future of people. If the industrially advanced nations understand the need to visualize the future so that it holds no unpleasant surprises in store for them, how much greater is the need for Third-World countries to do so? Suffering as they do from underdevelopment in many areas—economic, social, political and cultural—these countries cannot afford *not* to think ahead and to strive for a future that can ensure their progress, raise their living standards and improve their position in the world arena. Over and above this need, which certainly expresses the aspirations of the peoples of these countries, there is the fact that a passive attitude will not stop events from happening or changes from occurring. Change is a fact of life and events are constantly moving, both on the domestic and foreign fronts. Thus failure to strive for a specific vision of the future does not simply mean a perpetuation of the status quo, but could well result in a reduction of the present cultural level of society or the imposition of violent changes on society at exorbitant social cost.

When a society sets itself a number of goals for the future, it does not necessarily follow that the shape of its future will correspond to these goals. This will depend to a large extent on who takes the decision in that society's name, what his interests are and to what degree he is aware of these interests, on the interwoven results of his decision and their long-term effects, on his grasp of the realities of that society and of the world surrounding it and on how consistent the ends are with the means he uses to achieve them.

All this underscores the importance of future studies aimed primarily at trying to envisage the different shapes it can take according to different assumptions regarding social reality and its historical roots, the potentials available and the different ways they can be put to use, an awareness of the issue of the future, the declared targets, the actual processes changing society without its members being aware of the results of these processes, the reciprocal relations between the economic, social, political and cultural structures prevailing internally (on the one hand) and externally (on the other), etc. If the future bears no relation to the present but lies in the realm of the occult, to descend on society without warning, our people would have no option but to resort to soothsayers who profess to have knowledge of the supernatural, as the ancient Greeks resorted to the oracle of Apollo at Delphi. But now that we have explained the process of shaping the future and the effect of the present on its configuration, we have no choice but to conduct wide-ranging and in-depth research in the domain of future studies.

Developmental thought in most Third-World countries over the last three decades subscribed to a naïve understanding of development, namely, that it was no more than a remake of the historical growth of Western capitalism. This approach completely ignored the historical dimension of development. Western capitalism took shape in conditions which cannot recur, the most prominent of which are the technological advance, control of the Third-World's natural and human resources, and opening that world's markets to its products, overcoming the problem of poverty through settler colonization in North and South America, Australia, New Zealand and elsewhere. In Canada, the USA, Australia and New Zealand, this migration succeeded in displacing the original inhabitants and in furnishing the manpower (which these new societies could not otherwise have provided) to develop the huge resources of the newly-discovered continents. Although these conditions can obviously not recur in today's world, Western developmentalists postulated that it was possible to 'catch up' with the industrialized countries in a reasonable span of time. This goal has since been proved a myth. In face of the crisis of development in the Third World, a number of its intellectuals have sought, with the help of some intellectuals from industrialized countries, alternative strategies for development. New concepts of development emerged in the seventies, such as self-reliance, meeting the basic needs of the masses, the necessity for active popular participation in development, the social and cultural (not only economic) dimensions of development, etc. On the international level, the seventies witnessed a concerted effort by Third-World countries to adjust their relations with the industrialized countries. All these new concepts assume different policies and options from those hitherto prevailing in the Third World in general. The effects of adopting all or some of these must of necessity be reflected in the shape that the future of the societies adopting them will take. In other words, to hold that the future of any Third-World country will assume a unique shape is to depart from the premiss that there is one exclusive model of development, namely, that which proceeds along the lines of the Western model. Once we discard this premiss, the future becomes an open question and can take any one of a multitude of shapes. Then too, any real adjustment of relations between Third-World countries and industrialized countries will certainly change the shape of the future.

Others can shape our future

The need for futures studies by Third-World countries is more important today than at any other time because these countries have become part of an international order which governs their options to a great extent. This international order is a relatively new phenomenon in the long history of man. For the past tens of thousands of years, people have lived in scattered societies of different sizes and with different customs; they were always self-sufficient and had very little contact with other societies except through either invasion or trade. None of the old empires controlled more than a limited area of the globe, and none tried to impose one socio-economic system on the societies it had brought under its domain. The rulers of these empires were content to collect the economic surplus of these societies (basically in the form of tributes in kind) and did not think of merging them all into one social system. Even the Romans, for all their passion for organization and legislation, made a distinction between their civil law, the *jus civilis*, and the laws of the Roman-ruled provinces, the *jus gentium*. As for the European explorers who travelled to far-off places, they were motivated by curiosity and a yearning for knowledge, not by a desire to accumulate wealth. These explorers came back from their travels with more tales of the wondrous things they had seen than any material objects. As late as the end of the fifteenth century, the 'world' for the inhabitants of the Mediterranean basin meant first, their immediate neighbours in Europe and the Middle East, then India and China. World trade was limited to a few luxury items and was conducted more in the form of sporadic transactions than on a regular basis.

Things remained this way until, with the growth of capitalism in Western Europe, the Europeans embarked on an enterprise unprecedented in the history of mankind: nothing less than the conquest of the entire face of the globe. The riches pillaged from the conquered lands contributed to the process of primitive capital-accumulation which enabled wealthy Europeans to invest in transforming inventions—at that time limited to the manufacture of gadgets for the amusement of kings and princes—into means of production.

This process gave birth to modern mechanized industry with its two basic characteristics: an insatiable appetite for energy and raw materials and an endless need for bigger markets. Imperialism was a way of appeasing fledgling industry. It is generally accepted that the industrial revolution took place in the last quarter of the eighteenth century; during the following century, imperialism succeeded in casting its shadow over the whole world.

Thus, though operating through several empires, imperialism managed to unify the world under one socio-economic system: capitalism. The purpose here was not to collect 'tributes' as the old empires had done but, instead, to extract primary products and sources of cheap energy as well as securing markets for the colonial power's manufacturing industry. In other words, the aim was to establish productive and reciprocal links between the economy of the colonies and that of the colonial powers. Thus for the first time a world economy emerged, based on the complementary nature of the two economies, the colonial and the colonized, the course of each one affecting that of the other. This led some Western writers and politicians to talk of 'interdependence' between the centre and the periphery of the world economy. In fact the complementary nature of the world economy favoured those who initiated it and resulted in the concentration of industrial growth in a limited number of countries at the expense of others. Underdevelopment is thus not the result of historical stagnation or lethargy. It is not as though the colonies were left to their own devices and then failed to develop. Rather, their economic development was determined in the manner that could best serve the interests of imperialism. Underdevelopment does not denote a lack of economic growth as much as it does a distorted and dependent growth. The other side of the same coin is the growth of Western capitalism and its domination over the world.

Despite the success of the national liberation movement since the fifties, particularly as regards achieving political independence and eradicating old colonialism from all but a few limited areas (notably the settler colonialism in Palestine and South Africa), the world economy is far from reflecting an equitable image, unlike the equitable image reflected in the UN General Assembly. We live in a world economic, political, social and cultural system with a centre—made up of a limited number of Western countries—which controls the system and imposes its policies on the periphery, i.e. the Third-World countries. The centre has many means of control at its disposal, forming what are known as power structures, whose tentacles spread to envelop our nations despite their political independence. There is first of all the military factor, whether used to attack or threaten Third-World countries or to sell them arms so that they are tied to the sources of their weapons. Then there are the elements of economic power: industry, technology, money. There is no need to speak at length here of the effects of these elements on attempts at development in the Third World. And, last but not least, there is the West's control of mass information and communication media, from its monopoly of five 'international' news agencies to the sources of news published by our local press, from cinema and television material to advertisement, etc.—a control which enables it to shape tastes, opinions and values in Third-World countries in the interests of Western capitalism, by plugging the lifestyle of the consumerist society and so glorifying Western civilization that it comes to be regarded as the only viable model of civilization.

Thus Third-World countries are linked to a world system whose mechanics operate automatically for the benefit of the centre and to the detriment of the periphery. This system fosters the centre's exploitation of the periphery's natural and human resources and the periphery's subordination to the centre, whatever the wealth the periphery may dispose of, however much it may spend on investment and despite all its efforts to modernize. In fact, the world system operates in much the same way as the solar system which has a host of planets revolving around a large star according to the laws of gravity. It is clear then that, unless Third-World countries get together and try to shape a future that will leave them less vulnerable to exploitation, the very dynamics of the world system—with some assistance from various forms of direct or indirect intervention—will determine the shape of that future for them, according to what best serves the interests of the dominant powers at the centre of the world economy. The irony is that all this is happening at a time when the ruling élites and most intellectuals in the Third World believe they are choosing for themselves freely and rationally. But in any rational choice there is a time dimension which is often overlooked, namely, the links between past and present in the context of which the choice is made and the future effects of the accumulation of decisions determined.

We can shape our own future

Whatever the mechanics of the world system, they are not so strong as to cancel out the will of the Third-World nations. After all, they were able to become aware of their own strength, and rid themselves of occupation and direct forms of foreign domination. Through a struggle that took many forms, the countries of the Third World managed to achieve their independence even though the military balance of power was not tilted in their favour. Indeed, the military might of the industrial countries is much greater today than it was in the days when they conquered India, or even when they divided the Ottoman Empire among themselves after World War I. What is called for today is an awareness that real development means liberation from economic and cultural imperialism. The concept of development which prevailed throughout the last three decades was misleading for the Third World, in that it made development dependent on aid and investments from the industrial countries. Yesterday's enemy, against whom the people had fought, became the benefactor who would save them from underdevelopment in spite of the fact that such an underdevelopment was the result of imperialist domination in the first place. New concepts of development could open up new vistas for the future. The different development paths would have to be thoroughly studied, their effects analysed and their effectiveness tested, as a prelude to elaborating strategies that could lead to a future which would respond to the legitimate aspirations of all our nations.

The industrial countries attach a great deal of importance to future studies, despite the fact that they have built up their socio-economic system as an integrated whole which cannot be substantially deflected from its course except at a prohibitive cost. The industrialized societies are witnessing a growing wave of discontent with their present lifestyles. The current trend is to move towards lifestyles which would restore human beings to their rightful place as master, not slave, of the machine and its products, and which would strike a balance between the material and non-material needs, protection from environmental pollution and the danger of depleting natural resources. 'The quality of life' is regarded as a new objective, as opposed to the consumerist ethic based on 'quantity of things'. Third-World countries, on the other hand, are still at the beginning of the road and therefore their range of options is wider and the cost of adjustment is much less.

For example, if a certain technology pollutes the environment the industrialized countries are forced to invent means of countering this pollution at a cost which, though not inconsiderable, is nevertheless much lower than the cost of replacing the offending technology and shutting down the plants. Third-World countries, on the other hand, are free to choose a clean technology right from the start. This is one case where underdevelopment could be a blessing in disguise. Furthermore, industrial concentrations are usually accompanied by giant urban centres, which create insurmountable problems. A very recent example was the near bankruptcy of New York City, which was narrowly averted only by decreasing the municipal services it provided to its citizens. Surely this should encourage Third-World countries to devise development strategies that would strike a better balance between overall rural development and a polycentral urban growth. The list of examples is endless.

The question is no longer one of having to choose from preset development models. Indeed, model 'fetishism' is a thing of the past, as we shall explain in more detail in Part III. Contemporary developmental thought now holds that each society must follow its own path to development, a path determined by its cultural heritage, natural resources, socio-economic structures and relations with the outside world. There are no longer theoretical answers to such questions as whether to choose between capitalism or socialism—the issue of development is much too complex for that. Those who opt politically and socially for the capitalist system must search for the elements of success offered by that path in the context of the realities of their own society and not base their choice on admiration for the success of capitalism in the West or on an uncritical acceptance of the economic and social theories of that system. Similarly, those who opt for socialism must understand that it cannot be imposed by a political decision and that it is a long-term process of economic, social and cultural development, subject first and foremost to the realities of the society applying it.

A political choice does not in itself solve development problems, nor does it automatically determine a clear vision of the future—unless it is simply a Utopia; hence the multiplicity of development paths and the need to acquire a thorough and open-minded understanding of reality. In this context it becomes obvious that the capitalism of Japan is different from that of the USA and that the socialism of China is different from that of the Soviet Union. These cases are cited deliberately because they have attracted the most attention and affected Third-World countries to varying degrees.

The Arab nation with all its countries, rich and poor alike, is an integral part of the Third World. Its citizens must try to visualize the future and search for different development alternatives which can lead to that future. Possibly the Arab countries are privileged in this respect by a cultural homogeneity and in that they aspire to a kind of economic and political unity. This qualifies them to undertake a collective effort in the area of studying the future. This makes it all the more necessary to make them aware of the importance of such studies and to determine both substance and methodology in the Arab context.

Notes

1. See, for example, Herman Kahn and Anthony J. Wiener, *The Year 2000, a Framework for Speculation on the Next Thirty-Three Years*, New York, Hudson Institute, 1967; Fred Warshofsky, ed., *The Twenty-First Century: The New Age of Exploration*, Twenty-first Century Series, New York, Viking, 1969; James T. Martin and Adrian R. D. Norman, *The Computerized Society, an Appraisal of the Impact of Computers on Society over the Next Fifteen Years*, Automatic Computation Series, Englewood Cliffs N.J., Prentice-Hall, 1970; Arthur B. Bronwell, ed., *Science and Technology in the World of the Future,* New York, Wiley, Kreiger, 1970; Gerald Feinberg, *The Prometheus Project: Mankind's Search for Long Range Goals*, New York, Doubleday, 1969; and Romanian Academy of Science, *The Revolution in Science and Technology and the Contemporary Social Development,* The Romanian Academy, 1977.

   For evaluations of technological outlook, see, for example, Gordon R. Taylor, *The Doomsday Book*, London, Thames and Hudson, 1970; Victor C. Ferkiss, *Technological Man, the Myth and the Reality,* New York, Braziller, 1969; John D. Garcia, *The Moral Society: A Rational Alternative to Death*, New York, Julian Press, 1971; and Roberto Vacca, *Il Medievo Prossimo Ventura*, Rome, 1971, translated into English under the title, *The Coming Dark Age*, New York, Doubleday, Anchor Books, 1973. In direct opposition to the veneration-of-technology school, stand the works, of the well-known author, Ivan Illich, whose most famous book is *Medical Nemesis: The Exploration of Health*, New York, Bantam, 1977.
2. See Part I.

PART I

GLOBAL MODELS AND THE ARAB FUTURE

This part will set out to illustrate how others see us, more specifically, how the Arab region is perceived in futuristic exercises undertaken by non-Arab institutes and research groups. In line with the purpose of this book, we shall review and evaluate the various studies available on the future of the region with a view to determining how qualified they are to investigate the alternative futures of its development.

The first chapter of this part introduces the reader to the methodologies and concepts which we shall use in our evaluation of future images of development in a given country or in the Arab region as a whole. It distinguishes between the various methodologies used to treat futures issues, and briefly examines how the concept of 'investigating the future' has evolved over the years before moving on to review some images of the Arab region as seen by others. These examples are drawn from what are known as 'global models', the construction of which was a very popular and widely publicized activity during the seventies.

Chapter 2 can be regarded as a brief overview of global modelling works in general, with special emphasis on the sample selected for our purpose. We shall first submit these models to a critical review both from a Third World perspective and as regards their quality and technical competence to explore the future; secondly, we shall evaluate to what degree their divisions and structures adequately represent the Arab region, and thirdly, we shall assess them in terms of how ambitious, objective and comprehensive are their investigation of the Arab future several decades hence and to what extent we can be satisfied with the relative position allotted to the Arab region in the new map of the world put forward by these models.

2 CONCEPT OF INVESTIGATING THE FUTURE AND CRITERIA FOR SELECTION OF GLOBAL MODELS

1. Different methodologies used to address futures issues

The writings in circulation contain many terms and concepts related to attempts to portray 'future images' of all or some aspects of economic and social life. We shall try here to distinguish between some of these inasmuch as they touch on this book. But we should first bear in mind that it is rare for those writing in the area with which we are concerned, namely, economics and sociology, to agree on the same term for the same concept. Indeed, sometimes one term can mean very different things. The problem is compounded for the Arabic-speaking reader by the fact that many of the terms used are foreign in origin, with no Arabic equivalent other than individual attempts to translate them, where, it might be added, more effort is expended in deriving than in agreeing on a standard translation.

To begin with, this chapter is concerned only with those attempts to depict images of a relatively distant future, with a time horizon extending at least to the turn of the century. The methodologies to be discussed in this chapter will include neither *long-term planning*[1] nor *prophecies.*[2] The former involves a conscious intervention to reshape socio-economic structures through a set of integrated policies formulated by a central authority which disposes of the means to pursue and follow-up these policies and to create the objective conditions necessary for their implementation. Thus long-term planning is suitable only in countries or groupings of countries which exercise a measure of central control of economic life. As for prophecy, this is based on the naïve notion that the future is pre-ordained and that all we can do is to reveal that future. Obviously, one can talk of prophecy when dealing with individual beliefs and practices, but not in relation to administration and practice at the level of a state or a group of states.

Those concerned with futures issues have learnt from experience that medium- or long-term planning, as well as the elaboration of policies and programmes involving several time horizons in countries without a sufficient degree of central control, require more extensive background material than projections, predictions or futures analyses. An extensive background of futuristic information would be very useful in charting the most stable path to the future, by revealing the perils and bottlenecks which can be avoided by adopting the necessary policies in time. Most writings in this domain tend to resort to the technique of projection in its simplest form, by extrapolating past trends and relationships as computed from past statistical time series. We prefer using forecasting as a more serious and realistic technique by which to portray a detailed picture of the future without neglecting the different linkages and feed-back effects of the total system under study.

Given the complexities of the political-social-economic total system, the increasing degree of uncertainty over the future, and the failure of both *mechanical extrapolation* and *forecasting techniques*, to capture the dynamics of the future, the need arose for new methods and techniques. At best, we can make conditional forecasts,[3] (or scenarios), based on the dynamics of the main variables and their role in shaping the future, leaving the remaining details to subsequent stages of planning, in which we search for appropriate policies to achieve the desired trends of the main variables. The most we can hope to do is to express the total system in the form of sub-systems. We can never reach the ultimate stage of representing them accurately and objectively in one total integrated system with all its linkages and interactions. In other words, we make a sort of prospective analysis, beginning with a set of selected assumptions—whether explicit or implicit—in the hope of reaching a rational assessment of future prospects.

Thus investigating the future is a systematic scientific endeavour aimed at formulating a number of conditional forecasts comprising the main features of the situation in a given society or a group of societies. Extending slightly beyond twenty years into the future, it departs from some specific assumptions about the past and the present to investigate the impact of futuristic elements injected into society. Thus exploring the future does not exclude the possibility of investigating the nature and size of the basic changes which must occur in a given society for that society's future to take the desired shape.

The term *futurology* as it evolved in the West was used to denote projections of component elements of the future going much further in time than had hitherto been customary. It is historically associated with the promotion of 'technological innovation' by writers who perceived technology as the most important single variable in shaping images of the future. As to the term *prognosis*, which is widely used in Eastern Europe, this describes efforts to build up extensive backgrounds of futuristic information necessary for any long-term planning activity.

We should also note that all these techniques and methodologies draw upon a limited number of tools suitable for long-term analysis. These techniques can be divided into four main groups: intuitive, exploratory, normative[4] and, finally, feedback models.[5] In fact, all futures studies use a combination of these four techniques in different degrees according to the nature and purpose of the study.

2. On exploring the Arab future

Before attempting to explore the future of the Arab region, we will try to identify a number of elements relevant to this exercise.

(1) Any scientific investigation of the future must stem from a thorough grasp of the past and the present, that is, of the effect of the underlying factors which shaped the features of the past and present. The success of any such attempt depends to a great extent on the current state of the art in this field. Accordingly, investigating the future is a dynamic and continuous process which is greatly affected by the development of the state of the art.

(2) It should be borne in mind that scientific attempts to explore the future do not produce either prophecies or specific details of future events. No one at the beginning of the twentieth century, for example, could have possibly foreseen the momentous events or the scientific and technical achievements that have made their mark on the shape of our world today. By the same token, who can claim to

foretell the future state of affairs in a given country or group of countries some fifty years hence? At best, futures studies can shed some light on certain features of alternative futures, especially as they relate to events, actions and human aspirations. In other words, they can help draw us closer to the best of the available alternative futures.[6]

(3) The tools by which we can explore the future should derive from an analytical–theoretical view. In fact, these tools are simply more precise formulations of, and not replacements for, such a view, helping only to quantify expectations. An explicit ideological perspective ensures a comprehensive view and a conscious grasp of the dynamics of progress. Thus while quantitative tools can help us understand a theory and its application, they cannot in themselves serve as a basis on which the theory can be built.

(4) It is now widely accepted that scientific endeavours to explore the future are in themselves beneficial to society, in that they sharpen awareness of future problems and challenges thus allowing people to play an active role in shaping their own future.

(5) Exploring the future is of crucial importance for Third-World countries, in view of the fact that development is now recognized as a process of profound socio-economic structural change which, as such, takes much longer than the time horizon normally assigned to long-term economic planning. By focusing on the interaction between the various facets of the socio-economic system, exploring the future helps us understand the process of development in its complexity.

(6) One obvious reason for the importance of exploring the various dimensions of the future is the *sequential nature* of socio-economic events and developments, in the sense that any delay in taking the appropriate decisions to achieve the desired targets does not imply an equivalent time-lag in achieving these targets but could mean a much longer delay, or, even, a failure to reach them altogether.

For example, if devising new forms of mass participation is important to propel the development process forward, delaying such forms for a period of, say, ten years, would mean that the state of underdevelopment would continue for the same length of time so that, if participation were to begin after the ten year delay we would need either to work longer or harder—or both—to achieve the same targets.

(7) In the case of the Arab region, many development problems relevant to the Arab future cannot be envisaged other than in the very long term. For instance, such futures issues as exploiting oil resources, the use pattern of oil revenues and their impact on post-oil Arab societies, Arab integration and its central role in developing the region, must be placed in the context of long-term analysis.

Although the future of the Arab region is of paramount importance, both in the region and beyond, exploring that future has yet to be undertaken in a truly scientific fashion. In the following pages, we shall illustrate this point with reference to the global models selected for review.

Without serious efforts to explore the various dimensions of the Arab future, any attempt to address issues related to that future cannot rise above the level of speculation or, at best, rational expectations based on logical abstractions.

(8) The current disarray in Arab ranks vividly underlines the wide gulf separating hopes from reality thus breeding a sense of frustration and despair. However, in the following discussion, we shall adopt the view that the Arab region constitutes a historical-cultural entity, as conceived of in modern pan-Arab thinking which dates back to the twenties.

Indeed, one can attribute the present crisis to a lack of any future vision embracing common Arab aims. Perhaps one advantage of probing the various dimensions of the Arab future is that it can help free the Arab mind from the inhibitions and susceptibilities, fed by narrow national interests and suspicions, which stand in the way of genuine Arab development and co-operation. A long-term outlook would reveal the decisive difference between the results of today's choices and the options of the near future, between Arab fragmentation and the persistence of socio-economic underdevelopment on the one hand and, a serious move towards Arab unity and the achievement of overall development with the effective participation of Arab masses on the other. Any rational attempt to investigate the future of the Arab region must, if it is to rise up to its historical responsibility, take this difference into account when mapping out current and future courses of action conducive to regional development within the framework of a unified Arab world.

(9) As has already been mentioned, once the theoretical framework has been elaborated, our ability to explore the future depends on the use of appropriate quantitative tools, which may well take the form of sophisticated mathematical models.[7] Sophistication here can take one of two forms: either *horizontal*, represented in the wide range of problems addressed; or *vertical*, represented in the interplay of a large number of elements needed to guide the policy-maker in making his decisions. This second form was the main driving-force behind recent efforts to evolve new concepts and theories in the field of total systems analysis.

If we take the time factor into account, the quantitative tools required would acquire a high degree of vertical sophistication as a result of the conflict which may arise between the behaviour of the time paths of variables in the short and longer term respectively. In other words, as indicated by Forrester[8] the sophisticated total systems models are counter-intuitive, simply because the time-space relationships they contain are complex and hard to determine.

Thus it becomes increasingly difficult for the individual policy-maker to grasp all the elements of a given situation and to weave them into a system of causal relationships. This led to the development of a new generation of quantitative models designed to rationalize the process of decision-making with an eye on the future.

Building such models is no easy matter, for, while the first operation of identifying and enumerating all the relevant elements might be relatively easy, the second, of trying to weave them all into a coherent system, is much more difficult. As in the case of counter-intuitive models, the results derived from these new models depend, to a great extent, on the structure of the model. Accordingly, the validity of a model's result depends on its representation of the decision-maker's attitude. Moreover, the conscious—or unconscious—bias that goes into building a model affects the conclusions it reaches and the policy recommendations it makes. This factor must be borne in mind in respect of any model. There is a tendency to take for granted the conclusions drawn by a model, to accept them as absolute truths even outside the context in which they were presented, without due regard to the structure and biases of the model itself.

3. The movement of global modelling and futures studies

The earliest attempts to look at the future scientifically can be traced back to World War II, when a number of institutes were set up in the United States to conduct futures studies on military strategy questions. But it was not until the onset of the sixties, when futures studies broadened their perspective and came to adopt a more global outlook, that they acquired the importance and renown they now enjoy. The sixties saw a spate of futures studies and reports in the West, while planning agencies in countries with centrally-planned economies began systematically to build up more extensive background material for their planning activity. These forerunners of futures studies as they have since evolved were, for the most part, full of shortcomings, but they served to build up a certain amount of experience and new techniques which, together with a number of external factors, greatly enhanced the quality of futures studies. The conditions which favoured this development were:

(1) the development of a broader data base;
(2) an improvement in the understanding of socio-economic relations, thanks to new contributions to economic theory and developmental thought;
(3) the appearance of the computer and the spread of its use allowed for new opportunities to subject elaborate and complex systems and models to mathematical computation;
(4) a succession of crises of a global nature, economic and otherwise, underlined both the need to explore the future and the impossibility of doing so by employing a hasty, piecemeal approach.

It was not long before 'exploring the future' acquired enormous importance, not only at government level, both individually and collectively, but also for international organizations, scientific institutes and multinational corporations. Perhaps the most important—certainly the most famous—activities in this sphere were those undertaken in the early seventies by the Club of Rome.[9] An informal organization that grew out of a meeting held between a group of top intellectuals and business men at the invitation of Dr Aurelio Peccei, an Italian industrial manager and economist, the Club of Rome became the prime mover behind global modelling activities.

The approach adopted by the Club of Rome was much closer to the more mature understanding of exploring the future, in that it dealt with the world as a total system, made extensive use of the computer and undertook a long-term analysis of world problems. It also dealt with relations between the world's rich and poor, and spoke of world resources as the common property of mankind and the world's future as its collective responsibility.

Although we do not want to pass hasty judgements on the interests and concerns of the intellectuals and business men from whom the Club of Rome's membership is drawn—a question we shall be dealing with when we come to evaluate the global models put out by the Club—some general remarks are in order here. An initial observation is that the first report to the Club of Rome, published for general readership under the title of *The Limits to Growth*, mentions in a foreword that Dr Aurelio Peccei 'is affiliated with Fiat and Olivetti and manages a consulting firm for economic and engineering development, Italconsult, one of the largest of its kind in Europe'.

Another remark we would like to make here is that an enriching factor was added to global modelling activities by Third-World thinkers, who elaborated some provocative new ideas in the area of alternative development. This enrichment was continued when groupings of developing countries, like the Group of 77, began to call for more equitable relations with the industrial countries.

Bearing in mind that 'interest in global models could go beyond affecting public opinion . . . to formulating the policies of future',[10] we shall come back to these points later.

Finally, it is well worth recalling here the words of Mahbub ul Haq[11] on the question of global modelling activities: 'In your world, there is concern today about the quality of life; in our world, there is a concern about life itself which is threatened by hunger and malnutrition . . . In our world, anxiety is not about the depletion of resources, but about the best distribution and exploitation of these resources, for the benefit of all mankind rather than for the benefit of a few nations . . . You can afford to be concerned about polluted beaches; we have to worry a lot about the fact that less than 10 per cent of the population in the Third World has even drinkable water'.

4. Selection of most relevant global models

Global models have been presented to the reader as attempts to represent the world, with all its economic and social phenomena, as a 'total system', thereby improving our understanding of the world *problematique* and helping us explore the future and its various interconnected parts. Hence the distinctive feature of this type of modelling activity—the attempt (or claim) to go beyond the partial approach—and our interest in reviewing these models and appraising their effectiveness as tools with which to probe the future of the Arab nation.

To choose from among the many global models available, we were guided by a number of selection criteria:

(1) how comprehensive is the geographical coverage of the respective model;
(2) how extensive is the range of issues it addresses;
(3) how far does the model attempt to synthesize the interaction and linkages between; various phenomena and variables;
(4) is the model's time horizon longer than 10 years?

In the light of these criteria, global models of a *sectoral* nature, such as energy or *food* models, were dismissed, as they deal with only one problem, on a world-wide or regional basis. We also excluded some analytical studies of the future which did not make use of the global modelling approach that allows for a quantitative assessment of international linkages.[12]

We should point out, however, that our selection of these global models for review and appraisal does not mean that we shall not, in the course of discussion, draw on some of the data contained in any of the models which were excluded in accordance with our selection criteria. The Appendix table to Part I sums up the main features of the various global models selected for our analysis, as well as a number of the most important ones excluded from our sample.

We can on the whole distinguish between two generations of global models: a *first generation*, which treats the world as an homogeneous whole, best exemplified in the work of Forrester and Meadows which culminated in the 'World 3' model on which the *Limits to Growth* report was based; *a second generation*, which sought to divide the world into regions and which grew out of the controversy provoked by the publication of *Limits to Growth*. The main argument advanced against this model was that it was inadequate, both in terms of structure and data base, to sustain the conclusions reached by the report.[13] Furthermore, some of these conclusions were not based on solid grounds, as pointed out by some critics.[14] Thus each model of the second generation claims to be an improvement on its predecessor. Among the second generation models are the Mesarovic–Pestel multi-level model, which served as the basis for *Mankind at the Turning Point*, the Latin-American global model built by the Fundacione Bariloche in Argentina, which served as the basis for *Catastrophe or a new Society?* and the UN global model constructed under the supervision of Professor Wassily Leontief, which served as the basis for *The Future of the World Economy*.

Two other models belonging to this same generation but which did not enjoy the same renown are the SARU model, built by the Systems Analysis Research Unit of the UK Department of Environment, headed by Peter Roberts, and the FUGI model, developed in Japan under the supervision of Kaya and Ownitchi. The first served as the basis for another model elaborated by the Interfutures study commissioned by the OECD, whose conclusions we have included among our sample.[15] Unfortunately, despite the good design of the Japanese model and the advanced quantitative techniques which went into it, we were unable to include it in our sample because of the lack of sufficient references.[16] Moreover, the Japanese model's relevance for our purpose is limited by the fact that the time horizon for most of its projections (or conditional forecasts) does not extend beyond ten years.

Before concluding this brief introduction to the models that will be the object of analysis in the following pages, as well as to a number that have been rejected, it should be mentioned here that we were unable to include an important futures study which reached the authors after this chapter had been completed. Prepared essentially by the US Government's Council for Environment Awareness, this three-volume study was published under the title, *The Global 2000 Report to the President of the United States: Entering the Twenty First Century.*[17]

Notes

1. These are forecasts which depart from a set of predetermined assumptions about the future.
2. This approach depends essentially on personal intuition based on experience, and the set of assumptions implicit therein are not derived from a model of relationships and interlinkages.
3. This approach sets out to explore the future of relations as established in the past, through an explicit model of relationships and interlinkages.
4. The normative approach is a conscious intervention to change the course of the future according to present targets and *a priori* value judgements.
5. Known as feed-back models, these claim to permit clear identification of all phenomena and dynamics, taking account of past relations and of the objective reasons that will impose themselves to change future courses. This claim is grossly exaggerated, as we often find these models used for different purposes, as, say, exploratory or normative tools.
6. Indeed, the absence of futures studies of this kind, of any serious discussion of the different methodologies which can be used to explore the possibilities of shaping a better future for the Arab region and the failure to keep abreast of global modelling activities constitutes a threat not only to pan-Arabism but to Arab existence as such. This view is shared by some leading Arab planners, such as Mohamed Labib Shukeir, Ismail-Sabri Abdalla, and Mohamed Mahmoud El-Imam. See Mohamed Labib Shukeir, 'The Need for New Types of Studies on Arab Unity', *Al-Mustaqbal Al-Araby*, Year 2, Issue No. 10 (November 1979); Ismail-Sabri Abdalla, 'Comments on Working Paper of 3-Man Committee Selected by the Committee of Experts on a Strategy for Joint Arab Economic Action' in: *Proceedings of Pan-Arab Conference on a Strategy for Joint Arab Economic Action, 1, Baghdad, 6–12 May 1978*, Beirut, Arab Organization for Studies and Publishing, 1978, and Mohammed Mahmoud El-Imam, 'Global Models', in: *Proceedings of the Annual Scientific Conference for Egyptian Economists, 4, Cairo, May 1979,* Ismail Sabri Abdalla *et al.*, eds., *Economic Development and Social Justice in Contemporary Developmental Thought with Special Reference to the Case of Egypt*, Cairo, Egyptian Society for Political Economy, Statistics and Legislation, 1981.

7. For a detailed discussion of this issue, see the Introduction of the following research paper: Nader Fargany and Aly Nassar 'Global Models and Development: The Role of Models in Exploring Images of the Future of the Third World', in Abdalla *et al.*, eds., *Economic Development and Social Justice in Contemporary Developmental Thought with Special Reference to the Case of Egypt.*
8. J. W. Forrester, *World Dynamics*, Cambridge, Mass., Wright Allen, 1971.
9. *The Limits to Growth: A Report to the Club of Rome* (1968).
10. See S. Cole 'The Global Futures Debate, 1964–76,' in: Christopher Freeman and Marie Jahoda, eds., *World Futures: The Great Debate*, Falmer, Brighton, University of Sussex, 1979, pp. 28–9.
11. See Mahbub ul Haq, *The Poverty Curtain: Choices for the Third World*, p. 82, New York, Columbia University Press, 1976. (Translator's note.)
12. Two of the most important studies excluded from our sample are Jan T. Tinbergen, Co-ordinator, *Reshaping the International Order*, London, Hutchinson, 1977, otherwise known as the 'Rio Report', and Willy Brandt and Anthony Sampson, *North-South: A Programme for Survival*, London, Pan books, 1980, otherwise known as the Brandt Commission Report.
13. See, for example, H. D. Scholnik, *On a Methodological Criticism of Meadows' World 3 Model*, Bariloche, Buenos Aires, Fundacion Bariloche, 1972, and H. S. D. Cole *et al., Thinking About the Future: A Critique of the Limits to Growth*, London, Chatto and Windus, 1973.
14. Compare John Maddox, *The Doomsday Syndrome: An Attack on Pessimism,* New York, MacGraw-Hill, 1972.
15. (sic) See Organization for Economic Co-operation and Development (OECD), Interfutures, *Facing the Future, Mastering the Probable and Managing the Unpredictable*, Paris: OECD, 1979 (henceforth cited as *Facing the Future*).
16. No complete translation of this Japanese study exists. Perhaps the most accurate review and summary can be found in the following reference. *Technological Forecasting and Social Change*, **6**, 3 and 4 (1974), and A. Onishi, 'The Global Macro-Economic Model', in: G. Bruckmann, ed., *Global Modelling Review*, Laxenburg, Austria, International Institute for Applied Systems Analysis (IIASA), 1980.
17. G. O. Barney, study director, *The Global 2000 Report to the President of the United States: Entering the Twenty-First Century*, Vol. 1., Washington, D.C., US Government Printing Office, 1980, (3 vols).

3 THE ARAB REGION AS MIRRORED IN GLOBAL MODELS

This chapter will attempt to highlight the main features of the models referred to above and the results to be drawn from them, and should not be regarded as a detailed description of such models.

1. The Club of Rome model: *The Limits to Growth*

Concern in the West with what came to be called 'the world *problematique*' and the anxiety at crises looming on the horizon, led to the development by Forrester and Meadows of a series of models designed to serve as quantitative tools by which to formulate the policies conducive to the survival and well-being of the world system through averting expected crises.[1] These models looked at the world as an homogeneous mass constrained by natural fixed limits, and defined some variables or sub-systems interacting to form the global system.[2]

Forrester and Meadows reach the conclusion that the exponential growth in some sub-systems under consideration comes up against 'fixed' natural limits and warn that this will lead to the collapse of the world system in less than one hundred years.[3] They see the first signs of collapse in the gradual deterioration of the value of an index representing the quality of life, followed by a fall in the size of population as a result of rising mortality rates. To avoid such a fate, Forrester and Meadows advocate setting deliberate checks on Third-World population growth and on capital formation to reach a state of future equilibrium.[4]

Without doubt, *The Limits to Growth* was a pioneering attempt in that the builders of the model dealt with the world as an integral whole within the framework of a comprehensive model of human and material resources. The time horizon in this endeavour, which occasionally went beyond one hundred years, was the natural result of a global outlook encompassing the effects of industrialization, poverty, environmental damage, etc.

At any rate, it would be wrong to belittle the significant contributions of the *Limits to Growth* team, whose report was a warning that when catastrophe struck, it would affect everyone without exception. They also stressed that the prevailing pattern of industrial activity as it affected the environment would lead to collapse. But most important of all, perhaps, is their work in perfecting the techniques of building the total systems model, which can be counted as a truly outstanding scientific contribution in this area. As we shall be dealing in this and the following chapter with many of the criticisms levelled against the report, we should perhaps briefly mention here its basic recommendations and the main issues which provoked such heated debate.

Where Malthus neglected 'technical progress' when he compared population- and resource-growth in his early attempt at probing the future, *The Limits to Growth*, while acknowledging technological progress, was unduly pessimistic as to the role it could play in solving the world *problematique*. Having decided that technological achievements would not keep pace with the level of needs to be satisfied, the authors of the report advocated setting a limit to growth. It is not surprising that this should have been the conclusion reached by a report that did not address distributional problems, either between regions of the world or between rich and poor. Indeed, the report did not accord much importance to other than pure economic issues.

In sum, we would like here to point to some other characteristic features of this endeavour. There is a tendency to generate established accounting indicators, whether in respect of macro-aggregates or of industrial activity. There is also a tendency to present a fairly disaggregated picture of industry and services. The dynamics of the inter-relations between worldwide phenomena are emphasized. Due to the reliance on a weak data-base, many of the values it used in prediction were pure guesses.

For all its gloomy outlook for the future, the report's estimates of world resources were unduly optimistic in terms of its own assumptions. Perhaps one reason for this paradoxical result is its neglect of the resource–price relationship. Another shortcoming is that the report saw the main issue as being one of fighting environmental pollution, by spending more, rather than of avoiding pollution in the first place.

2. The Mesarovic–Pestel model

Although the group led by Mesarovic and Pestel set out to achieve the same goals as Forrester and Meadows, they used a more sophisticated methodological approach, evolving a system of models that covered ten regions of the world interlinked through flows of international trade. In addition to this horizontal division of the world, the models incorporate, at least theoretically, a vertical division through the interaction of various levels: individual, collective, demographic, economic, ecological, geographical, natural and technical.

These models evolved in two forms: one to analyse the *world energy* situation (especially oil); the other to study the *world food* situation. In both cases, a group of models linking different sub-systems for each region were first built up. The systems of each region were then linked to those of the others through a network of international trade relations. The first form includes sub-systems for demography, economics and energy, while the second includes sub-systems for demography, economics and food. In addition to dividing the world into regions and to the higher level of disaggregation in the sub-systems compared to the Forrester–Meadows model, the Mesarovic–Pestel model elaborated a new interactive formula between man and the computer that facilitates the computer's use in policy analysis.

Following the first two basic forms of these models, a fifth sub-system was developed for *raw materials*, designed primarily to study two basic metals: copper and aluminium. The system of models was also designed to allow for the division of one of the basic ten regions into a number of sub-regions. Efforts continued to develop a 'second generation' of the Mesarovic–Pestel models, which embodied a number of refinements over the first generation variety.[5] Unlike the Forrester–Meadows attempt, the Mesarovic–Pestel models could be used 'in formulating recommendations with an immediate bearing on the decision-making process . . . and explicitly spell out the theoretical basis of the model'.[6]

The main results of the first version were published in *Mankind at the Turning Point*. In response to the criticism levelled at Forrester and Meadows for treating the world as an homogeneous mass and their concept of 'undifferentiated growth', Mesarovic and Pestel came up with the concept of organic, or differentiated, growth across different regions of the world. According to this concept, crises in world systems could be overcome through changing the horizontal composition of these systems in the model, that is, by changing the relations between the regions of the world, or through changing their vertical composition, that is, by changing economic, demographic and technical relations within these regions.

Except that they were more detailed and elaborate, the findings of the Mesarovic–Pestel models were not fundamentally different from those reached by Forrester and Meadows.

The most important of these findings was that the short-term perspective of world problems is a deceptive one. But Mesarovic and Pestel also subscribe to the 'collapse' theory, which they maintain is inevitable, albeit only in some regions of the world, for different reasons and at different times, but with repercussions extending to the whole world. They hold that crises can only be averted through regulating world population growth, through co-operation rather than confrontation between the various regions of the world, through establishing a new international economic order and through evolving a new world system for resource allocation.[7] The model gives specific examples of the desired forms of co-operation between industrialized and developing countries, citing in this connection some scenarios of co-operation, mainly in the field of energy, in an attempt to show the advantages of co-operation over confrontation.[8]

Recalling that the point of departure of this group's work was the criticism levelled at *Limits to Growth* for dealing with the world as a 'monolithic' whole and for neglecting the diversity between world regions and levels, we are entitled to ask why their findings did not differ from those of Forrester and Meadows. Mesarovic and Pestel, who set out to construct a model that was more representative of world development and that could serve as a guideline to the methods and policies required to face the world *problematique*, did in fact succeed in elaborating a more sophisticated model. Why then did they come up with practically the same results? The reason could perhaps lie in the nature of the 'mathematical model' and its inability to express social aspects which are of extreme importance in investigating the future. It could also lie in the fact that the co-operation imperative and the distribution of roles between the regions of the world and between the poor and the rich are not the type of conclusions to be drawn from a mathematical model but are conclusions to which the sponsors of the model are receptive at the outside.

Without doubt, this endeavour added a great deal to our fund of technical knowledge in the area of systems analysis and studying the interaction between regional systems. Also, it reached a number of well-intentioned conclusions, namely, that the world *problematique* can be resolved through co-operation rather than confrontation; that the greatest obstacles to co-operation are the short-term gains that might be obtained through confrontation; and that the developed industrial countries must help the developing countries not through the sale of products but through the transfer of investment funds, to help them produce by and for themselves within the framework of a new international division of labour.

In conclusion, we would like to mention briefly the main features of this endeavour.

(1) Devoting much space to the global energy crisis, it nevertheless confined its treatment of the issue to having the energy sector govern the other elements of the model. What this means in application is that if a shortfall should occur in energy resources, it would inevitably entail a proportionate drop in production in certain sectors.
(2) Though much concerned with citing demographic data for each region of the world, it fails to study the dynamic relationship between demography and development. Further, its concern with the issue of demography is limited to calculating the workforce, population ratio and, occasionally, migration levels, while it does not see the link between death-rates and food shortages in regions with protein- and calorie-deficiencies.
(3) The study talks of the flow of goods from a world pool of resources and products while totally neglecting bilateral relations between regions—an oversight that is not

redeemed by the model's attempt to link imports to GNP, or by its representation of the exports of each region as a share of global exports. However, this oversight does not affect the other parts of the model.

(4) In its representation of the labour market and the phenomenon of labour migration, the study uses a special model to deal with the Middle East and North Africa regions.

(5) The mathematical equations in this model are extremely simple, covering neither the feedback effects between variables over long spans of time nor the effects of price changes, except through capital coefficients and through that proportion of production directed towards investment in producer goods.

(6) The model's attitude to environmental issues is similar to that adopted by its predecessor, first, in that it reduces the problem to one of removing the effects of pollution rather than avoiding it in the first place, and, second, in that it represents environmental issues through a sub-system that is practically isolated from other sub-systems.

(7) The point of departure in the calculations used in the various scenarios put forward by the study is the determination of the volume of foreign aid and rates of investment for each region in the light of available resources.

(8) The criteria used to determine what the model considers to be the advantages enjoyed by the Middle East and North Africa are the region's financial surpluses in the industrialized countries, rather than the development of the region's own capabilities and the capital accumulation conducive to its development.

3. The Fundacion Bariloche model

Among the many global models available, the Latin American world-model, built by the Fundacion Bariloche in the Argentine, stands in a class apart. Unlike the works of Forrester and Meadows or Mesarovic and Pestel, which claim scientific objectivity and ideological neutrality, the Fundacion Bariloche model freely admits an ideological bias in favour of the Third World and adopts a normative approach to the international order.[9] It deplores the deteriorating conditions of today's world, which it attributes to exploitative and unjust establishments, both on a global and national scale. Noting that the misery, which other models predict will soon engulf the whole world, is a condition already familiar to most of its inhabitants, the team which elaborated this model advocates a new, socialistic society based on mass participation, where private ownership of means of production would not be an instrument of privilege and domination or consumption an end in itself, but where production would be geared to meet basic needs determined collectively. Thus the Fundacion Bariloche model openly adopts a theoretical stand based on recent trends in developmental thought in Third-World countries.

The studies conducted within the framework of the model's research programme demonstrate that the 'natural limits' which other global models, such as *Limits to Growth*, claim to be insuperable, are in fact not so rigid and can be bent through increased knowledge.[10] The purpose in building the model was to show, in quantitative terms, the feasibility of establishing the proposed new society and in particular, of satisfying mankind's basic needs in the way of food, housing, education and health. In other words, the aim was to show that the threatened collapse of the world system could be averted if new policies designed to establish the new society were adopted.

The model divides the world into four regions, one for the developed world and three for the developing countries (Africa, Asia and Latin America). It consists of three main sub-systems: population; food in the world economy and allocation of resources. When talking of Third-World countries, the model stresses the importance of development in a regional framework, asserting that 'a group of Third-World countries can achieve a high degree of collective self-reliance by pooling their domestic resources'.[11]

From the technical point of view, the Latin American model is characterized by two main features: first, the presence of mutual inter-relations between sub-systems and constituent elements in a more comprehensive manner;[12] its adoption of an optimization approach in respect of the allocation of labour and capital among various economic sectors, by maximizing an objective function whose basic arguments are life-expectancy at birth and an index of quality of life (the proportion of GDP devoted to the consumption of goods and services in excess of the quota allocated to the satisfaction of basic needs).

According to the conclusions drawn by the model from its scenario of an alternative concept of international solidarity, the basic needs of the earth's inhabitants can be met within a period of sixty years, starting at 1980, if the advanced countries would allocate as little as two per cent of their GDP in the form of untied aid to Africa and Asia. In this logic, it appears unnecessary to heed the call of previous models to curb population growth in the Third World, an enterprise which is in any case not feasible in the absence of suitable social and economic conditions. By the same token, the collapse predicted by the doomsday models is no more than an outcome of the perpetuation of outdated forms of socio-economic organization prevailing in today's world.

The calculations made by the team on the basis of the model are instructive in showing the positive role that can be played by a more egalitarian form of social organization on both the local and global levels in the long-term preservation of resources to satisfy the needs of future generations. Two-thirds of the world's inhabitants live in abject poverty, while the remainder practise conspicious consumption, although they are now waking up to the destructive effects of such wasteful patterns on nature and the environment. In this connection, the Fundacion Bariloche team criticizes both the western and eastern European patterns of consumption. Calling for a more 'idealistic' society, the team identifies some features of this society in the area of social justice and popular participation.[13] But if man is ever to reach this society, it can only be through a conscious normative process—hence the importance of the mathematical model which, by comparing what is with what could be, can help guide us along the transitional path towards a better future. The calculations of the Latin American model are particularly relevant in this respect. The authors of *Catastrophe or a New Society* hold that the advanced countries, though capable of attaining higher levels of affluence, must be forced, for the sake of the common future of mankind, to curb their rates of growth and to accept new international relations. The 'population problem', a central issue in similar exercises, is less prominent in this study, which considers the central issue to be, instead, the need for a more equitable distribution of incomes and for developing countries to build independent economic structures geared to meet the basic needs of various regional groupings among them.

According to the model, this would allow Latin America to meet the basic needs of all its inhabitants by the year 2000, while Africa can achieve the same target by 2008. Asia, however, would have to develop its agriculture substantially if collapse were to be averted. But the study warns that the present distribution of resources among the regions of the world will delay achieving the desired goal by at least two generations.

Finally, the other main features of the Latin American model were that: it treated the pollution issue in a deliberately low-key fashion—according to the model, the cure for environmental degradation lies in social organization, in shunning the western pattern of consumption and in independent technological development; it amalgamated all the criteria of meeting basic needs into one 'composite' indicator, namely, life-expectancy at birth; it attempted to chart a course towards the ideal society but it failed to spell out either time paths or detailed policies, confining itself simply to laying down the conditions necessary to achieve that society; it neglected trade flows between different regions of the world, with the exception of the material mobility of capital assets; it did not allow for a good degree of disaggregation of the industrial sector.

4. Leontief's model of the world economy

Among the most important global models was the one used to analyse the input–output relationship underlying the structure of the world economy in a study conducted under the direction of Carter, Leontief and Petri. Commissioned by the United Nations Organization in 1970, the study sets its sights on the strategic considerations adopted by the UN in 1970 for the second development decade. The model divides the world into fifteen regions, and builds an 'input–output' table comprising forty-eight sectors for each region. The regions are linked to one another through international trade flows in more than forty categories of commodities, services and capital flows. The study was concerned mainly with the disparity in welfare standards between the developed and less-developed parts of the world, measured in terms of per capita money income, nutrition, pollution and anti-pollution measures,[14] energy and raw materials. The last three subjects were represented by more than one sector in the input–output table of each region, while UN demographic projections were used to estimate the size of future populations. The degree of progress in production techniques was reflected in the model by assuming the actual technical coefficients of advanced countries in the future structure of less developed countries. This analogous approach is implicit throughout the model, which assumes the same degree of pollution as that now degrading the environment of the developed industrial countries in depicting the future of the less-developed regions of the world.[15]

The future of the world economy was discussed in the form of eight scenarios, incorporating changes in production techniques, levels of production and consumption and the structure of world trade in such a way as to represent alternative development paths for the world economy starting from the base year (1970) until the year 2000.[16] The study made a broad analysis of the conditions accompanying such alternatives and the requisites for development as a function of: availability of food; possibility and cost of fighting pollution; necessary investments; the industrialization process; changes in the structure of world trade; patterns of international aid; and the need to establish a new international economic order.

The main conclusions drawn by the study in respect of Third-World development were that:

(1) even if the minimum development targets fixed for the less-developed countries in the world development strategy (6 per cent of the annual gross product) are attained, as long as the advanced countries continue at the same rate of growth, this would perpetuate the current level of disparities in per capita incomes until the year 2000;
(2) the gap in per capita income between the rich and poor of the world, which now stands at around 12.1, can be reduced to 7:1 by the year 2000, under the following conditions:[17] (a) that developing countries achieve an average growth rate in per capita income of 4.9 per cent per annum, which requires an investment rate of approximately 30–40 per cent, as well as other radical changes; (b) that population growth follow the low or medium projections of the United Nations.[18] (c) that the advanced countries reduce their per capita income growth rate from the level of 4 per cent

when gross per capita output exceeds the level of 4000 dollars per annum;

(3) no natural or technical limits stand in the way of accelerated Third-World development during this century—such limits as do exist are political-social-institutional in nature, whether in the less-developed countries themselves or in the world order;

(4) the key to solving most of the pressing problems plaguing Third-World countries lies in bringing unexploited land under cultivation, in doubling the actual productivity of land (both, though technically feasible, would require radical changes), and in establishing heavy industries in the various regions of the world;[19]

(5) maintaining an adequate supply of mineral resources until the end of the century is a problem not of scarcity but of misuse, inadequate prospecting activities for additional reserves and maldistribution between the regions of the world;

(6) environmental pollution will not pose a serious threat until the end of the century, and in the meantime, 'technological' solutions can be devised to cope with the problem;

(7) the way to solve the problem of balance of payments deficits is by establishing a new international economic order, and, in the case of developing countries with chronic deficits, to reduce their imports of manufactured goods.

From a technical viewpoint, the model exhibits a number of characteristics worth noting here. It is considered a special case in terms of the method of algorithm used as, unlike other global models, it starts with investment as an exogenous variable and from there proceeds to calculate levels of production, or vice versa. It allows for a high degree of disaggregation of the industry and energy sectors. It uses the 'input–output' model in place of the simple formulas of production functions used by other models. Its calculations, though showing the relationship between food production and mortality rates, completely neglect all internal dynamics, such as the relationship between income distribution and policies to limit spending, as well as external dynamics related to import policies, that is, it is hard to consider the model as serving the targets of meeting basic needs. It deals with international trade flows through the mechanics of the world market, and fails to take bilateral relations and sub-regional market arrangements into account.

5. The SARUM model

The SARUM model of the world, constructed by the UK Department of the Environment, tried to avoid some of the defects of other models, specifically the weakness of the data base used, and the failure to specify the theoretical basis on which the model is built.[20]

The team behind this endeavour set out to evolve a simulation model resting on a consistent theoretical basis and departing from analytically acceptable relations by which to study the future of world resources. Their model gives special importance to the effects of natural-resource depletion and technological change on the future economic balance and welfare of the world. As developed at a preliminary phase,[21] the model divides the world into three categories according to per capita income levels. The first category is exclusive to the United States, the second includes the rest of the industrialized world and the third covers the developing countries and China. By allowing for a large degree of sectoral classification,[22] the model is able to make a detailed analysis of supply and demand for food, as well as to control the degree of consistency of proportional growth across different industries. The neo-classical approach used in building the model makes 'the world operate as an integrated free market system, with no distinction between an individual working in management and striving to maximize profits, or a country striving to maximize 'economic surplus'.[23]

The model also assumes an unhindered labour mobility between sectors and regions, and does not allow for the determination of population size in the long term. It also neglects such vital issues as pollution. Still, it does exhibit some positive features, such as regional divisions and a developed data base.[24]

Among the conclusions drawn by the model is that the chances of the Third World acquiring a significant share in world industrial production are slight.[25] On the other hand, its expectations with regard to the future food situation in the Third World are among the most optimistic put forward by any model.[26] This is due not only to its superior data base, but also to the fact that, from the start, it deliberately emphasized high levels of agricultural investment in developing countries, by resorting to the most optimistic assumptions regarding the possibilities of horizontal and vertical expansion of agriculture in such countries.[27]

From the technical viewpoint, the main characteristics of this endeavour can be summed up briefly. Its approach to the agricultural sector is among the most comprehensive yet attempted by any model. It allows for a high degree of disaggregation for the activities of the industrial sector. It is obviously concerned with the relationship between consumption and income distribution. It is concerned with bilateral trade arrangements between the different sub-regions within its tripartite division, as well as with the terms of trade and the mutual effects between international trade and the other parts of the model.

6. The Interfutures study

Commissioned by the Organization for Economic Co-operation and Development in 1975, the Interfutures study set out to investigate 'the future development of advanced industrial societies in harmony with that of developing countries'. Presenting itself not as a forecasting exercise but as an analytical exploration of alternative futures the study draws upon the expertise of a large number of experts and analysts and relies to a lesser extent on quantitative models.[28] In its depiction of alternative futures, it focuses on economic and technological factors without, however, losing sight of social and political aspects.

More than any other model, it sets out to make specific policy recommendations on which the OECD's member-states can draw in making decisions of a long-term nature,[29] especially as regards energy policies and policies related to co-operation[30] in the field of technology transfers.[31] As far as external investments are concerned, the model uses a more detailed approach than the SARUM model by constructing five alternate scenarios for the future.[32]

The results of these scenarios were particularly useful in formulating some policy recommendations concerning the future of energy, industrialization and the importing of machinery and capital equipment. The model subdivides the world into twelve regions, thus allowing for meaningful comparisons with the regional results of the Leontief and Mesarovic models. Within each region, the model specifies eleven sectors, enabling it to use a certain degree of disaggregation for the industrial sectors, particularly those branches producing capital goods, construction and other manufacturing industries. In the agricultural sector, the disaggregation specifies subsectors of food production, land reclamation, irrigation and basic agricultural inputs.

In respect of Third-World countries, after a brief survey of their likely futures and of concepts of the North–South Dialogue in the various scenarios, the study comes up with a number of predictions: the middle-income developing countries stand a good chance of growth if the advanced industrial countries provide them with markets and part of their financing requirements,[33] while for the poor developing countries the chances of growth are nil.[34] For Third-World countries as a whole, dependency on food imports will increase.

Accordingly, the study recommends that the advanced industrial countries assist developing countries in acquiring appropriate technologies, compatible with the conditions of their societies and environment.[35] In the meantime, the world will witness a higher degree of internationalization of industrial activities within the framework of a new international division of labour, based on a concentration of scientific research, technological development and information systems in the countries of the North and the relocation of a substantial part of conventional industries in those of the South. With this re-deployment of activities between North and South, the study sees the share of developing countries in world trade increasing from the level of 12 per cent at which it stood in the early seventies, to 18–22 per cent by the turn of the century (excluding crude oil in both cases). Finally, the study points out that the anxiety now afflicting the world system will remain until the share of OPEC oil in the total supplies of world energy is significantly reduced,[36] and exhorts the advanced industrial countries to reduce their growth rates in anticipation of the expected increase in growth rates of the less-developed countries.[37]

7. The Arab region in global models

Despite all the differences and variations between the many countries making up the Arab nation, global models should have classified these countries in their regional sub-divisions of the world as one distinct entity. More than one argument can be advanced to justify this approach.

(1) The international community, through its various agencies, has, on many occasions and in various spheres, agreed to deal with the Arab nation as one entity.

(2) Given that most global models set out to probe the future of various world regions and, indeed, to recommend specific strategies and policies for these regions, it would appear more logical if, in formulating their visions, model builders took such factors as historical and cultural homogeneity, unity of language and geographical and resource complementarity into account.

Compared with some country groupings classified as regions in various global models, the Arab countries have more in common in terms of history, language and culture, not to mention the remarkable interdependence of natural, human and financial resources.[38]

(3) Taking the size of the population of the Arab region relative to the total world population as our criterion, we would find it representing a very high ratio as compared to other regions of the world considered by global models as distinct regional entities. At present, the Arab region accounts for some 3.9 per cent of the world population and is expected to rise to 4.7 per cent by the turn of the century. This ratio, while slightly lower than the relative ratio of the population of the Soviet Union, will be higher than that of the United States.[39]

In addition to this enormous human potential, the Arab region contains huge resources of energy, both renewable and non-renewable (53.8 per cent of proven world reserves of crude oil,[40] about 13.5 per cent of proven world reserves of natural gas[41] and unlimited solar energy), vast land areas, (more than one-tenth of the land surface area of the globe), cultivated land (plus about 3.4 per cent which can be cultivated under prevailing economic and technological conditions,[42] and 4.4 per cent which is potentially cultivable).[43] To these can be added phosphate[44] and iron-ore reserves.[45]

But more important still is the profound desire for Arab rapprochement, solidarity and integration, even for political unity in one form or another. This powerful latent desire for unification was behind the establishment of the League of Arab States in 1945, and the proliferation of an extensive network of specialized Arab agencies and organizations (official and semi-official).

Surely all these indicators warrant a treatment of the Arab nation as one distinct region within the framework of any global model.[46] In fact, to date, the manner in which the Arab region is depicted in most global models raises a number of doubts and reservations, first, because the Arab region is inappropriately represented and, second, because some of its characteristic features are deliberately overlooked.

As the success of any model depends largely on its ability to discern the factors likely to cause most impact on the future of development, as well as on its accurate representation of the specific nature of the society under study, those engaged in modelling activities should elaborate models capable of capturing the structural changes required in developing countries rather than simply resort to a standard model applicable to all world regions, developed and developing alike. For example, the structural changes expressed in a model dealing with the Third-World regions should pay more attention to human development issues such as skill-acquisition and improvement, workforce mobilization and allocation and the role of indigenous technical innovation.

While it is true that all these issues raise certain questions relating to type of leadership, ideology and forms of mass participation which are difficult to express in quantitative terms as part of the formal structure of a model, they can at least illustrate the normative character of the model. A model which sets out to chart a course of action and to fix the requirements necessary to attain the targets of meeting basic needs in the long term, can express such requirements in terms of the quantitative constraints on available resources and of the relationship between material development and saving policies on the one hand, and income distribution on the other. In order to express the required structural changes, the model would have to rearrange the sectoral mixes in the national economy in order to sustain a new production structure geared to the satisfaction of basic needs of the population. Such changes would also be reflected in the technical coefficients of production and the use pattern of natural resources.[47]

Education, for example, represents one of the main inputs in the process of development in that it helps mobilize the individual's productive and innovative capacities. Identifying the structural changes to be brought to the educational system in line with development targets should not be confined to specifying future trends of *enrolment ratios* at different educational levels or *illiteracy ratios* within different age groups, as was the case in most global models. Instead they should spell out more clearly the respective roles of different educational channels in achieving long-term social aims and in expanding and upgrading indigenous technological capabilities.

In most cases, global model builders were, understandably enough, conditioned by the dynamics and patterns of growth in their own countries and preoccupied with considerations and problems with a more direct bearing on the future as conceived in terms of the experience of these countries. On the other hand, any plausible global modelling activity dealing with the future of developing countries would have to depart from a clear and explicit understanding of the feasible and desirable features of the development process in such societies.

This confirms our thesis that any process of development represented in a model should emanate from a clear theoretical vision, over and above the internal consistency in the formal structure of the model. Unfortunately, however most global models resorted to the *analogous approach*, extrapolating the present structures of advanced industrial countries onto the future of Third-World countries. By focusing on the mechanical extrapolation of basic economic structures, such global models were unable to accommodate processes of social, political and economic restructuring in developing countries. As tools by which to explore the alternative futures of Third-World countries, these models were consequently inadequate. That is not to say, however, that some global models did not reach the conclusion that the main constraints in the way of sustained growth of Third-World economies were political, social and institutional in nature, whether at the country-specific or global level.[48] But, for all that, none of these models, with one exception, saw fit to incorporate these specific constraints—whose existence they themselves admit—into their assumptions, structure or scenarios.[49]

To take due account of these social political and institutional structural changes in building a model would require a clear ideological stand on the part of the model builder. It is difficult to expect a group drawn from the advanced industrial countries, with their own interests and concerns, to adopt theoretical stands attuned to Third-World aspirations.[50] This is graphically illustrated, for instance, in the widely divergent conclusions reached by the Fundacion Bariloche model, constructed by a group of Third-World economists, on the one hand, and by the Mesarovic–Pestel model on the other. Such very different outcomes only go to show that global models can in no way be regarded as neutral tools.[51]

8. Perception of the Arab region in global models

A closer look at how the Arab region fares in global models would reveal that most of these models tend to regard the region in the long term as an *oil and fuel depot*.[52] This view helps to explain the reluctance of global models to address the region as a distinct entity,[53] in total disregard of social, economic and political realities and of the recognition by the international community of the potential and aspirations of the Arab nation.

Thus we find non-Arab countries classified in regional divisions containing Arab countries or, conversely, certain Arab countries excluded from their appropriate regional location. Indeed, none of the scenarios put out by global models ever bothered to undertake an analysis of likely forms of future co-operation between Arab countries taken as an integral whole.

For example, in the United Nations' model for the future of the world economy, known as the Leontief model, the Arab countries are split between two of the fifteen regions of the world covered by the model. This division is indicative of the 'oil depot' view of the Arab region held by the advanced industrial countries. In this logic, the Arab oil-rich states were amalgamated with other non-Arab oil-states in the Middle East and Africa region, while other relatively rich non-oil Arab countries were lumped together with similar countries in Africa and other regions.

Another case is the Mesarovic model, where Cyprus and Iran could have been removed from the North Africa and Middle East region and Mauritania, Somalia and Sudan introduced, to make it a purely Arab region.[54] By the same token, the Leontief model could have excluded Iran, Nigeria and Gabon from the region labelled 'oil countries of the Middle East and North Africa' and Israel and seven African countries from the region labelled 'Arid Africa', and re-classified the countries remaining in the two regions as one Arab region. The regional classification of the Interfutures study, for its part, could have, by the simple removal of Iran and Israel from the eleventh region and insertion of Somalia and Mauritania, come up with a purely Arab region.

It could be said, in defence of these arbitrary divisions of the Arab region, that the oil countries exhibit similar socio-economic features which set them apart from the non-oil countries—Arab or non-Arab. The truth is that the model completely dismisses any possibility of integration among countries of the Arab region.

However, to give the Interfutures study its due, it does, contrary to other similar exercises, acknowledge the existence of a distinct Arab entity. In its analytical section, the study makes explicit mention of the 'Arab world' and of the diverse resources in which it abounds.[55] It admits that the 'Arab world' is unique among Third-World regions in that it displays a distinctive cultural homogeneity backed by a political awareness revolving around the idea of one nation. This being so, the 'Arab world' could be expected to figure prominently in any future arrangement of inter-regional co-operation, although, as the study is quick to point out, many political and social obstacles stand in the way of such a process.[56] Unfortunately, the Interfutures study did not pursue this line for reasoning, nor did it explore the future prospects of Arab regional co-operation.[57]

9. Selected images of the Arab region in forecasts of global models

At this point, it might be useful to look at some of the future images of the Arab region as portrayed by global models, with a view to identifying the basic assumptions on which these views reside, to ascertain how far they take Arab goals and aspirations —inasmuch as they acknowledge them at all—into account, and how satisfactory the future achievements and welfare levels of the Arab nation appear in the results put out by these models.

The fact is that no global model, not even when, like those put out by the Club of Rome, it sought to identify aims, made any real attempt to probe deeply into the distinctive goals and aspirations shared by all the Arab countries. The treatment accorded to the Arab region by the Laszlo report to the Club of Rome, entitled *Goals for Mankind*, is a case in point.[58] This report dismisses the goals of Arab[59] governments as short-sighted, those of Arab intellectuals as flights of fancy, and those of the remaining strata of the peoples of the region as individualistic and socially unfruitful.[60] The report did not deign to propose alternatives to these 'short-sighted' government goals, and completely ignored the fact that the aims propounded by some intellectuals, more representative of the majority of the region's peoples, can be translated into alternative socio-political policies which are not only eminently feasible, but, perhaps, even more realistic in the long term.

In this respect, the Long-Term Planning Group for Arab countries,[61] based at the INP in Cairo, set out to compile a list, as it were, of declared Arab goals, gathered from many long-term Arab plans and programmes, both country-specific and regional. Interestingly enough, a declared common goal was to reduce Arab dependence on the outside world through instituting domestic structural changes. It is also worth noting that, unlike many global model builders, most Arab intellectuals formulate the goals of development for the Arab nation in the light of recent trends in developmental thought, and with an eye on the need for revolutionary change.[62]

One would have thought that, after three decades of experimentation in development, global models would have been more attuned to the real needs of the majority of people in the long term. Unfortunately, however, apart from the Fundacion Bariloche model, which set itself the goal of proving that satisfying the basic needs of Third-World countries is feasible and attainable in the foreseeable future, all other global models were more concerned with protecting the interests of the North, while maintaining an open dialogue with the South. Their view of future Third-World development is limited to the projection of prevailing western patterns of industrialization, urbanization and lifestyles onto the future structures of developing countries.

A number of examples can be cited to illustrate this point. The Leontief study, whose terms of reference are the western pattern of industrialization and the material norms of development, holds that the real problem lies in promoting relations and exchange between developed and developing countries.[63] To this end, the study recommends that the developing countries should allocate something between 30 and 35 per cent of their Gross Regional Product (GRP) for investment purposes in order to reduce the gap in per capita income between advanced industrial countries and developing countries to a ratio of 7:1, while relying less on foreign finance and more on trade to reach this result.[64]

In its scenario for the year 2025, the Mesarovic study[65] puts the maximal price for crude oil at 'around 50% higher than the initial oil price' (in 1974). In calling for the uninterrupted supply of Arab oil at high levels to the advanced industrial countries, the study points to such advantages accruing to the Arab region as the maximization of the amount of excess revenues that can be used to accumulate wealth outside the region (i.e. the advanced industrial countries). According to the study, any alternative course of action, such as limiting production to a level below the demand—whether or not this provokes retaliatory measures from the advanced countries—would result in a lower GRP and a lower level of wealth accumulation.[66]

In other words, the study is asking the Arab region to accept the depletion of its resources for the sake of preserving lifestyles in the advanced industrial countries in exchange for a 'permanent' role in the new energy industry through the setting up of solar energy plants in 'North Africa and the Middle East'.[67]

In another study which they conducted on the cost-benefit analysis of human resources mobility within the Arab region, the Mesarovic team adopted the same approach as that used in the scenario analysis contained in the *Mankind at the Turning Point* study.[68] For example, the study envisaged the most beneficial future for a country like Egypt as lying in the continued exportation of Egyptian labour to the Arab oil-rich countries. This view was sharply criticized by the Cairo group for Long-Term Planning for Arab Countries as neglecting many of the socio-economic aspects associated with the phenomenon of labour migration, in both the country of origin and the host country, and thus making for a partial and mechanical outlook to the dynamics of the process of inter-Arab migration. The Cairo Group's critique is perhaps best borne out by the negative impact that the large-scale export of Yeminite labour has had on that country's domestic economy.

Another application of the Mesarovic methodology can be seen in a study undertaken by the same team under commission by UNIDO,[69] which argues that if countries of the Middle East region were to increase the price of oil by an average of 3 per cent per annum until it reaches a level 150 per cent higher than the 1974 reference level, and assuming that the level of world demand for the region's oil stands at 14 billion barrels per annum, an equilibrium level of oil production can be struck. On the other hand, should world-demand rise above such a level, as is expected by the turn of the century, then the advanced countries would have two options: either to counter this by raising prices of food and manufactured goods while stepping up research efforts for alternative substitutes for oil, or to resort to a more co-operative approach by calling on countries of the Middle East region to supply them with their oil needs without putting any ceiling on levels of oil production and to recycle the accumulated surplus to the industrial world, in exchange for part of this surplus being invested in producing hydrogen through the use of solar energy, which is available in abundance in the Middle East, and exporting it to the developed world.[70]

10. Images of the Arab future emerging from computations of global models

In this section, we shall present some examples of the prognosis of future developments given by various global models dealing with the Arab region.

One difficulty we shall be facing here is that none of the models, as previously indicated, deals with the Arab region as an integral whole. In some models, where the countries of the Arab region are scattered among many regions or strata (for example, the Fundacion Bariloche and the Mesarovic models) it will be virtually impossible to get round this difficulty. We are thus left with the results of only two models to contemplate: the Leontief model and the SARUM model, as embodied in the Interfutures study.

Let us begin by comparing some of the results drawn from the computations of the basic scenarios in the Leontief study as they relate to the two regional divisions comprising the Arab countries[71] with those comprising advanced countries, such as 'North America' and 'Japan', in the light of selected socio-economic indicators set forth in Table 3.1.

Table 3.1 Some socio-economic indicators taken from the Leontief model—scenario X* for the years 1970 and 2000

Indicator	Year	Oil countries of Middle East	Arid Africa	North America	Japan
Annual growth rate in GRP (%)	1970 2000	9.0	5.5	3.3	4.9
Share in total global GNP (%)	1970 2000	1.1 4.0	0.8 1.0	32.9 31.0	6.2 6.5
Share of manufacturing industry in GDP (%)	1970 2000	11.3 31.0	33.6 35.9	39.3 38.4	44.7 46.1
Balance of trade (US $ billions at 1970 prices)	1970 2000	5.3 4.5	0.6 16.2	0.2 39.1	2.6 56.6
Daily per capita calorie supply (thousand/day	1970 2000	2.0 2.9	2.5 2.5	3.2 3.2	2.4 3.2
Daily per capita protein supply (gm/day)	1970 2000	53 92	72 78	96 100	71 117

*Standard scenario.

It is clear from the table that the wide gulf now separating the non-oil Arab and African countries from the oil-producing countries, on the one hand, and that separating the oil-producing countries from North America and Japan, on the other, will still be there at the beginning of the twenty-first century. The GNP growth-rates projected for the non-oil countries by the Leontief study are lower than those expected to be achieved by the oil countries, which are expected to achieve a more diversified economic structure by the turn of the century (through increasing the contribution of the manufacturing industry to the GNP), while the non-oil countries are expected to experience very little change in their economic structures. It also predicts that the non-oil countries will suffer from increasing balance of payment deficits while the oil countries will continue to enjoy a surplus until the year 2000 (though nowhere near the huge surplus expected to be realized by the advanced industrial countries).

In the final analysis, all this is reflected in the level of meeting basic needs of the populations living in the countries covered by the study. For example, while non-oil countries are not expected to show any notable increase in per capita food consumption over the next thirty years, the oil countries will approach the per capita food consumption level prevailing in the advanced industrial countries at the end of the same period. This only confirms the thesis that, in the absence of any compatability between the resources and potentials of the two groups of Arab countries, the 'welfare gap' between the rich and poor countries of the Arab region can only continue to widen.

In an attempt to draw some meaningful comparisons between indicators of future development for the Arab region as a whole *vis-à-vis* other regions of the world, as well as between the oil and non-oil countries of the Arab region, we rearranged the country classifications[72] adopted by the Leontief study in such a way as to reach approximate results for the Arab regions as a whole and for oil and non-oil countries taken separately.[73]

Table 3.2 compares some of the socio-economic indicators computed for Arab oil and non-oil countries respectively and for the Arab region taken as a whole with those computed by the Leontief model for the Soviet Union and North America for the same period (1970–2000).

As we can see from the table, the level of economic performance in the Arab oil countries will remain very low in comparison to that of advanced countries. Indeed, the per capita share in the GDP of oil countries is expected to stand at no more than half that of the Soviet Union and one-third that of North America in the year 2000. These percentages drop to 47 and 31 per cent respectively for *per capita consumption* and to around 45 and 27 per cent for the per capita share in the value of capital assets.

As to the comparison made between indicators of expected economic performance in the Arab oil and non-oil countries,

Table 3.2 Some socio-economic indicators taken from Leontief's model of the *Future of the World Economy* for the years 1970 and 2000

Indicators	Year	Arab oil countries	Arab non-oil countries	Arab region	USSR	North America
Indicators relating to meeting basic needs: daily per capita calorie supply (thousands)	1970 2000	2.0 3.2	2.5 2.3	2.3 2.6	3.2 3.2	3.2 3.2
Daily per capita protein supply (gm)	1970 2000	53 106	72 70	66 83	92 108	96 100
Level of employment (person/year) work per 100 inhabitants	1970 2000	10 59	8 15	9 30	47 50	40 51
Indicators of economic power: GDP (US $ billions, constant 1970 prices)	1970 2000	12 336	18 59	30 395	435 1992	1059 2721
Capital assets (US $ billions, constant 1970 prices)	1970 2000	9 720	17 89	26 809	738 4753	2252 7543
Balance of Trade (US $ billions, constant 1970 prices)	1970 2000	0.7 141.7	- 8.7	0.7 133.9	- 106	2 97
Indicators of economic performance: GDP per capita (US $ thousands, constant 1970 prices)	1970 2000	0.29 3.11	0.21 0.29	0.23 1.28	1.79 6.21	4.62 9.07
Per capita share of capital assets (US $ thousands, constant 1970 prices)	1970 2000	0.2 6.7	0.2 0.4	0.2 2.6	3.0 14.8	9.8 15.1
Per capita consumption (US $ thousands, constant 1970 prices)	1970 2000	0.16 1.74	0.15 0.22	0.15 0.75	1.10 3.68	2.97 5.54

this shows up the enormous disparity in the pure economic power wielded by each of these two groups of countries as reflected in levels of GNP and of capital formation. This disparity is also exemplified in the huge balance of payments deficit predicted for the non-oil Arab countries as compared to the steady increase in the level of balance of payments surplus for the oil countries, which is expected to exceed 140 billion dollars (at 1970 prices) by the year 2000.

The disparity would appear even more dramatic if we were to take the differences in population sizes between the two groups of countries into account. This would bring the value of the first group's GDP to less than 10 per cent of that of the second group in the year 2000, while the corresponding figure for the per capita share in the value of capital assets would stand at no more than around 6 per cent.

The disparity in levels of economic performance will also be reflected in levels of meeting basic needs, where the glowing prospects for the Arab oil countries are in stark contrast to the expected deterioration in levels of meeting basic food needs in non-oil Arab countries over the coming two decades. Despite a slight increase in the level of utilization of manpower by the non-oil Arab countries, this level is not expected to exceed 30 per cent of that prevailing in advanced countries in the year 2000, and about one-quarter of the level expected to prevail in the Arab oil countries in the same year.

Once again, we would like to stress that the disparities revealed by the model's computations are a natural outcome of the mechanics of economic growth assumed by the model, and of its distribution of Arab potentials between two separate groups of countries linked together only by trade flows—which are very weak at that point. There is no doubt that an effective compatibility between the resources of both Arab oil and non-oil countries can greatly enhance the level of economic performance of the non-oil countries, prevent the deterioration of levels of meeting basic needs and achieve mutual benefits for both groups of countries. The benefits accruing to the group of oil countries need not necessarily take the form of high levels of economic growth, but can be reflected in the development of indigenous technological capabilities and in the promotion of a liberated and independent Arab presence in international affairs—over and above the fact that the risks of instability in the region will be greatly reduced with the reduction of socio-economic disparities between the two groups of countries.

All the reservations we have expressed on the results drawn by the computations of the Leontief model can be summed up under one main heading, namely, its failure to consider the possibility of Arab integration, even at the purely economic level. If seen from a more general developmental viewpoint, which is only fitting when we talk of the dimensions of the Arab future, the model is found lacking in that it fails to address the issue of restructuring the socio-economic-political build-up at pan-Arab level in order to produce new, qualitatively different systems. The main benefit to be drawn from the previous analysis is that it highlights the dangers of allowing the present state of affairs in the Arab region to continue and confirms that any perceptive investigation of the region's future must go beyond mechanical extrapolations, which depart from the status quo and do not allow for significant structural changes.

While the Interfutures study was more concerned with socio-political aspects, the main quantitative results computed from the formal global model were couched in terms of economic indicators. For example, the study makes the following predictions regarding per capita share in GDP in three alternative scenarios dealing with the nature of the process of economic growth and social cohesion in industrialized countries and the relationship of these countries with the less-developed countries.

Scenario 1: Rapid growth and close co-operation among industrialized countries, a good measure of internal social cohesion and consolidation of relations between the countries of the North and South.

Scenario 2: Slow growth, and close co-operation among industrialized countries, greater degree of internal social disruption and, again, consolidation of relations between the countries of the North and South.

Scenario 3: Slow growth and close co-operation among industrialized countries, greater degree of internal social disruption and confrontation between the countries of the North and South.

As can be seen from Table 3.3, the region of North Africa and the Middle East is expected to suffer a decline in the level of economic performance proportionally greater than other less-developed countries (LDCs) as a result of the sluggish economic growth in industrialized countries. On the other hand, a confrontation between the industrialized countries and the LDCs would lead to a drop in the level of economic performance—again the burden of adjustment would be proportionally heavier on the countries of North Africa and the Middle East. This is indicative of how dependent the economies of the countries of this region are on those of the industrialized countries, and, again, assumes the perpetuation of the present international economic order.

Table 3.3 Per-capita share in GDP according to the three scenarios

Scenario	Per capita share in GDP (US $ thousands, constant 1970 prices)		
	Industrialized countries	North Africa and Middle East	LDCs
First	7.7	2.5	0.9
Second	6.1	1.9	0.8
Third	4.7	1.7	0.6

In terms of the quantitative and descriptive features of the study, the importance of the North Africa and Middle East region derives mainly from oil. The study also predicts that the region will adopt a neutral stand in international affairs between the advanced North and the less-developed South. None the less, the study made the following observations on the Arab region. An abundance and diversity of resources, together with a cultural homogeneity, opens huge possibilities for inter-regional co-operation which could be a basic determinant for the region's future. The excessive vulnerability of the development process to levels of fluctuation and performance in the advanced industrial countries was noted. There is a possibility of instability and socio-political upheavals which could result from the acute imbalances associated with the 'oil' or 'post-oil' eras. Unfortunately, however, the model did not incorporate these specific features of the Arab region either in its formal structure or in the conclusions it reached. All this leads us to wonder whether the 'images' and 'predictions' put forward by global models, which are neither satisfactory nor reassuring for most Arabs, are the only ones possible, or whether there might not perhaps be alternative and feasible images for the Arab future. These then are the questions we shall try to answer in Part II which will attempt to extract elements of future outlooks and strategic visions through a critical review of key Arab strategy documents prepared by or for specialized Arab agencies. It is hoped that, in this way, a complete picture will emerge of how the Arabs see themselves in the mirror of the future.

Notes

1. The builders of this model consider it sufficiently developed 'to be of some use to decision-makers'. We shall discuss the 'world system' which they consider worth preserving and the type of decision they consider should be taken. Compare Donella H. Meadows *et al.*, *The Limits to Growth*, New York, Universe Books, 1979, p. 20.
2. The number of sub-systems ranges between 5 in Forrester's prototype model (namely, population, capital formation, natural resources, the percentage of capital allocated to agriculture and pollution) and 15 in one of the versions of the 'Tregionalized World' model. Interaction between these sub-systems is weak, a common defect of global models being their neglect of several important relationships between sub-systems.
3. Mainly population, followed by industrialization, pollution, food production and, finally, resource depletion.
4. However, they do not deny that global equilibrium is a state where the basic material needs of each person on earth are satisfied and where each person has an equal opportunity to realize his individual human potential. See J. M. Richardson, 'Global Modelling (1): The Models', *Futures*, **12**, 5, October 1978, p. 388.
5. Actually, no single or fixed structure exists for this group of global models. The work begun by Mesarovic and Pestel was taken up by the consulting firm Systems Analysis Inc. (SAI) of Cleveland, which specializes in building models and selling them to decision-makers. See Mihajlo D. Mesarovic and Edward C. Pestel, directors, 'Present State in the Development of the Multilevel Tregionalized World System Models,' Systems Analysis Inc. (SAI), Cleveland, 1977.
6. Richardson, "Global Modelling (1): The Models', op cit., pp. 389 and 390.
7. Essentially in the Third World. But the study does not propose any effective or humane method to bring this about. Failure to take due account of the relationship between population growth and socio-economic aspects—as is the case with the first model in the series put out by Mesarovic and Pestel—is bound to lead to such simplistic proposals.
8. Note that the main features of 'co-operation' between the various regions of the world in this and subsequent models are determined *a priori* in the construction of the model. We shall discuss this in the coming pages. Even the policies necessary for the 'organic growth' referred to are obscure. Compare in this respect A. Peccei and A. King 'Commentary', in Mihajlo D. Mesarovic and Edward C. Pestel, *Mankind at the Turning Point, the Second Report to the Club of Rome*, New York, Dutton, Readers' Digest Press, 1974, pp. 203–6.

9. A claim that is completely unjustified. For commentators on global modelling activities, the ideological bias is quite clear. See, for example, R. Petrella, 'Ideological Basis and Impact of World Models: A Comparison', in: *Seminar on Future Forecasts and World Models, Rio de Janiero, 28 November–3 December 1965.*
10. According to the Fundacion Bariloche study, proven and probable reserves of natural resources must be assessed against prevailing economic and technological conditions, a notion that we shall discuss further on. Compare Amilcar O. Herrera, *et al., Catastrophe or a New Society? A Latin American World Model*, Ottawa, International Development Research Centre, 1976, pp. 27–34.
11. Ibid., p.9.
12. A notable refinement in the model is the linkage it makes between population variables and socio-economic conditions, so that the size of the population can be determined as an endogenous variable in the model, given the assumed initial conditions and from the behaviour of economic and social variables in the model (levels of meeting basic needs, including housing and education, are met by corresponding levels of income distribution). If we compare this with other models concerned with the relationship between growth and population, namely *The Limits to Growth* and *Mankind at the Turning Point*, we find the former concerned with the impact of availability of protein and calories on mortality and birth rates.
13. The main features of this 'ideal society': the satisfaction of basic individual and collective needs, and not profits, is what would determine the volume of production; property will be neither private nor state-owned.
14. This makes it the second model—after *The Limits to Growth*—which addressed itself to the issue of pollution, albeit in more detail, as it includes concrete proposals for pollution abatement.
15. Technical coefficients usually assume different values at different points in time. Such values are all derived with reference to the sectoral and technical economic structure of the United States of America.
16. All assessments of global models agree that these models are far from perfect and could do with a great deal of improvement. This is true most of all of the model constructed by Leontief for the United Nations, which needs to be substantially modified and developed.
17. In Leontief's study: Wassily Leontief *et al., The Future of the World Economy, Preliminary Report*, New York, United Nations Department of Economic and Social Affairs, 1976.
18. Notice that these medium projections made by the UN are close to Bariloche's expectations but higher than those of both *The Limits to Growth* and the Mesarovic group as regards total world population. But they are much higher than Mesarovic's expectations as regards the Third World, particularly Africa.

19. As a result, the computations of the UN model exceed the target of generating 25 per cent of total world production in the Third World. The projections of the Bariloche model come very close to that while those of Mesarovic fall far short of the pre-assigned target (around 19 per cent only).
20. Compare Richardson, 'Global Modelling (1): The Models', op. cit., p. 392–3.
21. The model was designed and its data base compiled in such a way as to allow for a finer disaggregation into ten regions, as in the Mesarovic model, or fifteen regions, as in the Leontief model. We shall refer later to a finer degree of disaggregation adopted by the SARUM model, in our review of the Interfutures study.
22. The model comprises thirteen sectors in each area, bound together by an input–output model. Price mechanism will determine trade flows between the sectors, after allowing for transport cost and tariff and non-tariff barriers. See OECD, Interfutures, 'Summary of Global Models Intermediate Paper: FUT/DW/SI/A—Current Research and World Models', November 1976, p. 9.
23. The model makes a good effort to express the relationship between the shares of different socio-economic groups in nutrition as compared to national averages. More important is its attempt to go beyond published national statistics by supplementing these with field studies in poor areas.
24. Compare P. C. Roberts and D. Norse, 'The Problems of Food Production in Certain African Countries', in: IIASA Symposium on Global Modelling, 2nd Laxenburg, 1976, *MOIRA: Food and Agriculture Model*, ed. Gerbart Bruckman, Laxenburg, Austria, IIASA, 1977.
25. Much less than the target set by the Group of 77, which the SARUM study considers too ambitious as it fails to take into account the limits on the resources of developing countries.
26. For example, it predicts that the per capita calorie intake per day in the year 2000 will be around 3130 (as compared to 3000 predicted by Bariloche and 2600 by Leontief).
27. For example, the SARUM study predicts that the maximum level of productivity of tradition crops per hectare stands at 7.6 metric tonnes, as compared to around 4.0 metric tonnes in both the Leontief and Bariloche models. The SARUM study's predictions of cultivable lands in the world also went beyond the maximum levels predicted by other models (between 2400 and 3200 million hectares).
28. OECD, Interfutures, *Facing The Future*, p. 405.
29. Special emphasis is placed by the study on the high relative share of wages in total production in OECD countries as well as on pollution resulting from industrialization. Such emphasis is reflected in the type of working relationships proposed with the Third World, which we shall refer to further on. The reader could refer in this respect to

Part 3 of the following document: OECD Interfutures. 'Research Project on the Future Development of Advanced Industrial Societies in Harmony with that of Developing Countries', Draft Final Report, January 1979 (henceforth cited as 'Research Project',).

30. To illustrate the degree of interdependence between the different regions of the world, the study points to the special importance of Saudi oil for the economies of most countries.
31. OECD, Interfutures, 'Research Project'.
32. OECD, Interfutures, *Facing the Future*, pp. 329–30.
33. Ibid., p. 408.
34. Ibid., p. 408.
35. OECD, Interfutures, 'Research Project', part IV, p. 65.
36. OECD, Interfutures, *Facing the Future*, p. 410.
37. Ibid., p. 470.
38. For a full discussion and statistical review, see Nader Fargany: *Wasted Potentials: A Study of How Far the Arab People have Progressed Towards Their Aspirations*, Beirut, Centre for Studies on Arab Unity, 1980. The book discusses in detail Arab potentials in the way of human and land resources and oil revenues as well as the first signs of shortage in mineral resources and food supplies in the long term. This shortage is the subject of another important document, Mohamed Mahmoud El-Imam 'The Future of the Arab Development Process in the Context of International and Regional Variables', Arab Planning Institute, Kuwait, 1980, pp. 53–9. This document summarizes discussions of a group of experts who met at the invitation of the Arab Bureau of the UNDP.
39. *World Population Trends and Policies*, New York, 1979, vol. 1.
40. Petroleum Economist, *OPEC Oil Report*, 2nd edn., New York, Nichols, 1979.
41. Ibid.
42. Food and Agriculture Organization (FAO), *Production Yearbook*, 1977, Rome, FAO, 1978.
43. H. Linnemann *et al.*, eds., *MOIRA: Model of International Relations in Agriculture*, Amsterdam, North Holland; Elsevier, 1979.
44. According to statistics of the General Secretariat of the Council of Arab Economic Unity, the share of the Arab region in total world production averaged 22 per cent over the period 1970–74.
45. Iron-ore in Mauritania alone can cover the future needs of the entire Arab region. See Aziz El-Bendary, 'The Industrial Future of Arab Countries up to the Year 2000', in: *Research Project on Industrial Development*, Cairo, National Planning Institute, 1979.
46. Perhaps the only exception is the Interfutures study, which explored the effects resulting from internal socio-political changes within the industrial countries.
47. The experiment of the Fundacion Bariloche illustrates how the structure,

parameters and types of constraints could differ from one model to another, according to whether the model sets out to search for a future course of action aiming at the satisfaction of basic needs.

48. In addition to the clear references in Leontief's study that the determinants of growth are political, social and organizational in the first degree, and in *The Limits to Growth* that opposing blind progress requires drastic changes, many global and sectoral studies prove this point, such as the food model known as the MOIRA model. See Linnemann *et al.*, eds., *MOIRA: Model of International Relations in Agriculture.*
49. The Bariloche model. However, to be fair, we should mention also the Interfutures study which in addition to assuming socio-political changes within the advanced industrial countries, paid some attention to exploring the interaction of such socio-economic changes between them. But it confined itself to the existing pattern of relationship between these countries and Third-World countries.
50. For a stimulating discussion of the ideological foundations of the works of the Meadows group, see J. Galtung, 'Limits to Growth and Class Politics', *Journal of Peace Research*, 1973.
51. V. C. Rideout, 'Mathematical Modelling of Socio-Economic Resource System', in: *Proceedings of the Wisconsin Seminar on Natural Resource Policies*, Madison, Wisconsin, Wisconsin University, Institute for Environmental Studies, 1978, p. 257.
52. It can be said that the regional divisions of the world in both the Mesarovic and the Leontief models were made 'on an oil-basis'. See Fergany and Nassar: 'Global Models and Development: The Role of Models in Exploring Images of the Future of the Third World', p. 26–7.
53. We notice here that *The Limits to Growth* treated the world as one whole and that the SARUM model treated the developing world as one entity.
54. This is close to the 'Middle East' region in the division of the FUGI model. As a result, the outcomes of the scenarios for oil countries always represent relative gains for the advanced industrial countries in terms of the GRP. Compare: I. H. Abdel-Rahman, 'Concepts and Practice of Future Studies Using Models in the Arab Region', Regional Office for Education in the Arab countries, Beirut, 1980, p. 96.
55. See OECD, Interfutures, *Facing the Future*, pp. 216–22.
56. Ibid.
57. The 'North Africa and Middle East' region in the model includes all the Arab countries with the exception of Sudan, Somalia and Mauritania which, together with Iran and Israel, were included in the region of 'Black Africa'.
58. One of the main reports to the Club of Rome. The author relied on a series of dialogues with Arab intellectuals and Arab officials,

undertaken during field trips to the region as part of his attempt to identify the goals and aspirations of different regions of the world. See G. Laszlo *et al.*, *Goals for Mankind: A Report to the Club of Rome on the New Horizon of Global Community*, New York, Dutton, 1977.

59. The Arab region was incorporated into the region labelled North Africa and the Middle East in section 2 of Chapter 6 of the Report, which makes detailed references to Algeria, Saudi Arabia and Egypt.
60. Ibid.
61. The Long-Term Planning Group for Arab Countries, Memo No. 40 entitled: 'Goals and Objectives', National Planning Institute, Cairo, November 1976.
62. See, for instance, the set of features identified by Yusif Al-Sayigh for the requirements and objectives of real development in the introduction of his book: Yusif Al-Sayigh, *The Determinants of Arab Economic Development*, London, Croom Helm, 1978.
63. El-Imam 'Global Models', p. 15.
64. Ibid., p. 15.
65. Mesarovic and Pestel, *Mankind at the Turning Point: The Second Report to the Club of Rome.*
66. The worst sanction.
67. This would come about by economic forces, without any intervention by political authorities. Compare El-Imam, 'Global Models', p. 11.
68. Systems Analysis Inc. (SAI), 'Cost/Benefit of Human Resources Mobility: Example of Scenario Analysis', Cleveland, 15 December 1976, a study stubmitted to the Mesarovic group to the Arab Fund for Economic and Social Development.
69. United Nations Industrial Development Organization, (UNIDO), 'The Implications of Global Models for Developing Countries'.
70. It should be noted that the Mesarovic group does not consider its task complete with the publication of its studies, but assigns to itself an educational role *vis-à-vis* the Third World. This was the lesson drawn by the Cairo group from their dealings with the Mesarovic group, and was noted by a number of commentators on global models, referring to the work of Mesarovic and his group. See Richardson, 'Global Modelling (1): The Models', p. 389.
71. The standard scenario assumes the median population projections made by the UN; high income targets for both developed and less developed countries, (leading to a gap in per capita income of the order of 7:1 only in the year 2000) and low estimates for natural resource availabilities.
72. See Fergany, *Wasted Potentials*.
73. In the case of the first set of indicators, the values assigned to the 'Oil Middle East and North Africa' region were taken to represent the

typical average value of the indicators assigned to the Arab oil countries, and the values relating to the 'Arid African' region were taken to represent the typical average values for non-oil Arab countries. As for the Arab region as a whole, the average value of the indicators was taken to be a weighted average, weighted by the share of population in Arab oil and non-oil countries to the total population of the Arab region as a whole.

As for the second set of indicators, a certain part was deducted from the value of the indicator to correspond to the share of Arab countries in the total population in the two basic regions (assuming the regularity of the per capita share in the specific variables across the countries of the region) in order to reach the values proper to oil and non-oil Arab countries respectively.

Appendix: A brief profile of the most important global models

Model	*Principal document*	*No. of world regions*	*Region/s in which Arab world appears*	*Technical methods used*	*Main variables as determined by models*	*Time horizon*	*Function*	*No. of sectors per region*
Forrester/Meadows models, known as Limits to Growth	Donella H. Meadows, *et al.*, *The Limits to Growth,* New York, Universe Books, 1972.	1	The world	System dynamics	Population, energy & mineral resources, agricultural production, non-agricultural production, environmental pollution	Extends beyond 20th century	Exploratory, computing different scenarios for growth	5
SARUM, UK Department of the Environment	P. Roberts *et al.*, *Report on the SARUM Model,* in: IIASA Symposium of Global Modelling, 4th Laxenburg, 20–23 September 1976, SARUM and MRI: Description & Comparison of a World Model & a National Model, ed. Gerhart Bruckman, Oxford, New York, Pergamon Press, 1978.	3(A)	Region 3	System dynamics, Econometrics	Energy & minerals, demand & production for agricultural and non-agricultural commodities, prices, trade flows	End of 20th century, in application of Interfutures team	Exploratory, computing different scenarios for growth	13 or 16
Fundacion Bariloche (Latin American World Model)	Amilcar O. Herrera *et al.*, *Catastrophe or a New Society? A Latin American World Model*, Ottawa, International Development Research Centre, 1976.	4	Regions 3 (Africa) & 4 (Asia) except for Lebanon, which is included in Region 1	Operational research, optimization techniques, econometrics	Population, consumption of food, agricultural production, demand & production of non-agricultural commodities, time horizon required to meet basic needs	Time horizon to meet basic needs determined in model	Normative, investigating possibility of meeting basic needs	5

Mesarovic or Mesarovic-Pestel	See Works of Long-Term Planning Group for Arab Countries, National Planning Institute, Cairo							
	Mihajlo D. Mesarovic & Edward C. Pestel, *Mankind at the Turning Point: The Second Report to the Club of Rome*, New York, Dutton; Readers' Digest Press, 1974.	10 or 17	Regions 7 (North Africa & Middle East) & 8 (rest of Africa)	Systems dynamics econometrics, input/output analysis	Population, energy & minerals, agricultural and non-agricultural production, trade	Extends beyond 20th century	Exploratory, computing different scenarios for growth	9
Leontief, or UN World Model	See Works of Long-Term Planning Group for Arab Countries, National Planning Institute, Cairo							
	Wassily Leontief *et al.*, *The Future of the World Economy, Preliminary Report*, New York, United Nations Department of Economic & Social Affairs, 1976.		Regions 10 (oil countries of the Middle East & North Africa), & 12 (Arid Africa)	Input/output analysis	Energy & minerals, demand & production of agricultural & non-agricultural commodities, trade, extent of pollution	Till end of 20th century	Exploratory, computing different scenarios for growth	48

(A) Region 1 represents the United States, Region 2 mainly the EEC countries plus the Soviet Union.

Notes:

The following works are excluded, although they are usually included among studies of a futuristic nature.

Herman Kahn and Anthony J. Wiener (USA), *The Year 2000, a Framework for Speculation on the Next Thirty Three Years*, New York, Hudson Institute, 1967; Joseph J. Spengler (USA), *The Economist and the Population Question*, Princeton, New Jersey, [n.p.], 1966; Paul R. and Anne H. Ehrlich (USA), *Population, Resources, Environment Issues in Human Ecology*, San Francisco, Freeman, 1970; Robert L. Heilbroner (USA), *An Inquiry into the Human Prospect*, New York, Norton 1974; Robert L. Heilbroner (USA), *Business Civilisation in Decline*, New York, Norton, 1976, London, Boyars, 1976; Rene Dumont (France), *Utopia or Else?* trans. Vivienne Menkes, London, Deutch 1974; E. F. Schumacher (UK), *Small is Beautiful: A Study of Economics as if People Mattered*, New York, Harper and Row, 1973, London, Blond and Briggs, 1973; Yoichi Kaya *et al.* (Japan), 'Global Constraints and a New Vision for Development', *Technological Forecasting and Social Change*, **6**, 3 and 4 (1974); Elena D. Modrzhinskaya and C. A. Stephanyan (USSR), *The Future of Society: A Critique of Modern Bourgeois Philosophical and Socio Political Conceptions*, Moscow, Progress, 1973; V. Kosolopov (USSR), *Mankind and the Year 2000*, Moscow, Progress, 1976 and Herman Kahn, W. Brown and L. Martel (USA), *The Next Two Hundred Years: A Scenario for America and the World*, New York, Morrow. 1976.

A more extensive coverage and review of global models and future studies can be found in the following.

S. Cole, 'The Global Futures Debate, 1975–1976' in: Christopher Freeman and Marie Jahoda, eds., *World Futures: The Great Debate*, Falmer, Brighton, University of Sussex, 1979; J. M. Richardson, 'Global Modelling (1): The Models', *Futures*, **12**, 5 (October 1978); Richardson, 'Global Modelling (2): Where to Now' *Futures*, **12**, 6 (December 1978); Organization for Economic Cooperation and Development (OECD), Interfutures, 'Summary of Global Models, Intermediate paper: FUT/DW/SI/A—Current Research and World Models', November 1976, and OECD 'Intermediate Results: Review Phases A and B; A Comparative Evaluation of World Models', April 1977.

PART II

IMAGES OF THE ARAB FUTURE AS REFLECTED IN ARAB STRATEGY DOCUMENTS

In this, the last quarter of the twentieth century, the Arab nation is at a critical stage in its long history as it stands at a crossroads with many different paths stretching before it. It faces formidable challenges which suggest hard times ahead but, at the same time, it harbours vast potential which offers hope of progress and development. To move from the crossroads is an imperative dictated by the nature of life and the demands of modern civilization, the only question being: what road to travel, which direction to choose? Whatever the answer, one thing is certain: the Arab world must deploy all of its potential if it hopes to stand up to these challenges and overcome them in the direction of progress and development.[1]

This text quoted above, which is taken from the introduction to one of the Arab strategy documents now in print, eloquently sums up the apprehension which weighed heavily on the Arab psyche throughout the seventies and which led to many serious attempts to form a set of strategic visions of the Arab future in various fields and sectors up to the year 2000. Within this framework, we shall try here to present, analyse and critically appraise a number of documents which offer strategic perceptions, albeit incomplete, encompassing various aspects of the Arab future. In all fairness, it must be said that these documents did not set out to present an overall picture of the Arab future but, more modestly, to envision joint Arab efforts in future. In this sense they represent a 'new endeavour' to achieve pan-Arab co-operation in the face of future challenges and as a reaction to a series of unsuccessful bids to achieve Arab unity or at least greater integration. The most important of the documents now in circulation are as follows.

Documents of a sectoral (or partial) nature

(*a*) a strategy for securing food supplies in the Arab countries (issued by the Arab Organization for Agricultural Development, 1977);

(*b*) a strategy for industrialization based on self-reliance and aimed at meeting basic needs (sponsored by the Industrial Development Centre for the Arab States, 1977–1978);
(*c*) documents of the first Arab Energy Conference (sponsored by OAPEC and the Arab Fund for Economic and Social Development, March 1979);
(*d*) a strategy to develop Arab education (issued by the Arab Organization for Education, Culture and Science, 1979).

Documents of a global nature and outlook

(*a*) alternative patterns of development and lifestyles in the Arab region (study commissioned by the United Nations Economic Commission for West Asia and the UN Environmental Programme, 1979);
(*b*) working paper prepared by a three-man committee selected by the committee of experts on a strategy for joint Arab economic action (submitted to the first pan-Arab conference on a Joint Arab Economic Strategy in May 1978);
(*c*) towards developing joint Arab economic action (the principal document presented to the eleventh Arab summit in Amman, November 1980).

These seven documents all deal with issues related to the Arab future. They explore avenues for strategic action in various fields up till the end of the twentieth century. Not all are considered 'official' documents in the strict sense of the word. Some, like the strategy for industrialization based on self-reliance and aimed at meeting basic needs, the documents of the first Arab Energy conference and the study on alternative patterns of development and lifestyles in the Arab region, were not actually issued by specialized Arab organizations. They do represent, however, the scientific and academic endeavours of Arab experts officially commissioned by specialized organizations to conduct these studies.

We should point out that the seven documents we have chosen are not the only available documents and studies which have tried to come up with some sort of strategic view of future Arab development in various spheres.[2] It is therefore necessary to specify here the set of criteria on which we based our selection of these, rather than other, available documents as the object of our study and analysis. Perhaps the most important of the guidelines we followed to determine whether they qualify as documents of a strategic nature can be summed up as follows:

(a) to what extent the issues they address are crucial and pressing from the point of view of their impact on the course of the Arab future;

(b) to what extent they adopt a strategic outlook to issues of a common Arab destiny;

(c) how perceptive they are in identifying and analysing the major challenges looming on the Arab horizon, especially in the areas of industrialization, agricultural development, energy, education and ecology;

(d) the degree to which they are representative of collective Arab thinking in these areas.

The strategic visions contained in the group of documents under study must be evaluated according to a unified system of norms, and from a single perspective, that of 'a continuous, overall, pan-Arab development directed at the masses, one that asserts the Arab cultural identity and can awaken the creative forces and ingenuity of Arab society'.[3]

To fix the elements of this unified system of norms, we set out below a number of secondary criteria which make up the system of norms adopted to evaluate the credibility of the strategic visions contained in the relevant documents:

the extent to which they adopt a comprehensive outlook to Arab development as a joint process within the framework of which the pattern and movement of development in individual Arab countries is part of the pattern and movement of the Arab whole and not the other way round;

the extent to which they assert the line of independence in the Arab development process, reject relations of dependency and stress the need to reinforce the components of Arab independence through collective self-reliance on a pan-national level;

the extent to which development priorities are perceived of as satisfying the basic needs of the masses and, accordingly, at preventing the socio-economic élites from reaping most of the fruits of development and modernization;

the extent to which they stress the democratic aspect of the development process, in the sense that the pattern of development would accurately reflect, in dynamic expression, the opinions, initiatives and contributions of various socio-economic forces and the initiatives of primary producers at the grass roots level, thus helping awaken and stimulate the creative forces of the greatest number of Arab citizens.

But, in the final analysis, the value of a *strategic blueprint* is measured not only in terms of how perceptive is its grasp of problems, needs and potentials or even of whether it identifies some milestone on the road of future strategic action. It must also put forward concrete proposals as to the 'mechanics' and 'modalities' of possible action which can bring the desired aims within reach. Thus one of the criteria which determined our choice of documents was whether, in putting forth its strategic perception, a document went beyond the diagnostic approach to propose concrete remedial measures.

Below we shall review, analyse and evaluate the seven strategic documents in question in light of the considerations and criteria mentioned above.

Notes

1. See League of Arab States, Arab Organization for Education, Culture and Science, A Strategy for Developing Arab Education, *Comprehensive Report*, Cairo: League of Arab States, Arab Organization for Education, Culture and Science, 1977, p. 18, Introduction to Chapter one.
2. An example that can be cited here is the extensive study conducted by a team of experts at Cairo's National Planning Institute, under the supervision of Dr Ibrahim Helmy Abdel Rahman. See: Ibrahim Helmy Abdel Rahman, Supervisor, *Looking to the Future of Industrial Development in the Arab World*, Cairo: National Planning Institute, 1976, general volume. See also the four studies on *Future Developments in the Arab Region Until the Year 2000*, commissioned by the Arab office of the UN Development Programme, and prepared under the supervision of the Arab Planning Institute in Kuwait.
3. This quotation is taken from: Ismail Sabri Abdalla, *Comments on Working Paper of 3-Man Committee*, in the Pan-Arab Conference on a

Strategy for Joint Arab Economic Action, 1, Baghdad, 6–12 May 1978, Beirut, Arab Institute for Studies and Publishing of the League of Arab States, Economic Department, General Secretariat of the Federation of Arab Economists, 1979.

4 FOOD SECURITY STRATEGY IN THE ARAB COUNTRIES[1]

1. Nature of the problem

The document approaches food security as a basic, indeed an indispensable, component of Arab overall strategic security and expresses profound misgivings on that score, which can be summed up as follows: will food-consumption goods continue to be available in the required quantities or to increase at the required rates—as well as overcoming the deficiency of such essential components as animal proteins in the actual diet?

The document notes that the Arab economy was rocked to its very foundations during the sixties and seventies when the Arab countries stepped up their imports of staple food products, notably wheat, a vital strategic crop. The situation worsened in the seventies, with the Arab countries forced to import half of their wheat-consumption demands. This trend extended to a wide range of foodstuffs, such as sugar, vegetable oils, meat and dairy products. Nor did the agricultural development programmes launched during the sixties and seventies succeed in closing or even narrowing the 'food gap'. Indeed, the gap has become so wide that it now constitutes one of the major challenges facing the Arab nation.[2]

The document warns that the problem of Arab food security has come to acquire an increasingly political character on the level of international relations, particularly with regard to wheat, where the world market is an oligopoly controlled by three main exporters: the United States, Canada and Australia. This leads the document to conclude that 'with the Arab nation's inability to produce enough wheat to feed itself, with the shortfall having to be covered by stepping up imports, with such imports obtainable from only a handful of countries which control the world grain market, the Arab food problem is no longer purely *economic* in character but has become a *political* problem of the first order'.

But perhaps even more dangerous, from a future perspective, are the implications of the lack of a 'food surplus' on growth and development processes in general, more particularly on the ability of the Arab countries to achieve urban growth and industrial expansion. For it is a well established fact in development literature that a steady increase in the volume of 'agricultural surplus' is a necessary condition to sustain processes of urban growth and industrial expansion and that, without this increase, there can be no urbanization and industrial expansion.[3]

This in turn confirms the basic developmental law that, in the absence of a domestic surplus in food products, expansion in processes of urban and industrial development would impose a heavy strain on sectors financing food imports (including that of foreign aid in the case of the non-oil producing countries).

Having thus diagnosed the strategic and acute nature of what it terms the *'food gap' challenge*, the document sets out to identify the main elements that constitute the Arab agricultural production crisis. These can be summed up as follows.

Firstly the limited area of agricultural farmland in relation to the population, making for a constant structural imbalance between population, on the one hand, and actual and potential agricultural resources, on the other. *Secondly*, for all that it is so limited, most of the area under cultivation must nevertheless rely on rainfall. The rain-fed farmland constitutes an estimated 78 per cent of the total area under cultivation, while the irrigated area amounts to only 22 per cent. This heavy reliance on rainfall means that Arab agricultural output varies considerably from one year to the next. Moreover, rain-fed land yields less per hectare than does irrigated land. *Thirdly*, the document reports the severely underdeveloped economics of *livestock production*. Livestock is generally used for social and tribal purposes in countries where it is plentiful, such as Sudan and Somalia, while in others, like Egypt, it is used for farm labour at the expense of dairy products and meat.[4]

Fourthly, farming techniques are outdated, and make very little use of modern production inputs, such as chemical fertilizers, insecticides, selected seeds, tractors and other farm equipment. This is reflected in the low yields of various crops and the decline of agricultural productivity, especially in food grains, the key Arab crop.

Also, not enough *industrial crops* are produced to allow the agricultural and industrial sectors to complement one another. Of the annual cropped area, 4.3 per cent is allocated to *fibre crops*, 5.5 per cent to *oil seeds*, 0.6 per cent to *sugar products* and 0.2 per cent to *tobacco*. Production from these yields is too low to sustain a significant level of industrial activity. Moreover, such activity as there is operates on a seasonal basis and for limited periods, thus never attaining the level of full capacity.

Finally, the low performance level of Arab agricultural production is due not only to a shortage in the natural and material resources used (or available) but derives to a great extent from shortcomings in the pattern of social and economic organization in the agricultural sector as a whole. Subsistence agriculture prevails in most Arab countries, where the pattern of land tenure is dominated by small scattered farms which, being geared to produce for family consumption rather than for the market place, do not set their production priorities in terms of such considerations as specialization, optimal geographical allocation or economic efficiency. The result is an increase in the volume of 'economic waste'.[5]

2. Elements of the proposed strategy

After diagnosing the state of Arab agriculture today, the document then attempts to identify the 'strategic elements' with which to face the problem of Arab food security. In a grim reminder that the problem is one touching on the very destiny of the Arab nation, the document warns that 'the only viable option before the Arab nation as it looks to the future is to improve its food situation, the only alternative being famine or, at least, complete dependency on the grain-exporting countries'.

The various avenues of strategic action proposed in the document all depart from a central idea: given the unequal distribution of land, water, financial, human, managerial and scientific resources among the Arab countries, the only way that large agricultural projects capable of propelling the wheel of development forward can be established and operated economically is for resources to be made available, in the requisite quantities and at the opportune time, from a pool of Arab resources.

This would apply in particular to large projects aimed at

improving agricultural performance, such as projects for the storage and transportation of irrigation water, for drainage, for the storage and transportation of harvests and different utilities of agricultural infrastructure. But the document points out that resource allocation at the level of more than one Arab country is feasible only if it is backed politically, because:

(a) enormous financial resources will be put to use outside the borders of the country furnishing such resources;
(b) one of the results of these large projects will be to replace some of the existing relations between the Arab countries by forms more in keeping with the new organic economic interrelations between them.

That is why the document stresses that a joint Arab effort, in the scope and composition envisaged, is impossible without political reinforcement at the highest level.

In defining the objectives of its proposed strategy for joint Arab action in the area of food development, the document does not attempt to draw up a comprehensive plan for the agricultural sector in the Arab countries, but only to set long-term production goals for some staple food products, such as wheat, the most important food import and the crux of the Arab food security problem. It adopts the same approach with respect to a number of other staples in the Arab food basket, such as sugar, oils, meat and concentrated fodder, fixing production goals on the basis of actual consumption needs and projected needs for these staples until the end of the century and in the light of how far agricultural productive capacities can be expanded to meet future Arab food needs.

With this in mind, the broad lines of the proposed strategy are directed at exploring how the Arabs can achieve the greatest degree of self-sufficiency in some staple food products without giving up any of the advantages they derive from the 'transformation possibilities' open to them through international trade operations. As the document sees it, the production goal for a given commodity can best be attained by breaking it down, as it were, into several partial goals which the Arab countries endowed with the appropriate agricultural resources would then undertake to achieve, each according to its respective resources and potential, plus such allocations as are determined for it by the sector of joint Arab action.

The document considers Arab self-sufficiency in wheat cultivation before the end of the century to be extremely unlikely, and accordingly, that the strategic aim should be to achieve high rates of growth in its production in order to narrow the 'wheat gap' to the point where it will no longer pose a threat to Arab food security. However, prospects are less bleak for edible oils, sugar, meat and concentrated fodder, in which the document believes the Arabs can become completely—or largely—self-sufficient by the turn of the century. But this depends on the goal set for developing wheat production and for developing some staples at the expense of others, taking advantage of whatever 'substitution' possibilities exist.

After defining the broad strategic aims, the document then goes on to propose the practical approaches by which the elements of the proposed strategy can be successfully implemented and the strategic aims realized. The most important of the practical approaches proposed for the successful application of the strategy of joint Arab action for food development can be summed up as follows.

The document recommends that all the Arab countries participating in the programme contribute in kind to the implementation of expansion projects, each according to its resources and to the possibilities of using such resources. More concretely, it suggests, for example, that food and agricultural expansion projects be set up in those countries where cultivable land and irrigation water are plentiful, while the oil states which are not so blessed could specialize in manufacturing fertilizers, insecticides, tractors, farm equipment and other production requirements. Such an enterprise would obviously entail the establishment of large, constantly-developing industries in the Arab countries with financial surpluses, rather than confining their participation in the proposed joint action to that of financing expansion projects in the non-oil producing agricultural countries.

It recommends that programmes of joint agricultural expansion be established on a sound economic basis, so that expansion efforts would be directed at the regions, projects and crops least costly and most economical to develop. This is a strategic consideration, necessary to protect Arab funds financing the joint ventures and ensure their recovery and servicing on a 'commercial basis' as well as to protect the

Arab consumer by providing food commodities at the lowest possible prices.

On the question of joint financing of agricultural development projects, the document proposes that this would take the form of participating in the equity capital of projects for the reclamation or cultivation of virgin land (horizontal expansion projects). Loans might be a more suitable formula in the case of vertical expansion projects in cultivated areas, where land is privately owned or held, so that the economic efficiency of its vertical expansion depends on decisions taken by landholders in the light of the loans which can be made available to them for projects to improve actual production. The document recommends that joint loan financing be undertaken by an Arab agricultural development fund (or bank) that would extend long- or medium-term loans in adequate amounts, at the same interest rates prevailing in world money markets for governments and organizations, against central bank guarantees and according to the requirements of vertical expansion projects.

If joint Arab action directed at agricultural development is to succeed, there must be a free exchange of agricultural products between the Arab countries. Also, steps would have to be taken to ensure that they consume what their sister countries produce in the way of alternatives to their food imports. This entails taking joint measures to separate the Arab market from the world market for agricultural products, along the lines of the agricultural policy of EEC countries, through tariff protection measures, subsidies and pricing.

On the development of the Sudan's vast agricultural resources the report states that if projects to develop land and water resources are set up, if production is intensified, crop cycles are improved and the use of livestock is rationalized, agricultural development operations could, by the end of the century realize surplus for export attaining 1.5 million tons of millet, 850 thousands tons of oil seed, 750 thousand tons of livestock and 650 thousand tons of fodder.

The strategy to increase wheat production should rely essentially on *vertical expansion*, since the increase which can be achieved through horizontal expansion is by necessity limited, even in countries where possibilities for horizontal expansion exist, such as Iraq. That is why the emphasis is on vertical expansion in countries lying within the Arab wheat belt, which includes Iraq, Syria, and Algeria. It is in these countries that the possibilities of forming a significant surplus for export are concentrated.

All these efforts to achieve incremental growth in the production of wheat as a strategic crop aim at stabilizing the size of the *wheat gap* and maintaining it below a certain point, suggested by the document at somewhere between 10 and 12 million tons at the end of the century.

3. A brief appraisal

The document adopts a rigorous scientific approach in its analysis of the problems besetting Arab agriculture, as well as in the concrete steps and practical strategic action it proposes to attain the greatest degree of Arab food security. It is also to be commended for underlining the political character of the deepening Arab 'food gap' and the adverse implications of this development, which is bound to increase Arab 'food dependency' on grain- and meat-exporting countries, irrespective of the ability of the Arab countries to pay for their food imports.

Thus the strategic line governing all the proposals put forward by the document is aimed at closing, or at least reducing, the food gap by attaining the greatest degree of Arab self-reliance in food production. Looking to the future of the Arab nation, with its vast and untapped potentials for developmental integration and self-reliance in the crucial area of food security, the merits of the document's approach are obvious.

However, if we have a basic reservation on the document, it is that it over-emphasizes the 'production dimension' in agricultural development processes and completely neglects the 'distribution dimension' as it relates to patterns of land-holding and income distribution between families and individuals, the impact of these patterns on 'food-consumption patterns' and the distortions and aberrations they produce which help deepen what the document calls the 'food gap'.

As we see it, Arab food security is not only a question of developing agricultural production to achieve food security on the Arab national or pan-national level, but also, and essentially, on the individual level for the ordinary Arab citizen. This entails addressing the issues of rationalizing consumption and improving income-distribution patterns in the Arab region, where some people are victims of malnutrition and others fall ill from overeating as a result of the wasteful pattern of food consumption. A comprehensive approach to Arab food security strategy must therefore include both the productive and distribution dimensions.

This emphasizes the importance of the effect that land-holding patterns in the Arab world have on the volume of agricultural production, the levels of productivity and future prospects of vertical expansion (mechanization, fertilization, agricultural intensification).

Thus neglecting the land-holding pattern within the wider framework of rural development is a shortcoming in the methodological approach which detracts from the accuracy of any future vision of agricultural development and food security issues in the Arab world.

By over-emphasizing the production dimension, the document is essentially resource-oriented, and, consequently, fails to take sufficient account of alternative approaches that can be envisaged within the scope of a wider range of land-tenure patterns and alternative patterns of rural development.

It can be said on the whole that the document deals with the problem of Arab food security as one of 'inputs' and 'outputs', completely disregarding the peasant's relationship with the land and the pattern of rural development in its broad sense. The question of bridging the 'wheat gap' on a pan-Arab scale—the focal issue of the document—is inconceivable in isolation from many dynamic issues which affect relations of production and emigration from the countryside to the city (e.g. Iraq). The document's main weakness is that it deals with the inherently dynamic issue of food security in a static context that is, assuming other factors to be constants.

It is our firm conviction that an analysis of the long-term prospects for Arab food security cannot be made without discussing patterns of rural development in all its dimensions: education, health and lifestyles in general. None of these key issues are addressed by the document.

Notes

1. This study was sponsored by the Arab Organization for Agricultural Development (Khartoum). We have relied here on the important

summary of the study prepared by Dr Sayed Gaballah, the main consultant of the study.

2. According to the study, during the period between 1962 and 1974, the annual rate of growth in Arab production of grain stood at 1.8 per cent, of wheat at 1.5 per cent, of maize at 1.9 per cent, of millet at 2 per cent and of barley at 1.5 per cent. These rates are all lower than the rate of demographic growth in the Arab region, while the rate of growth in wheat production in particular is no more than half that of demographic growth.
3. To illustrate this point, the study notes that the Arab country with the highest rate of self-sufficiency in wheat during the period between 1970 and 1974 was Iraq. Nonetheless around 10 per cent of the urban population of that country had to rely on imports to meet their basic food needs. Iraq is followed by Syria and Morocco, which enjoyed self-sufficiency in wheat at the rate of 75 and 77 per cent respectively during the same period 1970–74. But wheat imports continued to cover some 25 and 30 per cent respectively of the urban populations' consumption needs in these countries in the first half of the seventies.
4. As a result, milk production in the Arab countries suffers from both decrease and stagnation. Average annual production fell as low as 7.2 million metric tonnes in the period 1971-73, a drop due to both the limited number of dairy cattle and to the limited annual output per head.
5. True, the study did touch briefly on organizational and land-tenure patterns as impediments to agricultural development, but failed to give this question its due share of analysis—a serious omission when we recall that the different solutions to the agricultural question could have important implications for the shape of the Arab future.

5 STRATEGY OF INDUSTRIAL DEVELOPMENT TO MEET BASIC NEEDS

In preparation for the Fifth Industrial Development Conference of Arab States, the Fourth Conference of Arab Industry Ministers commissioned the Industrial Development Centre of Arab States (IDCAS), a specialized agency of the Arab League, to prepare a preliminary strategic study on the pattern of industrial development necessary to assure the basic needs of Arab citizens. The IDCAS study subjects the concept of 'basic needs' to close scrutiny and detailed analytical study in the light of known facts of the Arab situation, to test its validity as a point of departure for an alternative pattern of Arab industrialization strategy. The study departs from the premise that any objective requirement necessary to preserve human life and secure human welfare can be classified as a 'need'. In terms of this definition, the following needs were identified as 'basic needs'.[1]

A. Material needs

These include all needs in the fulfilment of which human or natural resources (or factors of production) must be used, and which produce on the consumer, either directly or indirectly, effects that can be measured. Accordingly, the list of material needs includes 'adequate' food, 'appropriate' clothing, 'decent' housing, transportation, education and health. It is interesting to note that, unlike most contemporary writings, the study classifies health and education as material needs.

B. Non-material needs

These are needs which can be fulfilled essentially through social and political re-organization, irrespective of available material resources. They can be grouped into two main categories. The first category relates to individual self-fulfilment, that is, reinforcing the individual's feelings that he can realize his full potential without frustration by providing him with basic freedom and moral incentives. The second category relates to society, that is, confirming its role in the life of each individual through various forms of collective expression and societal activities.

In the light of these notions, a number of applied studies were undertaken to estimate the size of the basic needs that would have to be met until the year 2000 in the three areas of food, clothing and housing, in order to determine the most appropriate industrial production structure by which they can be fulfilled. This makes it possible to determine the size and type of production requirements commensurate with such a structure, specifically, the size and composition of inputs from the primary sector (agriculture and extractive industries) and those required from the construction and energy sectors, thus casting light, in quantitative terms, on the intersectoral pattern that would emerge from a new strategy of industrial development based on the satisfaction of basic needs. To the extent that a new pattern of industrialization based on satisfying basic needs emerges, so too will a new pattern of development and, more generally, of lifestyles, begin to emerge.

We shall review here the conclusions reached by the studies already undertaken in so far as they relate to the dimensions and strategy of securing basic needs in clothing in the Arab world until the year 2000 as well as to the industrial inputs necessary to satisfy the Arab citizen's basic needs for housing in the year 2000.

1. Elements of strategy to secure basic needs in clothing[2]

The study first makes a general projection of the volume and type of an individual's basic needs in different groupings of Arab countries, on the basis of which it estimates the expansion required in clothing production to satisfy those needs. It confines itself to the textile products used in clothing, and does not discuss other products, such as leather.

The individual's average consumption norm of clothing products in the Arab nation was estimated at some 3.3 kilograms per annum. However, what this figure conceals is that enormous disparities in the levels of individual consumption of clothing exist between the Arab countries. The highest level recorded is in Qatar and the United Arab Emirates (25.7

and 19 kilograms respectively), while the lowest is in North Yemen (1 kilogram).

An analysis of the data on clothing consumption patterns in the Arab world reveals that cotton products rank first (58 per cent for the period 1971–75), followed by synthetic fibre products (19 per cent), ready-made clothing products (12 per cent), knitted products (2 per cent) and, finally, wool products.[3]

A number of normative calculations were made to estimate the level of consumption that would satisfy the basic needs of Arab inhabitants during the period between 1985 and 2000, departing from a number of simplified assumptions as to the criteria and components, the basic pattern of consumption of clothing products for urban and rural, over-fifteen and under-fifteen age-groups, respectively. Detailed estimates, by sex, age and environment were thus made for each grouping of Arab countries. Looking to the future, the study sees a number of important trends emerging in the relationship between consumption patterns and industrialization policies as outlined below.

Firstly, an increase in the use of *synthetic*, rather than *natural*, fibres is forecast, contrary to the present pattern of consumption, and despite the fact that the climate in most Arab countries is more suited to the use of natural fibres, especially cotton. The study attributes the shift principally to the fact that not enough cotton can be produced to meet future demands, expansion in its cultivation being restricted by various factors, such as the limited areas of cultivable land and the fact that other agricultural products, with relatively higher margins of profit, compete for the same areas. Another reason is that synthetic fibres offer a number of advantages, being light-weight, drip-dry, etc.

Secondly, the volume of growth required in clothing products as a whole was estimated as equal to the size of the gap between the level of production required to satisfy basic needs and the volume of actual production in the base year. This is on the assumption that no 'surplus for export' will be realized, in view of the growing difficulties which textile exports from developing countries are facing as a result of the import restriction policies pursued by the EEC countries and the USA on the one hand, and of growing competition between the developing countries themselves on the other.

Thirdly, the volume of *input mixes* required is estimated by reference to the actual pattern in their consumption (heavy/medium/lightweight fabrics), taking into account the expected increase in per capita income and the prevailing pattern of income distribution in each Arab country, in order to calculate 'income elasticity' of demand for each type of fabric. Once product mix and input mix have been determined, it is easy to estimate the required productive capacity in terms of machinery and equipment (taking depreciation into account). Thus the number of spinning mills, looms, knitting machines and sewing machines required to satisfy clothing needs were estimated. On the basis of this estimate, the volume and cost of required investments are estimated, as well as the size of the extra manpower required to operate this machinery and equipment, using technical coefficients which establish the man/machine ratio.

Thus a complete picture emerges of what the strategy to meet basic needs in the area of clothing requires in the way of basic raw materials and inputs, machinery, equipment, manpower, capital investments and extra agricultural land, as illustrated in Table 5.1.

2. Elements of industrialization strategy required to satisfy basic needs in housing[4]

This applied study casts light on the numerous problems, both quantitative and qualitative, which face the Arab nation in the area of meeting basic housing needs, and points to its obvious failure to bridge the gap between what it can provide on the one hand and the urgent needs it is required to meet on the other. This is particularly pressing for the low-income strata and even for the middle-income strata, whose situation has deteriorated as a result of the sudden and steep increase in housing costs and of the widening gulf between real incomes and the share which can be allocated to securing a home. Laying a groundwork made up of facts on the actual housing situation and of expectations on future needs in this area, the study comes up with a strategic vision of the industrial capacity, building materials and equipment required to meet basic housing needs in the Arab nation up to the year 2000.

Drawing on census findings, the study analyses housing

Table 5.1 Summary of requirements needed to achieve development in clothing production to meet basic needs for the year 1985–2000

Requirements	Production 1975	Increase 1975–1985		Increase 1985–2000		Total increase 1975–2000	
		Quantity	%	Quantity	%	Quantity	%
Inputs							
cotton (thousand tonnes)	737	346	47	346	47	692	94
wool (thousand tonnes)	40	20	50	31	78	51	128
synthetic fibres (thousand tonnes)	20	284	1420	158	790	442	2210
Machinery							
looms	3311	3390	102	2737	83	6127	185
spinning mills	57	65	114	49	86	114	200
knitting machines	3	10	333	21	700	31	1033
sewing machines	29	119	410	201	693	320	1103
Labour force (thousand workers)	480	247	51	383	80	630	131
Investments (US $ millions)		7338		6664		14002	
Agricultural land (thousand hectares)	1293	577	45	576	45	1153	90

Source: Mohamed Samir Badawi, Salwa El-Antari: 'Ensuring Basic Clothing Needs in the Arab Nation until the Year 2000', *League of Arab States, Industrial Development Center of the Arab States, Seminar on a strategy for industrial development and meeting basic needs*, Tripoli, 2–4 April 1979.

conditions in the Arab world today, in terms of housing capacity (whether fit or unfit for habitation), rates of occupancy and degree of overcrowding in dwellings and rooms, access to public utilities and the building materials employed. From all these indicators, the number of dwellings unfit for habitation in 1975 was estimated at approximately 7.2 million, that is 30 per cent of the total housing-stock in all Arab countries that year (see Table 5.2).

An arbitrary estimate of the individual's share of total housing capacity was made according to a 'housing criterion' fixed in terms of the space required for the basic functions performed in every household. This criterion was used to determine the size of the 'future gap' in the light of projected population growth and size composition of rural and urban family units. The housing units necessary to close that gap were estimated at 28.9 million, covering a minimum of 1.8 billion square metres or, using the median criterion prevailing in various countries[5] 2.3 billion square metres. These figures do not cover the needs arising from the 'repeated depreciation' of the existing housing stock.

The study considers the rates at which various building materials are likely to be used in future, according to type, quality and location of dwellings envisaged. On the basis of projected rates, it then estimates the building materials and construction equipment necessary to fill actual and future gaps up to the year 2000.[6] This applied study puts forward a number of interesting propositions in respect of an industrialization strategy oriented towards the satisfaction of basic needs and the achievement of self-reliance, the most important of which are summarized below.

(1) By its very logic, such a strategy will inevitably lead to a gradual discarding of certain building materials such as marble, plastic floor coverings and paint and to replacing imported material wherever possible by local substitutes (e.g. metal in place of wooden window-frames and doors, stone in place of enamel sanitary installations).
(2) It is necessary to increase the use of silt in bricks, to manufacture clay, chalk and sand bricks and to develop the stone industry as far as possible in order to reduce building costs, provide more employment opportunities and promote the use of simple building techniques.

5.2 Actual housing situation in the Arab countries and dwellings unfit for habitation (in thousands)

	Jordan	United Arab Emirates	Bahrein	Tunisia	Algeria	Libya	Syria	Sudan	Somalia	Iraq	Oman	Qatar	Kuwait	Lebanon	Egypt	Morocco	Saudi Arabia	Mauritania	Yemen	Democr. Yemen	Overall total
g dwellings																					
an	258	77	29	456	1307	230	493	430	105	880	8	14	118	228	2281	1147	433	20	100	88	9712
al	107	17	8	550	1001	150	603	2775	396	650	116	2	15	168	3717	1900	742	238	900	194	14249
	365	94	37	1006	2308	380	1096	3205	501	1530	124	16	133	336	6998	3047	1175	268	1000	282	23961
ellings																					
an	244	23	26	424	1230	155	406	300	105	440	6	12	100	223	2137	831	384	22	80	70	1218
al	101	5	8	330	941	108	525	745	296	65	93	2	13	165	3672	910	658	114	630	136	9522
	345	28	34	754	2176	263	431	1045	401	505	99	14	113	388	5809	1741	1043	136	710	206	16740
dwellings																					
an	14	54	3	32	77	75	87	140	-	440	2	2	18	5	1144	316	46	8	20	18	2494
al	6	12	-	220	55	42	78	2030	100	585	23	-	2	3	45	990	84	124	270	58	4727
	20	66	3	252	132	117	165	2160	100	1025	25	2	20	8	1189	1306	133	132	290	76	7221
dwellings (%)																					
an	5	70		7	6	33	18	30	-	50	8	14	15	2	35	28	11	27	20	21	26
al	6	71		40	6	28	13	72	25	90	20		15	2	1	52	11	52	32	30	33

ıdicates data unavailable.

(3) While the raw products used in building materials may not be available in each individual Arab country, they can certainly be found in the community of Arab countries taken as a whole. Similarly, much of the basic equipment used in building and construction work such as metal cutting, drilling and welding equipment, engineering equipment, cranes etc, is manufactured in several Arab countries. There is no technical difficulty by way of manufacturing or operating them. What is required is to standardize the production specifications of this equipment in the various Arab countries.

(4) The industrial structure required for housing produces *backward linkages* which play an important role in feeding a number of basic industrial activities. More specifically, it can be said that the industrial structure linked to housing operations feeds industry along two main lines: (a) a first line (which is direct), represented in such basic industries as the manufacture of building materials, and the manufacture of construction, transportation and handling equipment; (b) a second (feedback) line represented in sectors which must be developed to sustain the industries of the first line, such as engineering, electrical and ceramics industries.

(5) A survey of actual Arab potentials in all these sectors shows that most of the equipment required to operate them can be manufactured, with a few exceptions, in the area of heavy industries, e.g. iron rolling mills.

From a strategic perspective of the Arab industrial development process, it is advisable to distinguish between two types of industries: industries which must be established on a pan-national level to help achieve the Arab integration so necessary to face housing and other problems, e.g. iron and steel, non-ferrous metals, transportation equipment, engineering workshop tools, glass, porcelain, ceramics, bulbs, etc.; industries to be developed on the level of individual Arab countries, such as cement, stone-cutting, bricks, doors and windows, tiles, assembly of electrical appliances, stone sanitary installations, and galvanized pipes.

3. A brief appraisal

No one can deny that this collection of studies, which envisage new policies for Arab industrialization in terms of the satisfaction of basic needs, have, by concentrating on the technical aspects which the requisite industrialization structure would involve, successfully demonstrated how these policies could be made to work in practice. Admittedly too, they have proved the merits of a strategy geared to the satisfaction of basic needs as a practical approach by which to apply the policies of Arab 'collective self-reliance' in the industrialization field.

However, they are less successful when it comes to looking into the political and social conditions necessary for the success of this strategy, especially as regards the set of 'accompanying policies' in the areas of restructuring political power, of redistributing assets and incomes, and of commodity pricing and subsidizing. Without the introduction of such policies, it would be difficult to break the fetters holding back the process of satisfying basic needs for the bulk of the people, which, because of the prevailing pattern of wealth- and income-distribution, is in danger of never reaching the level of effective demand bolstered by the appropriate purchasing power.

If these issues are not handled within the scope of a more comprehensive outlook that embraces future policies and institutional aspects, the elements of such a strategy would remain nothing more than a collection of Utopian ideas incapable of cutting a path through the rough terrain of Arab socio-economic realities. More generally, a number of major questions, standing at the very core of the issue under study, still need more precise answers. By way of illustration, some of these questions are given below.[7]

Basic needs and self-reliance

(1) What will relations with the outside world be like (aid, trade exchange, etc), in the context of an industrialization strategy directed at satisfying basic needs?
(2) What is the relationship between a strategy of basic needs and self-reliance?
(3) Does collective self-reliance—seen from the angle of basic needs—differ radically from the usual patterns of co-operation and integration?

Basic needs and participation

(1) Does the satisfaction of basic needs represent a new formula for the welfare society applicable to poor countries?
(2) What are the appropriate mechanisms by which basic needs can be defined? What are the roles that technocrats, citizens and planners respectively can be expected to play? What form will the debate take, and what will be its likely outcome?

Basic needs and pattern of development and technology

(1) Can the present economic structure in the Arab countries fulfil basic needs? If not, what is the nature of the changes which would have to be brought to these structures? Would they be represented in strengthening internal links and weakening those with the external world or in a more equitable distribution of income?
(2) If the satisfaction of basic needs entails a more equitable distribution of income, can this be achieved without the use of a different technology?
(3) If there is a trend in favour of a different technology, how can this trend be articulated?

As far as futures studies are concerned, the central question is not one of investigating and demonstrating how to satisfy basic needs in the Arab context, but remains that of revealing the contradictions and problems that may arise when an industrialization strategy directed at this goal comes to be implemented within the framework of existing technical and technological relations, institutional and social conditions, outlook to development and the pattern of international economic relations.

Without a thorough discussion of these issues, the documents under review represent nothing more than an intellectual exercise and cannot be credited with evolving a strategy that can be applied to the complexities of Arab reality.

Notes

1. For further details see Ismail Sabri Abdalla (consultant for the study), *Basic Needs: Would their Analysis Lead to a Theory for Consumption?*, in League of Arab States, Centre of Industrial Development for Arab Countries, Seminar on a Strategy for Industrial Development and Meeting Basic Needs, Tripoli, 2–4 April 1979.

2. See Mohamed Samir Badawy and Salwa El-Antary, *Ensuring Basic Clothing Needs in the Arab Nation until the Year 2000*, ibid.
3. Ibid., p. 15.
4. See Yassin Abdalla and Mohamed Aglan, *Industrial Inputs Required to Satisfy Basic Housing Needs of the Arab Citizen in the Year 2000*, ibid.
5. The 'median criterion' is higher than the minimum criterion, as it is an average value closer to the criterion prevailing in the more prosperous countries.
6. The building material presently used in the Arab region can be classified into four groups: (a) material derived from stone, like cement, ceramics, brick, plaster, limestone, tiles, marble and rock; (b) material of metal origin, like iron and aluminium; (c) material of chemical origin, like veneers for floors or some insulating materials; (d) other material derived by assembling or crafting others (e.g. electrical or carpentry works).
7. Most of these questons were formulated in the introductory working paper, in: League of Arab States, Centre of Industrial Development for Arab Countries, Seminar on a Strategy for Industrial Development and Meeting Basic Needs, Tripoli, 2–4 April 1979.

6 PROCEEDINGS OF THE FIRST ARAB ENERGY CONFERENCE

Over the last decade the energy sector has come to play a very prominent role in contemporary Arab life. But to the same extent that they have come to rely so heavily on the oil sector and the revenues from that sector, the Arab countries, oil and non-oil producers alike, face a formidable challenge in the not too distant future, with their oil reserves expected to dry up by the end of the century, and with efforts to develop alternative—and highly competitive—sources of energy being stepped up world-wide.

A question with such enormous implications for the Arab future had to be approached in terms of a clear-cut strategic vision for the management of oil reserves in the Arab nation up to the end of the century, based on the dynamics of local and global variables affecting the supply and pattern of oil and energy use. Accordingly, and at the initiative of OAPEC and the Arab Fund for Socio-Economic Development, the First Arab Energy Conference was held in Abu Dhabi, UAE, 4–8 March 1979. This step was an important landmark on the long road towards formulating long-term strategies for energy and hydrocarbons in the Arab region. It was also the first reaction, on the level of joint Arab structure thinking, to the creation of the International Energy Agency, which co-ordinates and leads energy policies in the large industrial countries.[1]

The most important papers and studies presented to the conference dealt with three main topics, namely: evaluating the energy situation in the Arab countries (as regards both production and consumption); energy alternatives and options at both the global and Arab levels; optimal policies for oil production and pricing.

1. Evaluating the energy situation in the Arab countries

The studies on this topic all refer to an important and well-established fact, namely, policies for the production and export of oil in the Arab region reflected global energy policies especially during the period from 1950 to 1973.[2] One of the more crucial periods in modern history, it saw the shift from coal to oil, when the advanced industrial countries (especially the members of the Organization for Economic Co-operation and Development) came to rely more and more heavily on oil in conducting their economic life.

Thus the demand for oil outstripped economic growth, growing faster than the demand for energy in general. Most of the burden in meeting the growing demand for oil by the advanced industrial countries (with the exception of the Soviet Union and China) fell on the shoulders of the Arab oil-exporting countries. Thus whereas in 1960 the OPEC countries produced 23.7 per cent of the total global oil production of 18.6 million barrels a day, in 1970, when global production stood at 40 million barrels a day, they produced 35.5 per cent. By 1977, they were producing 40.5 per cent of a total global production of 49.1 million barrels a day.[3]

In terms of production, this forced depletion of Arab oil reserves is accompanied by the waste of associated natural gas. According to one OPEC estimate, the gas flared or vented is equivalent to approximately 70 million barrels of oil a day. This goes back to the early days of oil production in the Arab countries, and will no doubt continue until projects to exploit natural gas are established.[4]

In terms of consumption, domestic consumption of oil grew faster in the Arab countries than anywhere else in the world during the sixties and seventies, jumping from 18 per cent in 1960 to 33 per cent in 1976. By reference to the ratio of oil consumption to oil production, the Arab countries can be divided into three groups:[5]

(1) countries with an energy 'surplus': Algeria, Bahrain, Iraq, Kuwait, Libya, Oman, Qatar, Saudi Arabia, the United Arab Emirates;
(2) countries with an energy 'deficit': Jordan, Lebanon, Morocco, Mauritania, Sudan, Somalia, North Yemen, South Yemen and Djibouti;
(3) countries with an energy 'balance': Egypt, Syria, Tunisia.[6]

Of course, this classification in terms of 'balance' and 'surplus' only holds true in the short term.

Despite the scarcity of available information on how energy consumption is distributed among the various sectors in the Arab countries, the sector most heavily dependent on liquid fuel (benzine) is undoubtedly transportation, which exhibits a profligate fuel consumption pattern. All these facts call for a strategic re-evaluation of the policies and patterns of oil productin and consumption in the Arab nation today. All the more so in view of the established—and disquieting—fact that the rates of relative growth for oil production and consumption are less a function of sound policies for the management of oil resources dictated by considerations of Arab interests than they are the historical result of the policies of the international oil cartel.

2. Energy alternatives and options at both the global and Arab levels

There is almost unanimous agreement that the eighties and nineties represent a 'transitional period' in world history as far as energy policies and alternatives go, not least because the era of 'cheap energy' is irrevocably behind us.[7] Obviously the changes that will take place in the energy sector worldwide during this transitional period are bound to have far-reaching effects on the shape of the Arab future in the economic, political and social spheres.

Against this backdrop, the studies presented to the Conference on the technological options open to the Arab region focused on areas which can provide renewable sources of energy in anticipation of the post-oil era.[8] According to the studies, there are several alternative sources of energy which can be developed in the Arab region, such as uranium, electricity, solar energy and geo-thermal energy;

Uranium Its use in nuclear reactors makes it the second most important non-renewable source of energy after oil. According to a study presented by the International Atomic Agency, preliminary deposits of uranium are known to exist in Algeria and Somalia. Proven reserves have been estimated at around 34 thousand tonnes while probable reserves are estimated at around 53 thousand tonnes. There is also evidence pointing to the possibility of uranium deposits in Libya, Mauritania, Sudan, Egypt, Yemen and Saudi Arabia, with likely reserves estimated at between 150 and 500 thousand tonnes.

Hydraulic energy A renewable source of energy in that it is linked to the availability of water in a number of Arab countries such as Egypt, Sudan, Lebanon, Tunisia, Algeria, Morocco and Iran. On the other hand, its capacity is limited in comparison with other sources of energy. The total hydro-electric capacity that can be generated in the Arab countries is estimated at approximately 41 thousand megawatts/hour. Two-thirds of this capacity is either already in use or soon to be put to use, while the remaining third is still the subject of research and study.

Solar energy This is available without limitation, every single day the sun rises, to all Arab countries. It is an enormous, renewable source of energy. To realize just how enormous, one has only to consider the following facts: if the solar energy received at ground level in the Arab countries every year is translated into billions of barrels of oil they would need to use no more than 5 per cent of that energy.

Geo-thermal energy This is generated by the intense heat dicharged from the depths of the earth in the form of hot springs or steam. It is concentrated in belts running below the earth's crust, one of which passes through the Red Sea. Some effects of this are clearly apparent in the southern region, and indeed, throughout the entire Red Sea Basin, where hot waters that sometimes attain a temperature of 200 °C collect in depressions in the sea bed.

This review of alternative sources of energy only confirms the pressing need for a pan-Arab energy plan for the region as a whole that would continue to use the oil umbrella until other renewable sources of solar and nuclear energy have been developed, while at the same time strengthening this umbrella by prospecting for new oil-fields.[9] Under the protection of a reinforced oil umbrella, the Arab countries could adopt a comprehensive pan-national plan to develop solar energy and renewable nuclear energy which they would all, oil and non-oil countries alike, co-operate in implementing. This in turn entails a pan-national energy plan for the implementation of a number of mutually complementary investment options to which energy budgets would be allocated in each country, in proportions that could vary from one to the other.

These options would encompass investments in all four spheres, not as alternatives to choose from, but as options that complement one another in each individual country and on a pan-national level. Each Arab country should have an energy plan consisting of those options which best suit its particular case. From all these plans combined, a pan-national energy plan could be designed incorporating all four options for the development of sources of energy.[10] In short, then, the Arab nation is protected by an extremely solid oil umbrella which allows it to develop and produce hydro-electric energy wherever water-power resources can be found, to purchase nuclear reactors wherever population density and an industrial environment exist and to tap solar energy at will.

3. Optimal policies for oil production and pricing

Perhaps the most important paper presented by the Arab side on the subject was a study by Dr Fadel El-Galby and Dr Adnan El-Ganaby entitled 'Optimal Production and Pricing Policies for Oil'.[11] The authors reach a number of conclusions of a strategic nature, which we sum up below.

The world market for crude is full of constraints and shortcomings. Oil-price formation was never determined by market forces or by their free interaction. It would thus be illogical to sit back today and wait for market forces to form optimal prices for crude. In fact, prices in the past were simply the result of interaction between various pressure groups, and may well continue to reflect the relative strength of these groups in the future. In this sort of situation, it might be necessary to plan oil prices in advance.

In planning prices, it is not only the need to find a mechanism to maintain them at their real level which should be taken into account, but also the fact that *price elasticity of demand* will be very low in the short term. In the medium-term and long-term however, price elasticity may be greater for products which have a number of substitutes, such as fuel oil used to generate electricity. On the other hand, we find that the *income elasticity of demand* is very high, as it is the level of economic activity which determines overall demand for energy. Prices affect demand through their impact on the level of economic activity, on substitutes and on energy conservation policies.

Prices of crude could rise in the short-term to reflect the price level of finished products paid by the final consumer without this significantly affecting the volume of demand. Prices must also be directed in such a way as to become compatible in the long run with price planning goals, in the light of compensation and substitution requirements on the one hand, and considerations of depletion and exhaustion on the other. In the long run, prices must be oriented not only to conform to the total cost of alternatives (heavy crude and liquified coal) but also brought up to the level necessary for the systematic conversion from one specific type of fuel to another, taking into consideration the degree of depletion and relative scarcity.

The efficiency of oil prices from the standpoint of oil-exporting countries can be measured in terms of the economic development they can realize by converting oil revenues into stable investments and social capital. In this respect, levels of production and prices are directly linked to the development process. Thus oil resources should not be completely exhausted before the economy has reached the level required for sustained self-development without having to rely on oil revenues. In general, oil revenues can be maximized through the price of one unit of production and not through the total amount exported, and it is the interaction between the price, development and depletion (i.e. levels of production) which is the real axis of the exporting countries' policies. For these countries, price levels are linked to the burden of investments required to develop the strategic oil-extraction sector. The way out would be to link prices in the medium term to marginal costs, in order to compensate for the cheap barrel of oil evaluated at the replacement cost necessary to make available a new barrel at the margin.

The oil producers' choice of energy-intensive technological options and their policy of pricing oil products at a low level will lead to the rapid growth of domestic energy consumption. The increasing demand in the medium- and long term will begin to compete with export for a greater share of the total production. This problem must be taken into account when current production policies are being decided.

A number of new phenomena have also emerged, such as profligate consumption and deteriorating 'work ethics' as a result of the split between 'effort' and 'revenue'. These are bound to increase the high 'social cost' paid by Arab society as a result of the rapid inflow of enormous oil revenue.

4. A brief appraisal of the proceedings of the Conference

The many studies presented to the First Arab Energy Conference, whether technical, economic or social, all stress the urgent need to establish a joint Arab strategy in the domain of energy. The light cast on energy consumption patterns in the various Arab countries, whether in the oil producer/exporter states, those self-sufficient in oil or those having to import it, reveal how necessary it is to link the requirements of economic plans to the question of demand for energy, since any development plan must focus on this link and on rationalizing consumption and guiding it towards patterns that would serve economic development. However, the question of alternative energy was not exhaustively covered and a number of alternatives such as wind energy were not mentioned at all.

The formulation of a strategy for joint Arab action in the domain of energy, based on the papers and discussions of the Conference, required the formation of national energy committees in the various Arab countries to follow up energy questions, to help in planning the exploitation and development of energy, to compile the data so indispensable to policy-making and, in general, to serve as the pillars of the Joint Arab Energy Committee.[12]

For all their concern with the problems of Arab oil in the areas of production, consumption, pricing and development, none of the studies presented to the First Arab Energy Conference addressed the problems facing the Arab oil-producing countries in the context of changing world economic conditions, particularly those arising from fluctuations in the dollar exchange rate, the erosion of the purchasing power of oil revenues, the multiplicity of oil prices, etc. These are vital issues which no projection of the Arab economy, seen in the context of the world economic order, can afford to ignore.

The Conference also failed to give issues of the 'post-oil' era their due. Apart from the question of developing alternative sources of energy, it did not come to grips with the challenges of the post-oil world, notably in the area of creating and expanding the industrial base in the oil countries and in trying to see the present as history. For it is more than the material depletion of their oil that the Arab oil states will be facing in future. There will be the enormous problem of adjusting to the new realities, not easy for societies whose economic and social lifestyles are so closely linked to 'oil rents' and which depend so heavily on imports because of the accumulation of oil money in the form of foreign currencies. Such is the gravity of the challenge that these pure 'rentier states' will be facing in future that problems of the post-oil era must head the list of priorities in any attempt to scan the horizons of the Arab future.[13]

Notes

1. This agency was formed after the OPEC oil price increase and embargo in 1973 and 1974, and was joined by all the advanced industrial capitalist countries except France.
2. See, in particular, the following papers Abdel Aziz El-Watary, *Adjustment of World Energy Policies and the Effect on Arab Countries*; Ossman El-Gamaly, *Evaluating the Energy Situation in the Arab Countries*; and Aly Sadek, Hamdy Saleh and Mohamed El-Badrawy, *Predicted Demand for Energy from Arab Countries*; all in Arab Energy Conference, 1, Abu Dhabi, 4–8 March 1979, Conference Documents, Abu Dhabi, OAPEC, Arab Fund for Economic and Social Development.
3. See El-Watary, op. cit.
4. Ibid.
5. See Sadek, Saleh and El-Badrawy, *Predicted Demand for Energy from Arab Countries*, op. cit.
6. Egypt and Syria moved into the category of countries with an energy surplus in the second half of the seventies.
7. For further details in this regard, see Mahmoud Abdel-Fadil, ed., *Papers on the Economics of Oil*, New York, Oxford University Press, 1979.
8. Foremost among these can be cited: Adnan Mustapha, *Arab Nuclear Potential*; Aly Kittani and Mohamed Anwar Malek, *Solar Energy in the Arab Region*; Mahmoud Sayed Amin, *Technological Energy Options in the Arab Countries*; Ossman El-Kholy and Essam El-Henawy, *Energy and the Environment in the Arab Region.*
9. See Amin, *Technological Energy Options in the Arab Countries.*
10. Ibid.
11. This study was published in *Al-Mustaqbal Al-Araby*, **2**, 10, November 1979, pp. 33–49.
12. See *First Arab Energy Conference, A First Step on a Long Road*, OAPEC Bulletin, **5**, 4, April 1979.

13. For more details about patterns and problems of development in these societies, see Mahmoud Abdel-Fadil, 'Problems and Perspectives of Development Process in Oil "Rentier" States', *Arab Oil and Co-operation*, **5**, 3, 1979.

7 STRATEGY TO DEVELOP ARAB EDUCATION

Upon the recommendations of the Fourth Conference of Arab Education Ministers held in Sanaa in December 1972, a committee was formed to lay down a strategy for the development of Arab education. Its task, as defined in the resolution passed in this regard, would be to lay down a pan-Arab educational strategy which each Arab country could use as a guideline for its own education plan. The committee was formed for this purpose,[1] began its work in April 1973, and published a report at the end of 1976[2] under the title 'Strategy for the Development of Arab Education', which dealt with the following points: the will for change in Arab society; problems of Arab education: analysis and resolution; principles and perspectives of an Arab educational strategy conducive to progress and responsive to pan-national aims.

1. Aims and basic premises of the strategy

The report departs from the following two main propositions.

Firstly, that 'the best way to face the challenges of the scientific and technical revolution and to bridge the gap cutting us off from the mainstream of this revolution is by modernizing the Arab mind as a whole, thus enabling it to absorb the spirit of the age in its healthy expression, devoid of aberrations and negative aspects, and in all its dimensions: science, the mental discipline necessary for a rigorous scientific approach and the skills and techniques which can be applied and invested'.[3]

Secondly, that 'education' is one of many systems in society and cannot therefore be clearly seen in isolation from it. A proper understanding of education can only derive from an understanding of its relations with the other systems, economic, social, political and cultural, in society . . . for, like them, it is an offshoot of a bigger system, society, with which it interacts, affecting it and being affected by it in return.'[4]

The report stresses the role that education can play in overcoming problems of backwardness and fragmentation, in realizing overall development to ensure the dignity of man and in enabling the Arab nation to attain its objectives. It is in this understanding that the report addresses itself to a number of vital issues which it sees as touching substantially on the future of the Arab citizen, such as 'Arabization' and the need to confirm the Arabic language as a tool for expression, thinking, legislation and transactions. But first it lays a solid foundation on which to base the elements of the strategy it envisages for Arab education until the end of the century, by analysing the condition, trends and problems of Arab education today, with a view to coming up with answers to the following questions.[5]

Has Arab education managed to keep pace with the changes in society and to respond to the overwhelming will for change?

Has it achieved democracy of education and applied the principle of equal opportunities for education in its broadest sense?

Has it attained peak efficiency internally, in terms of its performance, and externally, in terms of its being tuned to society?

Has it assimilated the cultural attitudes that combine between 'authenticity and renewal'?

Has it been responsive to pan-national needs?

In an attempt to reply to these questions the report identifies some areas of weakness in Arab educational systems. The biggest problem it identifies remains the high rate of adult illiteracy[6] in general, and of female illiteracy in particular. The movement to expand education at the *primary level* in all Arab countries, whatever their political systems, did not as a rule proceed according to a clear plan. It was usually in response to the pressures of growing social demand for education in densely populated areas rather than to the real needs of such areas. The result has been an over-concentration of primary education in some areas and a scarcity in others, at the expense of social justice and cohesion. Despite a continued enrolment growth at the *secondary level* of education, attaining 25 per cent of youths in that age group in 1974/5 as opposed to 19 per cent in 1969/70, the main problem remains the limited and weak formation of intermediary technical cadres because secondary education, the main link in their formation, is dominated by an academic, theoretical character.

In the absence of a comprehensive blueprint for expansion of university and higher education, their expansion has proceeded erratically, without any clear direction or plan. This has led to duplication in specializations, with the result that shortages in teaching staff and elements of instability are now making themselves felt.

The educational systems prevailing in the Arab countries are geared to the examination system in its traditional form, which is based essentially on testing the ability to learn by rote. They are also encumbered with rigid curricula and insular schools which are detached from the problems of society, neither learning about nor dealing with them in a manner which could develop curricula by linking them to rich sources of knowledge, skills and means of production lying beyond the school perimeter.

The report deplores the lack of an Arab philosophy of education, which could steer efforts throughout the Arab world to expand in education and increase enrolments at different levels of education as 'expansion in education stems essentially from a general feeling of the importance of education, from a desire on the part of the masses to make up for educational opportunities they missed and from each Arab country's endeavour to consolidate its independence . . . But these feelings will be gratified only if the future demands of Arab society can be anticipated through the exhaustive study of available human and material resources and of the means of converting them into effective forces for real change in the Arab world'.[7]

The report also notes that, during the last few years, there has been an excessive concentration on school education in Arab countries and none at all on 'extra-school' education. This calls for a reappraisal of the Arab educational system and its extra-school patterns. At the same time, scientific research has been neglected, with the result that it is weak and dissociated from society's needs and, consequently, unable to establish a scientific Arab outlook and indigenous Arab thinking, in most cases continuing to rely on foreign sources and western models and formulas.

In short, education in the Arab world is based on imported systems which aim to perpetuate the system of 'educated élites'. Accordingly, the educational process does not extend to the whole of society (especially adults, women, rural- and nomadic-dwellers). Thus these systems are concerned with 'formal structures', making for weak links with development processes, practical aspects of production and life in general. They also express inadequately the pan-national aims and aspirations of the Arab citizen striving to liberate himself from the shackles of backwardness and to assert himself by helping shape the features of the Arab present and future.

On the basis of these given acknowledged facts, the committee set up to devise a strategy for the development of education in the Arab countries proposed the elements of what it called a 'strategy for the complete renewal of education within the framework of the overall development of the Arab nation', which aimed at overcoming the weaknesses in the actual educational systems and process. It would take too long to discuss in detail the principles and ideals underlying the strategy, so we shall confine ourselves to noting the pattern of priorities which determined the main areas to which the report believes the proposed strategic action should be directed. The following guidelines were used in selecting the areas most worthy of attention.[8]

> Areas which reflect the need to come to grips with acute problems in which reside the loci of weakness in Arab education in particular and to which can be attributed many of the negative aspects of Arab life in general. All attempts to solve them over the years have been unsuccessful, and these problems remain huge, with ramifications extending to major sectors in society.
>
> Areas which require concerted efforts, on both the national and pan-national levels, because of their importance in establishing or completing the necessary infrastructure for a take-off in education and its renewal within the framework of overall development.
>
> Areas falling within the global understanding of development, which entail the active participation of main sectors in society-workers, peasants and others—through various work opportunities and favourable social conditions.

2. Different approaches to the proposed strategy

In the light of these guidelines, the report suggests the following practical approaches to implement the proposed strategy.[9] Firstly, minimum educational opportunities should be provided for a large number of children and adults, especially those who did not have a chance to receive a basic education or who dropped out because of social oppression or economic destitution. The minimum could be limited to the primary level of education, but not for less than four years—thus reconciling two considerations: the limitations on the state's financial capacity and its duty to provide basic education to all citizens. The main aim here is to meet 'minimum needs' for education for young and old alike as an essential condition for the individual's participation in economic, social and political activities. These needs include learning on-the-job, in reading and arithmetic, and training in skills and expertise related to productive activities. This in turn entails reorganizing primary schools and developing new forms of extra-school educational programmes, more especially in rural areas with high drop-out rates.

Secondly, channels of secondary education should be diversified in accordance with development needs. Historically, secondary education is linked to higher and university education more than it is to social and economic developments, with the result that it is predominantly theoretical in character. Thus efforts must be directed at developing the secondary school and linking it closely to development needs and practical life, by injecting curricula with practical studies and technological subjects. It is also necessary to diversify the channels of secondary education by promoting secondary technical education in order to increase the number of technically-trained people who are in short supply in the labour markets of most Arab countries. Expansion in this area will help gradually overcome the present disparity between the outputs of the secondary education system on the one hand, and, on the other, the requirements of industrial development and the ability to cope with growing operational and maintenance problems arising from the continuous influx of modern machinery and equipment. The strategy also emphasizes the importance of enriching secondary education with studies of a technological character (properties of metals, technical drawing) through comprehensive schools and other formulae.

Thirdly, higher education should be updated by devising new models of higher education tailored to the requirements of overall development. The Arab countries should experiment with such formulas as small or medium colleges, environmental colleges, provincial and open universities, correspondence courses and rotating classes, with a view to adopting and developing those which best respond to their needs. They should also revise their present policies regarding overseas scholarships and the systems of postgraduate studies and research in the aim of developing new 'schools of thought' in Arab universities. Postgraduate students should be directed at studying Arab realities and problems, to acquire visions of the future through field-studies of the present. To co-ordinate efforts in this direction, the document urges that a 'centre or institute for the development of higher education' be established on a pan-Arab level, under the supervision of the Federation of Arab Universities, to undertake planning and coordination, to study the problems of higher education, to set rules of admission and to facilitate the exchange of professors, postgraduate students, documentation and information among the Arab countries.

Fourthly, the actual educational structure should be reformed because, from a strategic point of view, it is imperative that the educational philosophy be in tune with the concerns and problems of society. This would entail changing the content, tools and modes of education by improving curricula, giving special attention to science, modern mathematics and foreign languages and by improving school textbooks, one of the most important tools of education. At the same time, educational techniques should be developed. Within this framework, the document recommends that the Regional Centre for Educational Methods in Kuwait be given an important role to play in activating pan-Arab and national efforts in this direction.

Fifthly, Arabization is recommended, increasing and enhancing the use of Arabic. This issue is high on the list of the proposed strategy's priorities, in that it is inseparable from the issue of Arab authenticity and renewal as a whole. New methods of teaching the language in schools must be devised, and teachers, whatever their subject, should use classical Arabic in class. Institutes of higher learning should also participate by Arabizing subjects for which no Arab terminology exists as yet.

Finally, the document does not lose sight of the fact that, for its proposals to be adopted, expenditure on education must be increased and the disparities which now exist between the Arab countries, both as to the amount of public expenditure and the areas in which it is invested, must be reduced. Where, in some Arab countries, the rate of public expenditure on education is less than 3 per cent of GNP, in others it goes up to more than 6 per cent. Although this is a respectable rate for developing countries, the importance of education at this stage of Arab history makes it incumbent on the Arab countries to increase public expenditure in this area, especially on the pan-Arab level. To this end, the document calls on Arab countries in general to spend more on education and on some in particular to help their sister countries meet their responsibilities.

3. Different models for the application of the strategy

The document is not content simply to propose elements of a strategy to develop Arab education, but proceeds to put before us specific models which allow for a degree of flexibility in applying the proposed strategy in the various Arab countries according to their respective availabilities and needs. In application, the proposed priorities can take many forms, depending on the degree of development of the educational system in a given country and on its conditions, needs and potentials. The main criteria adopted in constructing the models were: population (the pattern of sparsity or density, of dispersion or concentration); geographical area (whether extensive or limited); degree of development of educational systems (whether recent or with a long history of achievements and related problems); resources (whether abundant or scarce, and the effect of this on the level of development).

According to these four criteria, the relative weight of the priorities referred to above could vary from one model to the next. The document defines the following models for the different groupings of Arab countries at the present stage as outlined below.

Model 1: This comprises countries characterized for the most part by scarcity of population, an abundance of resources, relatively young educational systems and disparate geographical areas namely, Lebanon, Kuwait, Qatar, Bahrain, Jordan, Libya, United Arab Emirates. On the whole, these countries have gone a long way towards providing and generalizing primary education and are expected to make it compulsory by no later than 1980. However, some of them need to generalize basic education for adults and to expand extra- and pre-school education in order to achieve democracy of education in its broadest sense, a goal they should try to reach by around 1985. At the same time, they should focus on educational reform, on improving internal and external efficiency and on devising suitable formulas for secondary and higher education that would respond to the requirements of overall development.

One of the elements in their strategy should be to affirm and consolidate joint Arab action from two basic premises: one stemming from their awareness of the need for such joint action and of their reliance on the expertise and experience of some Arab countries in the domain of education, the other stemming from a sense of responsibility, especially on the part of those countries among them with financial or human resources, to support joint Arab action.

Model 2: This comprises countries characterized for the most part by density of population, wide geographic areas, broad-based and diversified economics, uneven distribution of resources, by the development of educational systems over a long period in modern times and, accordingly, by experience in the domain of education. These countries are Egypt, Iraq, Syria and Tunisia.

Although these countries have covered a lot of ground in expanding and generalizing primary education, there is still much to be done before basic education is made available·to both children and adults. This they are called upon to achieve by about 1985.

An important priority of these countries should be to strike a balance between secondary and higher education on the one hand, and the different specializations required on the other, to devise new models for both levels of education, and to increase their internal and external efficiency in accordance with the demands of overall development. In the area of joint Arab action, they should develop an educational doctrine drawn from their long and varied experience and co-ordinate their efforts to make their expertise and experience available to other Arab countries on the one hand and, on the other, to seek the assistance of those among them with large financial resources.

Model 3: The countries in this model share the following general traits—a relative scarcity of population, a wide geographical area (with a few exceptions), weak resources (except in one or two cases) and educational systems at varying levels of development. These countries are Morocco,

Saudi Arabia, Sudan, Somalia, Mauritania, North Yemen, South Yemen and Oman. Providing general education for adults and children is still a long way off in all these countries, although the last few years have seen important efforts in this direction. Furthermore, education for women remains severely underdeveloped. The countries are called upon to provide basic education for all their citizens, male and female alike, by sometime between 1985 and 1990.

Those countries which, like Saudi Arabia and Morocco, are rich in resources, will have no difficulty in expanding and diversifying secondary education or in developing higher education to meet the overall development with the help of other Arab countries experienced in these domains.

As for the remaining countries in this Model, their expansion will depend on their ability to strike a balance between two factors: giving clear priority to democratizing basic education, on the one hand, and providing the technical cadres necessary for overall development on the other.

Joint Arab action is required to help these countries achieve their goals. They need to draw on the expertise and services available to a number of countries in Model 2 in order to develop their educational systems and base them on a distinctive educational doctrine. While some of these countries are hard-pressed for financial resources to develop their educational systems, others have financial resources to spare. Thus formulas and trends of joint Arab action in future can assume multiple forms of 'give and take' in this as in the other models.

Model 4: This is devoted exclusively to Palestine, the core issue for the Arab nation as a whole and the pivot of its confrontation with imperialism and Zionism. Victims of a tragedy that has gone on now for more than thirty years the Palestinian people, scattered as they are in different parts of the Arab world and beyond, nevertheless retain a strong sense of national identity. Deprived of their land, they have not been deprived of their vigour or of their will to fight for what is theirs by right. To this end, they have directed their efforts at educating their young in the face of heavy odds. Within the framework of the proposed strategy, the Model aims to lay down a comprehensive educational policy for the Palestinian people that is linked to their national aim to return to Palestine and establish a state on their land, as well as to guarantee a decent life for them with the assistance of other Arab countries. This policy sets itself the following strategic objectives.

(*a*) Guaranteeing the rights of all Palestinians, children and adults, to basic education; making child education compulsory and wiping out adult illiteracy for the Palestinians as well as for the citizens of their temporary host countries.

(*b*) Ensuring that the social, cultural and national dimensions are upheld in the education of Palestinians, young and old, in the occupied territories, and reminding international organizations and the world community of their responsibilities in this respect.

(*c*) Enabling Palestinians to take advantage of the opportunities for secondary and higher education available in the host country, fixing adequate quotas for them in the universities of that country and encouraging Palestinian children in pre-school and extra-school education.

(*d*) Enabling Palestinian professionals living abroad to take part in the struggle to liberate their land by returning to the Arab nation and helping develop education for their fellow Palestinians.

(*e*) Making the Palestinian cause the focal point in civics classes throughout the Arab world.

(*f*) Promoting two-way Arab action, in the sense that the many talented and experienced Palestinians can contribute greatly to the development of education in many Arab countries, while the Palestinians for their part need resources to develop the forms of education suitable for them. Their need will become all the greater if the Palestinian State is proclaimed in preparation for liberating the usurped land, for it must be built on a solid educational foundation and a new educational philosophy, both possible only through consolidating joint Arab action.

It can be noticed that the models devised by the document are quite similar, with no sharp lines of demarcation separating one from the other. None of them display distinctive traits or tends. In fact, the differences between them are less qualitative than they are relative, in the sense that they are linked to how developed the educational system is, to socio-economic conditions and to the balance between potential and needs in each model or in the various countries in a given model. Moreover, not only did these models not draw on specific data bases, contenting themselves with identifying features and trends only in the most general way, but the time horizons they envisage for the attainment of certain goals are limited in the main to the area of basic education, particularly as it relates to compulsory education for children and to eradicating adult illiteracy.

4. A brief appraisal

While we have nothing but praise for the considerable efforts that went into this document, and for its extensive coverage of aspects of education as they relate to issues of development and to asserting the cultural identity of the Arab people, we must point out that it failed to address a number of important questions vital to the Arab future. One such question is the 'plurality of educational channels' at each level of education. There is often a *duality*, even a *triplicity*, in the educational process in the Arab world, where three distinct and unrelated educational channels live side by side: religious education, public government education and private education in foreign language schools. This state of affairs can profoundly affect the course of the Arab future. By deepening the dichotomy in thinking and in cultural values among educated Arabs, it will produce a new set of contradictions that will bring about further anguish and 'cultural schizophrenia' in Arab life.

The document also fails to accord sufficient attention to a number of strategic issues related to democracy of education and the eradication of illiteracy—on this last question it limits itself basically to discussing 'alphabetical illiteracy', without touching on other forms such as 'cultural' or 'political' illiteracy, although these are closely related to the education of the citizen. The battle to wipe out illiteracy in all its dimensions is a battle for Arab emancipation which, as such, requires a degree of mobilization going far beyond the building of new schools or the opening of new classes.

Among the important issues neglected by the report in this area is the 'return to illiteracy' phenomenon which we are today witnessing in many Arab countries. Because many of the activities in which people are engaged in these countries do not necessitate reading and writing, this phenomenon is becoming more and more widespread. This underlines the importance of making what is called 'continuous' or 'renewable' education a basic component in a new Arab educational strategy to avoid slipping into the pitfall of illiteracy once again. Another loophole in the document is that it does not look seriously into the present and future dimensions of 'democracy of education' and such related problems as the emergence of new forms of education and cultural formation which, through various channels of communication such as television and official information media, have introduced deep distortions into the educational process. This entails devising policies to improve means of education and the content of textbooks with a view to linking schools to the environment so that educational activities do not acquire an élitist character.

This in turn entails developing educational techniques and means in line with an expanded educational framework that would include wide segments of the population on the work site or living in the shadow of deep economic privation. In this connection, we must point out that the report confused the concept of 'extra-school' education, which involves opening new classes to teach adults and eradicate adult illiteracy, with the concept of 'informal' education, which takes such forms as learning on-the-job, the 'open school' or the 'mobile school'. Possibly one of the reasons the report did not touch on these questions is that it approaches issues of education, learning and culture from a purely professional perspective. It seems the committee still subscribes to the notion that questions of education are the exclusive domain of educators, although some aspects of the radical changes proposed by this very document, and its recognition that relations between the social, economic, political and educational systems are closely interwoven, would seem to indicate that experts from other fields of specialization should have participated in laying down the strategy for Arab education, together with those who will benefit from the output of the educational process (people working in the domain of planning and development, those responsible for production units and other services) and those who may benefit from democratization of education (representatives of trade unions, peasants' organizations, women and youth).

Notes

1. The committee was formed, in consultation with the Executive Council of the Arab Organization for Education, Culture and Science, as follows: Dr Mohamed Ahmed El-Sherif (chairman), Mr Abdel Hamid El-Mehry, Dr Abdel Razek Kodwa, Dr Abdel Aziz El-Bassam, Dr Mohamed El-Hady Afifi, Dr Mohamed Rifat El-Faneesh and Dr Nagati El-Bokhary (members).
2. See League of Arab States, Arab Organization for Education, Culture and Science, *Strategy for Developing Arab Education*, Comprehensive Report.
3. Ibid., p. 22.
4. Ibid., p. 42.
5. Ibid., p. 51.
6. Although the rate of adult illiteracy varies from one year to the next and from one country to another—ranging from 90 per cent in some

Arab countries to 45 per cent in others—the average for the Arab countries taken together is close to 75 per cent. While the rate varies according to the different regions within one country and by sex, what is certain is that some 80 per cent of illiterates are found among the rural and nomadic populations and that the rate of female illiteracy is higher than that for males. Ibid., p. 71.

7. Ibid., p. 60.
8. Ibid., p. 137.
9. Ibid., p. 123.

8 ALTERNATIVE PATTERNS OF DEVELOPMENT AND LIFESTYLES[1]

Conducted as an assignment for the United Nations Economic Commission for West Asia (ECWA), this study confines itself, according to the terms of reference, to the countries falling within the ECWA region. However, the strategic issues it addresses are pertinent to all the countries of the Arab nation, both in the 'Mashreq' and the 'Maghreb'. The author of the study, Dr Ismail Sabri Abdalla, casts light on the relationship between development patterns in the Arab region on the one hand, and environmental issues, in their natural, biological, social and cultural dimensions, on the other.

It is the first study of its kind in that it gives an overview of the environmental issues arising from socio-economic development processes underway in the region. The study correctly points out that the environment and disruptions in the 'ecological balance' only caught the attention of researchers and policy-makers in the Arab region after these issues had come in for a great deal of attention and concern in the West. Indeed, Arab thinking in this area is merely an extension of western thinking on the issues of pollution and the problems arising from the depletion of natural resources (especially oil). This is all the more surprising in view of the fact that the Arab region is considered among the most sensitive to issues related to the development of man's relationship with nature, and to the environment in general, containing as it does vast tracts of desert, fertile river valleys and rich reserves of natural resources in the ground.

This leads the study to conclude that it is no longer possible to put off confronting a number of crucial issues relating to the environment and the balance between man and the elements of the ecosystems surrounding him. According to the study, this would entail raising public awareness, on both the official and popular levels, of environmental issues which have a direct and strong bearing on the future of the Arab individual; assessing actual development policies and practices in terms of sound environment management principles; identifying, whenever possible, alternative strategies of development and lifestyles that would allow for greater harmony between man and the various elements of his ecosystem, including the rational management of water, oil and other natural resources.

The ecological history of the region has been a tumultuous one, a drama of survival and growth in an inhospitable arid or semi-arid environment. The civilizations which grew and flourished in the region were linked to the river valleys of Egypt, the Fertile Crescent and the Maghreb. More recently, the discovery of oil in desert countries like the Gulf States, Saudi Arabia and Libya was crucial in shaping new patterns of lifestyles and development in these countries. Thus the 'dialectics of Nature' played a vital role in shaping the features of Arab history, past and present, and there is every reason to suppose that considerations dictated by their inexorable logic will mark the Arab future just as strongly.

The author points out that population movements throughout the Arab region were determined largely by relations of equilibrium (or disequilibrium) between man and his environment. Thus Arab migrations through the ages obeyed a general rule: away from the arid regions, where Nature was harsh and life difficult, towards the river valleys, where a more amenable Nature offered man an easier livelihood. However, the discovery of vast oil-wealth in arid regions (the Gulf States, Saudi Arabia and Libya) gave rise to new population movements in the opposite direction: from the river valleys towards the arid regions, where the 'black gold' bonanza offered opportunities for easier livelihood. This phenomenon has helped the components of modern urban life and new lifestyles to flourish, and has accelerated the tempo of growth in these countries.[2]

1. The issues

The document raises a number of vital issues touching on the future of the region's ecosystems. We refer to the five most important of these below.

(1) The need to develop relations between the inhabitants of

the Arab region and its natural resources, since agricultural expansion is a function of two determinants—availability of cultivable land with the required specifications and of water for irrigation. Each of these determinants is in itself an important component of the Arab ecosystem. It is clear that the expansion—or stagnation—of the Arab agricultural sector in future depends on our ability to increase the area now available for agriculture and to provide the water required in the manner proposed by the strategy for Arab food security reviewed earlier.

(2) Rapid urban spread and the strain it imposes on basic infrastructures which, unable to cope with increasingly heavy demands, deteriorate and, indeed, sometimes collapse entirely, as well as its encroachment on the 'green belts' surrounding cities and the green areas inside them, has severely disrupted ecosystems in Arab urban centres. The problem is further compounded by heavy congestion, making for a decline in housing and health conditions as the urban poor are crowded into shanty towns. At the same time the exhaust fumes given off by cars, which have grown in number and size with the influx of wealth and the new patterns of consumption and lifestyles that have invaded Arab life, are increasing atmospheric pollution. All this leads the author to observe that the region suffers from the negative environmental effects of both excessive wealth and extreme poverty.[3]

(3) Another issue, closely linked to this and with enormous implications for the Arab future, is the permeation of western consumption patterns into Arab society during the seventies, making for what the author calls a 'consumption fever', in which resources are squandered in consumption processes and in importing commodities totally unsuited to the Arab climate and cultural environment. Thus synthetic fibres are imported when cotton fabrics are more appropriate for weather conditions in the region, while high-fidelity stereophonic sound systems are used to listen to essentially monodic Arabic music. Perhaps the most glaring example lies in copying western styles of architecture, with their heavy use of glass, steel and aluminium, in climates where buildings should be designed to provide as much shade and natural cooling inside the buildings as

possible, in the manner of traditional Arab architecture before its distortion by the blind imitation of western architectural styles.

(4) The same issue comes up in the area of education, through its relationship with the historical, cultural and social environment of the Arab nation. The author speaks of the *dangers of equating modernization to westernization*, warning that processes of educational and cultural modernization that take the form of westernization will lead, in the final analysis, to the negation of Arab society's cultural identity and to the alienation of the Arab individual.

(5) Finally, the study stresses the need to reject pollution-generating and resource-intensive industries and techniques, especially at a time when the capitalist West is trying to export these industries, and with them pollution, to the Third World.

2. Recommendations

The study puts forward some recommendations of a general nature on how to deal with a number of questions closely related to the issues of environment and development. The most important of these can be summed up as follows.

(1) Sound planning and management of environmental resources, in the 'ecological' understanding of development, that is, that the evolution and growth of Arab development processes in future based on the evolution and development of the individual should proceed in line with the evolution and development of the ecosystem, and not in opposition to it or at its expense, as was the case in the past. This entails the sound management of environmental resources, as well as evolving 'economic accounting' systems capable of assessing costs and benefits of environmental quality. In other words, environmental issues and problems can only be dealt with within the framework of long-range overall planning, for, while it is difficult to measure environmental effects (whether positive or negative) at the micro-level of the individual project, it is far easier to do so at the level of the overall national economy or of a geographical region, in the framework of regional planning.[4]

Rational use of available natural resources, particularly water resources, the optimal use of which remains central to the future development of Arab agriculture; pastures, which are linked to the development and improvement of livestock wealth throughout the Arab nation; non-renewable resources now being rapidly depleted, notably oil. Use should also be made of hitherto unexploited natural resources, especially those of a renewable nature, such as solar energy, which is available in abundance throughout the Arab region. The study classifies the vast empty spaces of Arab land under this same heading, and notes that making rational use of such areas could help achieve a balanced development and reduce some of the enormous pressure on other areas which are overpopulated and whose ecosystems are severely strained.

(3) Suitable consumption patterns. A strategy based on satisfying basic needs could alleviate the incidence and acuteness of poverty, an ever-present danger that threatens to disrupt the man–environment–society balance. On the other hand, limiting conspicuous (especially profligate) consumption could help avert other kinds of danger to society and the environment, such as pollution from car exhaust fumes or architectural styles which disfigure the beauty of the towns and environment.

(4) Asserting cultural identity. Since lifestyles are known to be strongly affected by the prevailing set of cultural norms, any search for alternative patterns and lifestyles to replace the prevailing ones which have been imported from the West, must look for their roots among the components of the Arab socio-cultural heritage, where the group takes precedence over the individual as a means of ensuring the social continuum and which display distinctive patterns in architecture, art and folklore compatible with the historical specificity of the Arab socio-cultural environment.

(5) Popular participation and democracy are issues which appear central to processes designed to curtail degradation of the natural, social and cultural components of the ecosystem. The optimum policies and strategies which can strike a balance between man and the environment are those based on the complete awareness of citizens, through their active participation in decision-making processes at the

grass-root level. Many of the processes that we see degrading the ecosystem are the result of economic decisions guided by profit-maximization considerations taken at the macro level, which, being imposed without democratic debate, overlook the adverse effects of such decisions on the components and equilibrium of the ecosystem.

3. A brief appraisal

Although the study represents a first attempt to address environmental issues as they relate to processes of economic and political development underway in the Arab nation, it remains a highly abstract exercise. In this it displays a trait common to all pioneering works. As successful as it was in identifying critical areas which will have an enormous bearing on the future of the Arab ecosystem (natural-resource depletion; patterns of using water resources, land and pastures; urban spread; environmental pollution and its relations with patterns of consumption and industrialization), we feel the study did not sufficiently explore how decision-making processes, at the micro- and macro-levels, affect the components and elements of the ecosystem.

Accordingly, any futures study must understand the dialectical relationship between decision-making processes at the local, micro and macro levels on the one hand, and their effects in impairing (or protecting) the components of the Arab ecosystem on the other. We have absolutely no doubt that environmental considerations will be among the most crucial in determining possible images of the Arab future in the next two decades.

Notes

1. We relied in this review on the original English language version of the study Ismail-Sabri Abdalla, *Alternative Patterns of Development and Lifestyles in Western Asia: A Keynote and an Overview*, United Nations, Economic Commission for West Asia (ECWA) United Nations Environment Program (UNEP), Beirut, December 1979.
2. See, in this connection, Mahmoud Abdel-Fadil, *Oil and Arab Unity*, Beirut, Centre for Arab Unity Studies, 1979, Chapter 2.
3. Ibid., p. 91.
4. It must be pointed out here that environmental issues usually come up

in connection with such major projects as the building of dams to regulate a river's flow. A case in point is Egypt's High Dam, which has brought important changes to some elements of the prevailing ecological balance. For the side-effects of the High Dam and the possibilities of overcoming them see: Mahmoud Abdel-Fadil *Structural Effects of the High Dam on the Future of Development in Egypt*, in Studies in Planning, Beirut, Dar El-Quds, 1979 and Abdel Azeem Aboul Atta *Applied Study on High Dam Project in Aswan*, United Nations Economic Commission for West Asia, Co-ordinating Unit for Environmental Affairs, Beirut, November 1979.

9 WORKING PAPER OF THE THREE-MAN COMMITTEE SELECTED BY THE COMMITTEE OF EXPERTS ON A STRATEGY FOR JOINT ARAB ECONOMIC ACTION

This document was prepared by a three-man committee[1] selected by the committee of experts on joint Arab economic action (later known as the 'committee of twenty'), and was presented —as the main document—to the first pan-national conference on a strategy for joint Arab economic action held in Baghdad 6–12 May, 1978.

Its main concern is how the role of the *joint Arab economic sector*, which has grown around a multitude of specialized organizations, financing institutions and joint ventures, can be streamlined and developed. Although the funds allocated to this sector are quite substantial (the document estimates that they amounted to some 15.5 billion dollars at the time), the main complaint is 'the absence of any integrative vision that can raise [the joint sector's] benefits from the limited country-specific level to the pan-national level, which represents the only possible point of departure for an Arab economic base that is solid, modern, dynamic and conducive to growth and development'. The document here puts forward three questions of a strategic character.

Is it possible to formulate a vision of integrated joint Arab economic action?

Is there any incentive for the various Arab countries to adopt such a vision and work towards realizing it?

If the answer to both these questions is affirmative, what is the mechanism by which integration can be implemented?

1. Premises and incentives of joint Arab economic action

The premise on which the strategic concept is based is eloquently expressed in the document as follows: 'Any plausible strategy must depart from what is and not from what should be, for what is ideal in theoretical terms is not what is ideal in strategic terms, which is the optimal maximization of realistic chances.'

Translated into practical terms, the strategic line governing this document can perhaps best be expressed as an attempt to give 'oil capital' the leading role in any joint Arab economic action in future, and to make of it the real organizer of factors of production as they dynamically interact throughout the entire region. A look at some of the key passages in the working paper confirms this view: 'The first aim of any strategy for joint Arab economic action under the present circumstances must be to find a system of credible incentives which could convince the wealthy Arab oil-states to take the initiative in working towards the ultimate goal of converting "oil reserves" into "technological capabilities".'

Accordingly, a strategy for 'technological transformation' must give countries with financial resources and the readiness to invest these in joint ventures the right to choose the technologies and industries they wish to introduce into the region. In practical terms, this would entail giving them first option in three matters related to their exercise of this right. To begin with, they should be allowed to conceive for themselves the pattern of technology distribution on a pan-Arab scale. For example, if they should opt for establishing a fertilizer industry in the region, they should be allowed to decide the location and size of this industry, as well as when it should be set up. Such a right would not be given haphazardly: in exchange, these countries would have relinquished other technologies to other Arab states and would be committed to investing in these states.[2]

Within this framework, the paper gives a great deal of importance to what it calls the specifications of 'Arab consensus' and the incentives of joint Arab action, stressing that: 'Joint Arab economic action' must be placed in the context of country-specific development processes, that is, it must be seen as one of the basic elements in the development of each country. Regional organization is, after all, an extension of development processes in each of the countries within the region, which it promotes to a level higher than that which any one of them could have attained on its own, by introducing into these processes new dynamic elements in the domains of resources, markets and aspirations through the enormous increase which joint Arab action can bring to these domains. Joint action requires a degree of organization if it is to bring about such an increase. Also, to be successful, it must be geared to increasing both resources and aspirations simultaneously. For resources can increase without a corresponding increase in aspirations, in which case the size of the economy would remain the same and the additional resources would be wasted in domains which have no lasting effect. Aspirations can only be increased by expanding the horizons of national development, so that the aspirations of the state applying this development—for resources, markets and abilities—comes to encompass all, or most, of the Arab states.

Thus the paper sees the first incentive for joint economic action to be a political one—both national and pan-national in scope—in that, for the financing country, it is a way of consolidating its security against external dangers, while maintaining a climate of understanding within the Arab framework. In the light of these premises, the paper defines the following principles to serve as a guideline in determining the orientations of strategic action in the context of the sector of joint Arab economic action.

(1) The strategic action must be capable of maximizing Arab industrial and economic development and of generalizing it as widely as possible. This means that it must be economically justifiable and not based purely on analyses, deductions and abstract principles.
(2) Within this framework, it must be capable of attracting, assimilating and storing the greatest measure of technological capability as defined earlier.
(3) It must generate benefits which can be distributed fairly and evenly.
(4) Arab collective self-reliance must replace reliance on the outside world as much as possible.
(5) It must incorporate a system of incentives that would encourage the greatest possible number of Arab countries to participate.
(6) It must be geared so that the various Arab states complement one another as much as possible.
(7) It must contribute to maximizing Arab security capabilities in the areas of food, basic production and military production.

2. Main axes of joint Arab economic action

The paper defines the main axes of practical action within the framework of the strategy for joint Arab economic action.

(*a*) *Installing technology* In visualizing the future of joint Arab economic action, the document accords special importance to what it calls 'breaking the technological-backwardness barrier' pointing to the fact that all the Arab countries are aware that 'the technological barrier cannot be crossed by any individual Arab state acting alone. If even the most populous and industrialized among them, with the longest and widest experience in development, has been unable to penetrate the barrier and is still being pushed back each time they try, this means there was a missing link in its concept of development, namely, the factor of size: the size of the various resources required to break the technological barrier (human, natural and financial) and the size of the markets necessary to build the technological base that would make a breakthrough possible. While the importance of size in any industrialization process has often been mentioned in the past, it was always the economic aspect of size that was stressed, as expressed in the externalities it could produce. But more important is size as it relates to the resources required to build an industrial base with a market for its products.'

In this connection, the document stresses an important strategic fact that we consider to be the key to the development process in the Arab region, noting that 'as long as the Arab countries are striving to achieve real progress then they must realize the nature of technological capability and the fastest way of achieving it. For there is a real danger that a substantial part of the preparatory investment now being undertaken by many Arab countries can go to waste simply because it is being built behind the "technological barrier", so to speak. This danger is confirmed by Arab experiences from the era of Mohamed Aly in Egypt to the present day, when not a single Arab country has yet attained technological maturity or even come close to it. There have been instances when a society on the verge of crossing the technological barrier suffered a reversal that set it back to a level below the one at which it previously stood. In relative terms, the setback in such cases appeared still greater when compared with other societies.'

For an Arab take-off in this domain, the paper points out

that priority must be given to establishing complexes for the manufacture of productive and machine-tool industries. Similarly, the engineering sector, with both its consultative and productive branches must be encouraged, especially Arab consultative institutions (in the areas of design, production and construction).

While admitting that in the actual situation the Arab countries have no option but to resort to importing technology, the paper believes that in respect of technologies which are unobtainable from the world technological 'pool' or through buying 'industrial licences', rationalization and improvement are possible by setting terms and specifications for the partner and forms of partnership that would guarantee equality. The document also believes that there are available degrees of freedom for choosing the partner from countries which do not represent an imperialist threat, as the paper puts it, such as India, Spain, Italy, Switzerland, Austria and Sweden.

(*b*) *Industrial development* The paper states that: 'No direct step has been taken to date for industrial co-ordination between the Arab states. Nor have any collective steps been taken to strengthen industrial development in general or specifically. All efforts at industrial development are confined within the national framework, and are undertaken by each country in almost total isolation from what is happening in the other countries of the region'.

The paper believes that a strategy for industrial integration can be based on stimulating the demand for industries according to needs. The prospects here are promising. For instance, a growing demand will emerge for chemical fertilizers, pesticides, agricultural equipment, silos for storage of agricultural produce, refrigerators for food storage and transportation vehicles as a result of developing the agricultural sector. The development of this sector in the Sudan alone would be sufficient to form a market capable of developing all these industries. However, this would entail co-ordination between the processes of agricultural development and the formulation of industrial perspectives of a strategic character.

Similarly, the 'civil construction sector' offers wide possibilities for the development of a number of industries, especially in the field of building-materials, engineering industries and petrochemicals. Thus immediate efforts can be directed at establishing industries that can manufacture building-materials and equipment locally on a pan-Arab level. There is also the possibility of developing a solid basis for an Arab military industry, which can benefit from the enormous amounts spent by the Arab countries on importing military hardware. This industry would rest in turn on a developed base of engineering industries, thus confirming the characteristic of forward and backward linkages between the various branches of industry in any strategic plan for joint Arab industrial development.

The document believes that the first phase in the process of Arab industrial co-ordination should focus on future industries, while the second phase should be to co-ordinate between the existing industries at the proper time.

This order of precedence is due to the fact that most of the existing industries grew in the context of tariff protectionism policies, which raised the cost of production of these industries in comparison with the outside world. If we take into consideration the main factors which led the Arab countries to encourage industry (including providing the required work-force, achieving a degree of diversity in the structure of production, decreasing reliance on the outside world) we would realize how sensitive they are towards any measure that could affect the industries they have already established. In addition, future industries, even if they are set up under high tariff protection extending to all the countries co-ordinating their efforts, will mobilize some of the natural and human resources lying idle in these countries, thus contributing to the benefits to be derived from co-ordination.

As far as future industries are concerned, agreement can be reached between the co-ordinating countries on distributing a number of these industries among themselves, so that each one could get an industry that would provide it with given benefits and so that the industries selected for co-ordination would be established in all the concerned states in such a way as to internalize the advantages of co-ordination. To ensure this, assistance must be extended to the less-developed Arab countries when they come to set up the industries allocated to them. It might be useful if two institutions are established for this purpose: a financing institution, to extend low-interest loans (this task could be undertaken by the Arab Fund for Economic and Social Development); the other to handle contracting works, such as design, construction and maintenance.

(*c*) *Developing and vitalizing the trade sector* According to the document, 'basing the continuation of economic co-operation on the trade sector is important, because this sector can, in the context of the proposed industrial strategy, set up the establishments complementary to major industrial works, and vital to ensuring their growth and success. In other words, the investments generated by an Arab open trade policy could be transformed into technological investments'. Thus any serious attempt to vitalize and expand the Arab common market should be given every support.

The document stresses the importance of adopting a strategic line in the domain of strengthening and developing trade exchange between the Arab countries, based on liberalizing given commodities from all trade restrictions, that is, customs tariffs, currency regulations, licences of any sort. This document proposes liberalizing trade by exempting the following categories of commodities:

(1) All agricultural, livestock and raw materials, in accordance with the principle adopted by the 1953 Agreement, not only from customs tariffs but, more importantly, from administrative constraints, such as agricultural quotas, as well as from currency restrictions. This is necessary to ensure food security and complementary agricultural activities, as well as for agricultural development activities within the framework of the Arab Agricultural Development Authority. If we have been calling for a unified market for agricultural industries, there is all the more reason to call for a unified market for agricultural products themselves. It should be noted that only seven Arab states were parties to the 1953 Agreement which established this principle, while such countries as the Sudan, vital for the future of agricultural development in the region, all the countries of the Maghreb, Somalia, Mauritania and Djibouti, with its livestock wealth, did not participate.
(2) All commodities produced by Arab joint ventures, or by companies in which the share of any Arab holding company in the capital amounts to 15 per cent or more.
(3) All commodities produced by companies which pledge to make their shares negotiable in all the Arab states, without

granting preferential access to the nationals of any state over those of another.

(4) All technological products, that is, in which skill represents at least 60 per cent of the value.

(5) All intermediary products falling within the scope of co-operation between Arab industries, as well as all parts manufactured in Arab countries for assembly in others.

(6) All commodities which the general federation of any Arab industry agrees to liberalize, thus encouraging a new division of specializations within the same industry as a basis for such liberalization.

(*d*) *Facilitating capital flows between Arab states* The document holds that among the proposals worthy of study in this respect is the idea of establishing '*Arab investment zones*', that would be assimilated in the national build-up and the development plans of the states in which they would be set up, and where the party licensed to establish these zones would undertake to execute an overall plan for infrastructures and economical housing and buildings, taking such administrative procedures as may be required without touching on the sovereignty of the host state. If the idea is approved, Arab companies could be set up to establish and operate these investment zones, in which the private sector would be required to play an important role.

Still on the subject of encouraging capital inflows, the document deals with the question of developing the *Arab financial market* and proposes that, rather than rely for this on foreign banks, Arab banks could play an important role to this end. But, first, 'a regulatory financial body would have to be set up, to perform, on the regional level, the function that central banks play on the national level, viz., re-discounting bills of exchange and ensuring currency liquidity as required by banks. This is a pioneering concept which, if accepted in principle would have to be thoroughly studied and the necessary regulations and framework laid down'.

If stock markets are to play a role within the sector of joint Arab economic action, then, as the document points out, shares must first be made negotiable on a pan-Arab level. Arab joint ventures could make a percentage of their shares negotiable among Arab citizens (as in the case of the Arab African Bank), while at the country-level, governments could gradually allow the negotiability of a percentage of national companies' shares to Arab citizens. However, as the document itself admits, such an evolution would take some time.

(*e*) *Linking efforts within the sector of joint Arab economic action to processes of Arab solidarity in general* Among the most important new elements contained in the three-man committee's working paper is the attempt to formulate a strategic vision of how to tie-up efforts for joint Arab economic action to processes of Arab solidarity in general. Any strategy for joint Arab economic action which fails to address this question would face enormous difficulties, if not outright paralysis, in application.

The document maintains, and rightly so, that one of the main reasons for the current Arab crisis is the disparity between the Arab countries in per capita income levels. Obviously the reasons for convergence between societies with an annual per capita income of over 4000 dollars and others where the overwhelming majority of the population are forced to live on under 200 dollars a year, are fewer than reasons of divergence. The situation is complicated still further by the fact that, because of transient geographical and historical circumstances, *the distribution of wealth is in inverse proportion to the distribution of burdens and sacrifices.* Whatever the reasons for this disproportionality it has had effects and repercussions going beyond anything that could have been foreseen—or, indeed, imagined.

Thus the point of departure in any attempt to strategically link-up Arab solidarity to joint Arab economic action must be to redress the enormous disparity in income-levels between the 'affluent' and 'needy' countries of the region. This link-up can be effected at very little cost the oil countries, according to the document, which proposes that the Arabs assert their solidarity by imposing a 10 per cent surcharge on all oil exports (in co-ordination with OPEC), allocating the proceeds to a fund for Arab Economic Development, which the Arab oil states levying the surcharge could themselves administer. This assertion of the Arab identity would bring home to the outside world the commitment of the Arabs to the common Arab cause. At the same time, each Arab citizen would feel that he has a real, and not just a theoretical right, to Arab wealth, thus removing the sensitivities arising from the concept of assistance and charity, which generates feelings of superiority on one side and of inferiority on the other. An arrangement of this sort would be a real evaluation of services exchanged between the two sides and would express the worth of these services.

Pursuing the same theme, the document goes on to say that the proposed surcharge should remain above any new price determined for oil, something like an export *ad valorem* duty on Arab oil. This would provide the sector of joint Arab economic action with a stable source of revenue to finance the elements of the proposed strategy which, by redressing the balance between benefits and sacrifices on the pan-Arab level, would strengthen the ties of solidarity and the sense of common purpose among the Arabs.

3. A brief critique

The paper prepared by the three-man committee came in for a great deal of criticism, both during the first conference on a strategy for joint Arab economic action and in a number of subsequent papers and commentaries.[3]

The main lines of the criticism levelled against the paper were brilliantly summed by by Dr Youssef Sayigh[4] as follows: the working paper did not depart from an overall, consistent vision of what future the Arab region should choose for itself; it did not lay down a comprehensive, coherent strategy for action, limiting itself to partial approximations; it stuck closely to the concept of 'joint Arab economic action' sanctioned by the general secretariat of the Arab League, and did not attempt to to go beyond this concept towards more ambitious, global formulas, such as integration or unity; certain aspects related to the region's position and future in the new world economic order and to the question of reshaping the international division of labour were neglected by the document; the paper made its point of departure the actual situation and country-specific development plans. In other words, it proposes that the future be built on a foundation of the present situation, with all its effects and distortions.

To be fair, though, some of the paper's shortcomings were due not to an oversight on the part of the committee which drew it up but, as the head of the committee explained, to the fact that their major concern was to try and find a common ground, however limited, that would be acceptable to all Arab parties. To do so, the paper had, of necessity, to make many concessions and to back down somewhat from the ideal pan-national aims and aspirations towards which the Arabs strive in the area of integration and joint Arab economic action, departing rather from a minimum programme of joint Arab action. This could gradually change through 'the grid of the present Arab system', bearing in mind the apprehensions and inhibitions of Arab governments in the light of the pressures to which they are subjected. This is clear when the paper affirms the necessity of opening the field to the private sector, driven by the profit motive, and of providing the institutional framework and appropriate climate in which it can flourish.

Notes

1. Composed of Borhan El-Dajany, Sayed Gaballah and Antoine Zahlan.
2. See *Report of the 3-Man Committee* in: First Pan-Arab Conference on a Strategy for Joint Arab Economic Action, 1, Baghdad, 6–12 May 1978, p. 99.
3. It is interesting to note here that during their deliberations, the members of the strategy experts committee (known as the 'Committee of Twenty') were divided between two trends:
   (a) one was for adopting a comprehensive liberation-oriented developmental outlook, irrespective of how acceptable this might be to the Arab governments;
   (b) another argued that the Committee's recommendations should be confined to what was possible in the medium-term, in order to achieve the greatest degree of joint Arab consensus. It was this trend which prevailed in the report of the three-man committee.
4. See Youssef Sayigh, 'Arab Economic Integration and Protection of National Sovereignty', *Al-Mustaqbal Al-Araby,* **1**, 6, March 1979, pp. 35–6.

10 TOWARDS DEVELOPING JOINT ARAB ECONOMIC ACTION (STRATEGY DOCUMENTS PRESENTED TO THE 11TH ARAB SUMMIT CONFERENCE HELD IN AMMAN IN NOVEMBER 1980)

The declaration issued by the conference on joint Arab economic action held early in 1980 at Habaneya, Iraq, defined the targets of joint Arab economic action as outlined below.

* Emancipation of the Arab citizen and of his creative abilities so that he can effectively participate in, and reap the fruits of, the development process.
* Pan-national security, including intellectual, military, food and technological security.
* Standing up to the Zionist entity, which is colonialist in nature, organically linked to international monopolies, and which aims at crowning its expansionist designs by absorbing the Arab world itself.
* Accelerate overall development geared to realize the maximum degree of Arab collective self-reliance and of conformity between the various sectors and regions and to meet growing basic needs.
* Reducing the 'development gap' which exists in the Arab region, both between and within the various states.
* Economic integration towards Arab economic unity, with all this entails in the way of bringing about structural transformations in Arab economies and realizing the organic economic links between them, especially in the productive field.
* Establishing *a new Arab economic order* based on a complementary nature that is conducive to overall development and in which the pattern of the division of labour in the Arab region can realize the development and emancipation of the countries within that region and thus contribute to

the establishment of the new world economic order which aims at eliminating dependency, halting the depletion of the Third World's resources and establishing equitable, fair and dependable relations between the countries of the world.

1. Basic premises

In the light of these premises and targets, Dr Youssef Sayigh was assigned to form a working group to prepare a new strategy document on the perspectives of developing joint Arab economic action, for presentation to the 11th Arab Summit. A number of principal and supplementary[1] papers were prepared by the working groups formed, and we shall review and analyse below two of the principal documents having a strategic bearing: (*a*) the main general paper, entitled 'Towards Developing Joint Arab Economic Action', and (*b*) the draft framework of a pan-national plan for joint Arab economic action.

The main paper on developing joint Arab economic action departs from the basic proposition that 'development and security, in the wide sense of these words, together form a central and pressing need for the Arab region as a whole in this era, and a goal towards which joint Arab economic action must be directed as an essential part of joint Arab action in its totality. For in development and security reside the elements of resistance, in its economic expression, to the formidable challenges confronting the Arabs'.

The paper then proceeds to emphasize the importance of the organic interrelations and interaction between Arab developments and security in facing up to the loci of weaknesses in Arab society and economy, noting that they interact on two planes. 'A first, *horizontal*, plane, which is the influence each exerts on the other. Pan-national development in its multiple dimensions (most prominently, the emancipation of the Arab individual and the liberation of his abilities) provides the solid human and material base for pan-national security, indeed for the very destiny of the Arab region, while pan-national security in its various dimensions (which extend beyond the purely military dimensions), provides the protective shield for development gains and, again, for the very destiny of the Arab region'.

'The second plane on which interaction between Arab development and security operates is *the vertical plane*, which is the mutual effects and benefits between the national framework for development and security on the one hand and their pan-Arab framework on the other, if they depart from a sound understanding which ensures harmony and complementarity between them'.

While frankly admitting that it is concerned mainly with the economic aspect of joint Arab action, the paper nonetheless does not lose sight of the strong links between economics and other aspects of societal activities. At the same time, the paper diagnoses the loci of weakness in the Arab economy, on both the national and pan-national levels, as being the absence of a joint Arab developmental outlook with clearly defined goals and features, which departs from an overall vision determined by a system of planning or programming capable of realizing the greatest measure of interconnection and cohesiveness between the forces and institutions of production in the various sectors and in basic structures. More amazing still is that the 'development gap' between productive abilities and the development effort has become a common feature in most Arab countries. This underlines the importance of joint Arab action as the most effective mechanism by which to narrow this gap through a combination of national and pan-national efforts and a judicious allocation of human and material resources on the pan-national level.

The paper warns in general of great dangers that will be confronting the Arabs in future, and to which they must stand up in defence of their very integrity. The paper identifies the most important of these dangers as: insecurity of Arab food supplies; increased dependence on the advanced industrial world; disparities between countries in development capability and within countries in respect of economic performance levels and standards of living; eventual depletion of oil reserves, coupled with unpreparedness for the post-oil era; growing Zionist threat.

In the face of these dangers, the paper notes that the Arab future over the coming two decades can witness dichotomy, waste, maldistribution of resources, bottlenecks in the way of overall development and growing threats to pan-Arab security if the narrow national outlook continues to prevail.

On the other hand, the Arab culture could be more 'prosperous, secure and conducive to the realization of economic, social, and pan-national dignity if the scope of joint Arab economic action were to be extended and deepened on a sound basis along the guidelines of the visions and proposals that this paper puts forward.'

2. Programmes and activities

Perhaps the most important methodological innovation in this strategy document was the emphasis it placed on adopting a planning approach to integrated Arab development. As the document puts it, 'it is through the twin gateways of integrated development and region-specific planning that joint Arab economic action aimed at close integration must be approached.'

The main advantage of adopting a planning approach to integrated development is that it would streamline the sector of Arab joint ventures, which the document notes are being set up randomly, not according to 'a general and purposeful concept of the linkages—horizontal (geographical) or vertical (related to stages of development)—that would have to be established between Arab sectors and economies in order to accelerate development both nationally and regionally'.[2] 'The result has been that the distribution of human and financial resources among the economic needs of the region and the geographic distribution of projects have remained random, governed not by a clear system of priorities determined by a strategy and plan but by transient conditions and trends'.[3]

This leads the document to stress the need for efforts at planning on the pan-national level directed at laying down a regional development plan and following up its implementation. To be effective, such a plan would have to enjoy a minimum possibility of being at least as far as the sector of joint Arab economic action is concerned, while at the country level it could preserve *an indicative character*, serving as a guideline for the drawing up of national development plans. This could achieve a high degree of consistency and proportionality among country-specific plans in their regional dimension, and would enable them to benefit from the regional organization of the Arab economy. The document proposes that planning efforts (as one aspect of joint action) should be continuous, taking the form of five-year plans beginning in 1981.

The document cites a number of advantages that can be derived from adopting a planning approach to achieve integrated Arab development.

(1) Given that integrated development is achieved in many stages and according to priorities fixed by each stage, it is the planning approach which can determine these priorities in a scientific manner according to their importance and the stage of development.
(2) Through planning, linkages can be built up first between sectors and, secondly, between programmes, activities and various productive projects, in the light of their needs for factors and requirements of production and their precedence in the order of priorities.
(3) Planning is necessary for the geographical distribution of programmes, activities and projects among the various countries and in determining the patterns of relationships and forms of linkages (both horizontal and vertical).

Hence the document's insistence that the necessity of planning on the pan-national level must be emphasized, first as it relates to the sector of joint Arab economic action and moving gradually towards making the idea of an overall pan-Arab development plan acceptable, whether such a plan would be *imperative* in all its elements or only in some (namely, the sector of joint Arab economic action) while the other elements in the plan would remain *indicative*. Thus the principal strategy document and other related papers presented to the 11th Arab Summit came up with no more than the framework of a pan-Arab plan, or, rather, the broad lines of a framework. None the less, they certainly represent something new in the field of joint Arab action and an important contribution to the methodology of such action.

On the question of setting priorities for the first five-year indicative plan, the document considers it necessary to concentrate on programmes and activities in the following key spheres, as points of departure towards long-term strategic aims:

developing human resources;

securing food supplies;

energy;

technological security;

industrialization, giving priority to the following fields: basic industries, engineering industries (especially industries of capital goods), oil and petrochemical industries;

developing infrastructures in their various forms;

developing Arab financial markets.

Despite the detailed approach which the draft framework of the pan-national plan for joint Arab economic action adopts with respect to sectoral aims and programmes related to each of the proposed key areas of strategic action, its detailed proposals concerning programmes and activities are not, in our opinion, very different from those contained in the working paper of the 3-man committee presented to the first Arab conference on a strategy for joint Arab economic action.

What is new, however, in the principal strategy document presented to the 11th Arab summit is that it casts further light on the core issues in the area of Arab foreign economic relations in an attempt to investigate how these can be harnessed to serve Arab economic interests and basic pan-national problems. The document contains a serious discussion of a number of basic issues fixing the relationship of the Arab economy as a whole with the world economic order. Among the issues thoroughly discussed and analysed were: assimilating modern technology; importing foodstuffs; terms of trade for Arab exports and imports; oil and energy questions; Arab financial surpluses.

In the area of regulating the relations between the Arab economy as a whole and the world economy, the document determines the pivots of Arab strategic action as contributing to redressing the world economic order; contributing to correcting international terms of trade and economic relations; determining patterns of relations and dealings with the multinational corporations; consolidating the Arab presence in international organizations. Without a doubt, its emphasis on these aspects is an important contribution by this strategy document and distinguishes it from earlier efforts in this field, which tended to deal with the Arab economy as though it operated in a vacuum and not as a process that is organically linked to trends in the world economy, with all its distortions and mechanisms.

3. Proposed mechanisms

Any planning endeavour at the pan-Arab level must first determine the central organ that would undertake planning, follow-up and guidance without infringing on the independence of national and pan-national agencies involved in the formulation and execution of plans. In this connection the document, entitled 'Towards a Charter for Pan-Arab Economic Action', envisaged a general institutional/organizational framework for the mechanisms necessary in the areas of planning, execution and follow-up, based on the principle of centralized planning and non-centralized execution.

This document proposes that the task of pan-Arab planning be assigned to a Supreme Central Council which would, in addition to laying down the pan-Arab plan, supervise its execution and follow-up as well as determine the budget it would require. The proposed council must enjoy a high level of representation (for example, prime ministers) and wide prerogatives that can enable it to perform the enormous tasks entrusted to it. It would have to have a technical general secretariat, along the lines of the General Secretariat for Economic Affairs in the League of Arab states.

As to execution, this would be undertaken by existing development and financing agencies. The document proposes that the Arab Fund for Economic and Social Development be given an *executive function* in the field of infrastructural projects and a *supervisory function* in controlling the use of funds from a special account to be operated by the Fund and fed from the contributions of the pan-national budget. The role of specialized Arab organizations would be to formulate sectoral plans, identify projects, undertake required sectoral surveys and prepare pre-investment and feasibility studies of projects to be implemented according to the priorities of the pan-Arab plan.

The volume of financing required for the first 5-year plan (1981–85) for the sector of joint Arab economic action was determined at US $ 15 billion, phased out as follows:

first year : US $ 1 billion;
second year : US $ 2 billion;
third year : US $ 3 billion;
fourth year : US $ 4 billion;
fifth year : US $ 5 billion.

The resolutions passed by the 11th Summit Conference in this regard were disappointing. Only US $ 5 billion were earmarked for this sector, to be spent over a time span of 10 years, that is, at an annual rate of half a billion dollars on the average. The question is not one of haggling over the size of financing to be allocated to the development of joint Arab economic action through a series of pan-Arab 5-year plans, but is basically one of having the Arab oil states (especially the Gulf states) develop a strategic vision.

A narrow static outlook tends to underline a conflict of interests between oil and non-oil Arab states, in that national short-term and medium-term benefits are maximized, while the funds allocated to the sector of joint Arab action are seen as a constraint on the free use of national funds. The money that goes to the joint Arab sector is looked at in 'non-strategic' terms, more as a sort of moral obligation or a 'charity fund' set up to help the poor Arab countries and protect them from further deterioration. On the other hand, a scientific and rational assessment of the situation in the framework of a dynamic strategic outlook, which takes into account the depletion of oil reserves and upsets in the mechanisms of the world economy which are now absorbing the bulk of Arab financial surpluses, would clearly show that developing the sector of joint Arab economic action is the best line of defence and the best guarantee for the future of the affluent in the oil states. Only within the framework of this outlook does it become clear that the present 'sacrifice' of oil-wealth to develop the sector of joint Arab economic action will be compensated for by long-term benefits for the oil states when their oil reserves are running dry.[4]

However, the historic circumstance that we have chosen to call the phenomenon of the 'joint Arab hesitation', notably on the part of the oil states with 'surpluses', will not be resolved simply by demonstrating, with the tools of economic analysis used in discussing 'welfare propositions', that the oil states will reap enormous benefits in the long term if they invest their money now in developing the sector of joint Arab economic action. The historical resolution of such major questions, at the level of decision-making processes in the oil states is, in the final analysis, determined by conflicts of interest and pressure groups operating within these states, so that the pertinent questions become: from whose point of view is contributing to the development of the sector of joint Arab economic action a 'wise investment'? And who will be the beneficiary of this investment, whether in the short or long term?

4. A brief appraisal

While we have nothing but praise for the enormous effort that went into the set of strategy documents presented to the Amman Economic Summit, especially in enumerating and diagnosing the 'future dangers' facing the Arabs until the end of the century, we nevertheless believe that the urgency of these dangers was not sufficiently reflected in the formulation of aims and the fixing of programmes and practical activities in these documents.

In addition, their treatment of future problems does not articulate sufficiently the nature of 'external constraints' that may govern the course of the Arab future. Any discerning onlooker faced with the current state of Arab affairs cannot fail to see that some aspects of the future are practically mortgaged and predetermined by the actual patterns of consumption, production, financing and technology. It should also be noted that none of these documents contained any programmes of activities related to the aim of 'emancipating the Arab citizen and his creative abilities so that he can effectively participate in, and reap the fruits of, the development process', to use the words of the introduction to the principal document.

Moreover, despite the impressive efforts furnished in preparing the principal and supplementary documents to highlight the concept and feasibility of *indicative planning* as an approach to integrated Arab development, it is not clear where 'partial imperativeness' ends and 'total indicativeness' begins in the planning activities envisaged in the various fields.[5]

Any talk of planning as an approach to integrated Arab development remains vague and obscure if it is not translated into effective mechanisms and unless it pinpoints the 'areas of dispute' between the requirements of indicative planning at the level of the broad aggregates, and the requirements of imperative planning, which is concerned with laying down detailed programmes and specifying the orientation of development at the level of the component elements in Arab action.

Indeed, we would go so far as to say that the principal document presented in Amman showed itself to be out of touch with reality when it spoke of planning as a mechanism and a successful cure for the problems of integrated Arab development. The process of planning is not in itself a cure, and remains in the final analysis, subject to basic options decided upon at the highest political level. Planning as a mechanism (whether imperative or indicative) cannot replace a global developmental outlook, at the pan-Arab level, that should precede planning and guide efforts in this field. The document here is self-contradictory; on the one hand it departs from the current Arab economic situation, while on the other, it proposes the adoption of indicative planning as a mechanism, a proposal that would entail departing from economic and political conditions and relationships very different from those now prevailing. This would in turn entail more scientific efforts at both the theoretical and procedural levels, to ensure a greater measure of success for this kind of planning effort in the light of the complexities of Arab reality. This is particularly important in the field of pinpointing 'areas of conflict' that could arise between national sovereignties, as well as in the modalities of solving the contradictions that could emerge between planning at the country-specific and pan-Arab levels.

Notes

1. These were presented to the League of Arab states, General Secretariat, General Department for Economic Affairs, 11th Arab Summit Conference, Amman, November 1980, under the following titles: *Towards Developing Joint Arab Economic Action* (principal document); *Draft Framework of Pan-Arab Plan for Joint Arab Economic Action*; *Towards a Charter for Pan-Arab Economic Action*; *Economic Conditions and Relations Between the Arab Countries and Means of Consolidating them*; and *Using Arab Economic Relations with Foreign Countries in the Service of Pan-Arab Issues and Economic Interests.*
2. See *Towards Developing Joint Arab Economic Action*, (principal document), in: The League of Arab States, General Secretariat, General Department for Economic Affairs, 11th Arab Summit Conference, Amman, November 1980, p. 26.
3. Ibid., p. 27.
4. See, in this connection, Mahmoud Abdel-Fadil, *Problems and Perspectives of the Development Process in the Arab Oil Countries*, Section 3,

and Hazem El-Beblawy, *The Role of Oil Surpluses and the Third World*, in the Conference of the New Arab Economic Order, Los Angeles, July 1980, as summarized in: Ibrahim Nawar's rewiew published in *Al-Siassa Al-Dawleya*, 62, October 1980.

5. See, in this connection, the important work by one of the founders of the science of indicative planning in France, Pierre Massé, *Le Plan ou l'antihasard*, Paris, Gallimard, 1965, Chapter 1.

11 AN OVERALL APPRAISAL

There can be no denying the fact that every major field in the Arab nation is in urgent need of a strategy that would confront its many problems and issues, fix its objectives, articulate the principles and concepts that should govern its path and determine procedural ways and means of achieving its objectives. Such a strategy would have to be comprehensive and coherent in its own field and interlinked with other strategies in a manner that would make them comprehensive and coherent when taken together.

The range of vision in any strategy must extend from the reality in which it is formulated to the horizons of the future on which it sets its sights. A strategic outlook should therefore depart from a diagnosis of reality with its problems, contradictions and potentialities into a search for the developments and possibilities that the future holds in store. A strategic outlook cannot be *undimensional*, but should necessarily proceed along numerous paths and avenues. Accordingly, to think of the future is to think in terms of numerous scenarios and likely variants of possible images of the future.

A look at the set of key strategy documents that we have reviewed, analysed and critically evaluated in this chapter, shows that they share two main characteristics—a description of what exists (often incomplete) and a proposal of some (though not all) visions of the desired future.

Moreover, these documents lack two major dimensions. First, they are not clear as to the paths and mechanisms of transition from the actual situation with its problems and contradictions to the new vistas unfolded by the various strategic visions. If the strategies proposed in the fields of food security, industrialization based on satisfying basic needs, education, protecting and developing the environment, co-ordinating and rationalizing energy policies, developing the sector of joint Arab action, etc., are not to sink to the level of wishful thinking, unable to affect the dynamics of Arab society as it strives towards a better future, they must come up with a thorough analysis of institutional organization, of economic forces and strata, of political pressures which affect decision-making processes and of patterns of dealing with future problems.

We consider that the absence of this dimension represents the missing link in all the efforts at strategic thinking which we reviewed and analysed in the preceding sections. Indeed, it is hard to see how the strategic visions and outlooks contained in these documents can be effective and positive without a clear understanding of the *transitional paths* and *mechanisms*. The absence of any vision of these mechanisms and their functions implies the continuation of existing mechanisms, and, accordingly, the perpetuation of all the manifestations of backwardness and crisis, making the desired goals more remote than ever.

For example, when one of the documents under study states that the strategy it proposes is feasible only through political reinforcement at the highest level, it does not bother to explain how this political reinforcement can be forthcoming, or what obstacles can stand in its way.

Second, the partial strategies proposed in the various fields suffer from lack of linkages and organic cohesiveness between the components of the numerous strategies. A comprehensive look at the course of Arab society must, in future, emphasize as many of the interlinkages and mutual relations as possible between the programmes emanating from the various strategies in the fields of food security, industrialization, energy, environmental protection, technological development, etc. For a comprehensive vision of the future to be methodologically sound, it must look at social, economic and technical phenomena in their totality, see the interactions and interlinkages between the various aspects, build up into a consistent whole and stress the transition from the present into the future through these dynamics of change.

The areas of overlapping and elements of interpenetration in the partial strategies under review are shown in the following simplified matrix. Identifying these areas and elements in the various sectoral and partial strategies is a necessary condition of achieving greater harmony and coherence in future between the different component elements in various fields.

Most of the documents at hand are sectoral strategies, indeed,

Simplified matrix showing interrelations between various Arab strategy documents

Strategy document	*Food security*	*Industrialization aimed at meeting basic needs*	*Energy*	*Education*	*Environmental protection*	*Developing sector of joint Arab economic action*
Food security	○	Industrialization inputs required to achieve food security strategy	Extracting proteins from oil derivatives	a. Eradicating rural illiteracy b. Increasing woman's contribution to agricultural labour	a. Soil erosion b. Salinization c. Urban spread	a. Production scheduling in wheat belt countries (Syria, Iraq, Morocco, Algeria) b. Financing joint Arab agro-ventures
Industrialization aimed at meeting basic needs	Developing inputs required for textile industries to meet basic needs in clothing	○	Using economical forms of energy and fuel in industry	a. Providing middle-level technical cadres b. Developing extra-school education	a. Fighting pollution b. Linking the satisfaction of basic needs in housing to patterns of local architecture	a. Developing basic and engineering industries b. Absorbing and adapting modern technology
Energy	Rationalizing use of river water to serve 2 purposes: generate electricity & improve irrigation system to produce grain	Develop role of solar energy in industry	○	Developing studies and research on preserving non-renewable resources	Developing alternative sources of energy	Formulating joint Arab strategy in domain of pricing and production scheduling and of preserving and using oil revenues
Education	Developing new patterns for rural schools allowing for education and participation in production at the same time	Developing formula of technical secondary schools and comprehensive schools	Raising awareness of environmental issues and introducing them to economic calculus and educational thinking	○	Faculties of ecology	a. Arabization and Arabic textbooks b. Developing Arab scientific research on a joint basis
Environmental protection	a. Improving irrigation and drainage systems b. Halting non-agricultural exploitation of agricultural land	Replacing imported by local raw materials to prevent distortion to architectural patterns suitable for Arab region	Preventing rapid depletion of oil resources	Develop cultural and consumption values to preserve elements of ecological balance	○	a. Develop joint programme to protect Arab environment b. Joint programmes for sound management of water resources, pastures and cultivable land

they are sometimes limited to dealing with partial problems, such as food security. In many cases, endogenous Arab efforts to build strategic concepts were mere reflections of world interest in given problems, such as food, energy, satisfying basic needs, environment, etc. As such, some of these efforts were just attempts to indulge in new 'intellectual exercises' which had become fashionable all over the world. But, notwithstanding their shortcomings and limitations, these documents certainly helped cast light on problems of the Arab future and are, accordingly, worthy of discussion and critical assessment.

If we attempt a more comprehensive appraisal by reading 'across' the documents, as it were, we would find that they all affirm Arab co-operation and integration as the natural framework for future action in all fields. Though this is in itself commendable, the missing link in all the documents is their failure to determine the type of mechanisms necessary to connect actual and latent possibilities to the desired aims. Without this connection, strategic visions remain suspended in mid-air, with no relation to reality. Further, with the exception of the papers of the Amman Summit, all the documents deal with the Arab future as though it were moving in a vacuum, capable of moving at will and of shaping its own features in isolation from the web of foreign relations and the dependency of Arab society on economic, political and technological developments taking place in the context of the power structure governing the present world order. This obviously constitutes a serious shortcoming in any attempt to look at the Arab future, not to mention the fact that it isolates it from the common problems and concerns of the rest of the Third World.

In conclusion, the main criticisms we have against all these documents can be summed up as follows.

(a) They do not set a clear timetable until the end of the century, but confine themselves mainly to a normative outlook not phased through time.

(b) They failed to determine the nature of the mechanisms necessary for the transition from the actual to the desired situation.

(c) The strategic concepts and visions contained in the various documents are not consistent with one another due to the fact that they do not share a common outlook on development. Rather, the dominant feature in these documents is the techno-economic approach each adopts in its respective field.

Finally, we must point to an important issue related to the dynamics of the contemporary world surrounding us. Any attempt to map the Arab future cannot be made in isolation from these dynamics. Arab society, like any other society, is, in the final analysis a system that interacts and is affected by world systems and their future developments. The pace of change in today's world is extremely rapid in all fields of matter and life, in the nature of technical knowledge and in all areas of management and organization.

Any image of the Arab future is bound to be affected by discoveries of new sources of energy and by new forms of technical knowledge hitherto unknown to man. The future is full of promise and hope, but also carries the threat of hardships and crises. An awareness of these future dangers and challenges can pave the way to a better Arab future.

The difficulties of assessing, choosing and affecting the various courses which the future can take underline the urgent need for concerted efforts at scientific thinking and reflection that would approach the dynamically interacting issues of the present and their bearing on the future from a global point of view, as proposed by the Arab Alternative Futures project set up at the beginning of the eighties. Indeed, the more formidable the challenges and the wider the scope of concerns, the greater the need for broad-based study, reflection and research to identify the factors, variables, forces and trends that will affect the course of the Arab future, as well as to investigate alternative Arab futures, with all they present in the way of problems and challenges and all they hold in the way of promises and potentialities. In short, the future will be as bright or as bleak as the scenarios of likely Arab futures are successful today in their assessment of and preparations for the future.

Appendix: Summary of Arab strategy documents translated into programming language

Strategy document	*Implicit optimization problem*	*Implicit objective functions*	*Constraints*
Food security strategy	Minimization problem of one variable	Narrowing 'wheat gap' over the period between 1975 and 2000	a. Limited water resources b. Limited area of cultivable land c. Technical constraints imposed by nature of crop mixes
Strategy for industrialization to meet basic needs	Minimization problem of multi-variables	Narrowing gap between 'normative level' to satisfy basic needs and 'actual level' to satisfy basic needs in the period between 1975 and 2000 in domains of food, clothing and housing	a. Matrix of technical coefficients and inter-industry linkages inherent in production processes b. Availability of financial resources in foreign and local currencies c. Availability of adequately trained and suitably skilled workforce
Strategic problems addressed by first Arab energy conference	Problem of optimal dynamic transitional path from oil and hydrocarbon resources to alternative sources of energy	Maximizing long-term development effects of oil resources through formulating optimal policies for production and pricing	a. World demand for Arab oil b. Fluctuations in terms of trade for oil exports c. Expected time horizon for depletion of oil resources
Strategy for development of Arab education	Maximization of developmental and social effects of output of Arab education system by solving a series of maximization problems	a. Reducing stock of adult and child illiterates b. Maximizing output of secondary technical education system c. Maximizing inputs and outputs of extra-school education d. Maximizing research projects by Arab universities and higher institutes	a. Limited financial resources than can be allocated to education b. Degree of availability of required number of trained teachers c. Degree of availability of educational buildings, equipment and means

Strategy for alternative patterns of development and lifestyles	Problem of minimization of negative effects of growth processes on natural, cultural and social environment by solving a series of sub-optimization problems	a. Extending life-span of non-renewable resources (minerals and fuel) b. Maximizing livestock resources by optimizing use of pastures c. Reducing amount of water resources wasted d. Achieving ecological balance, including reducing atmospheric and water pollution	a. Patterns of industrial growth b. Patterns of urban growth c. Patterns of consumption growth
3-man committee's working paper on strategy for joint Arab economic action	A minimax problem in the sense of the game theory, whereby a balance should be struck between the maximization of growth at the country level and ensuring in the meantime the minimum chances of expansion of the sector of joint Arab economic action	a. Maximizing ability to store modern technological knowledge b. Maximizing Arab security capabilities in the areas of food, basic production and military industrialization c. Maximizing capital flows between oil and non-oil countries	a. Limits imposed by country-specific development attitudes and legislative systems in force at the country level b. Size of financial resources earmarked for the sector of joint Arab action c. Pattern of development of inter-Arab political relations d. Pattern of development of the Arab nation's relations with the outside world
Principal document on developing joint Arab economic action (presented to 11th Arab Summit)	A problem of gradual minimization of the gap between production capability and growth performance at the pan-Arab level	Expanding the area of joint Arab economic action that is subject to the rules of imperative planning at the pan-Arab level	a. Size of financial resources earmarked for developing sector of joint Arab economic action b. Extent of commitment to framework of pan-Arab plan at national and pan-national levels c. Degree of efficiency of existing mechanisms and institutions in operating sector of joint Arab economic action

PART III

TOWARDS ARAB STUDIES OF THE ARAB FUTURE

12 THE ARABS AT THE CROSSROADS

As we have seen from Part I, works devoted to global modelling and forecasting warn that the Arab nation is heading towards greater fragmentation and hold out no hope of a bright future for any part of that nation. On the other hand, as we have also seen from our critical examination of Arab strategy documents in Part II, it is widely held in many Arab circles that the natural and human resources of which they dispose are in themselves sufficient to assure the Arabs of progress. Nothing could be more dangerous than for the Arabs to lull themselves into a false sense of security by believing that an abundance of 'money and men' will necessarily lead to a rosy future. We should pause, therefore, to assess Arab potential on the one hand, and the challenges facing them on the other, to realize that the picture of the future can be a very different one indeed from that to which they aspire.

1. Arab resources: actuality and potential

When the subject of Arab potential comes up, the talk centres primarily on the vital role played by a number of Arab countries in producing and exporting oil, with special reference to the enormous financial surpluses accumulated by these countries, particularly after the adjustment brought to oil prices after 1973. Much is also made of the size of human and material resources, including cultivable land and mineral wealth. Special emphasis is laid on the ability of the Arabs to generate a momentum in the direction of progress and development if they optimize the mobilization of their human, financial and material resources and deploy them within a framework of regional co-operation and integration.

Important though these factors undeniably are, it would serve no useful purpose here to stress the size of the various Arab resources actually or potentially available—a point that has been repeatedly made in numerous works—in order to show the real potential for Arab progress at the present historical stage. All the more so in that the realization of cultural progress and comprehensive development by any society is not essentially a function of that society's material wealth nor of the size of its material or human resources—although these factors constitute constraints which must be taken into account. What the realization of these aims entails is, rather, an awareness on the part of the popular forces who will be the main beneficiaries of progress and comprehensive development, of the importance and necessity of changing existing conditions and a struggle to break the constraints imposed by existing structures and relations—economic, social and cultural—thus laying the groundwork for an efficient social organization capable of releasing human potential, of mobilizing and developing this potential, enhancing its capabilities and optimizing the use of available material resources.

It does not require an in-depth analysis of what many consider to be the main sources of Arab power and potential at the present stage to realize that these sources would not have been there in the first place—let alone come to exert so much influence on global economic and social relations—had it not been for the successes scored by the Arab struggle to eradicate colonial domination and its bases from the region, and to regain control over basic Arab resources. By the same token, many of the constraints and bottlenecks impeding the deployment of these resources towards realizing a comprehensive Arab renaissance can also be attributed to the reverses suffered by the Arabs in their struggle to follow through their liberation and to realize economic and political integration.

It follows then that Arab potential is dependent less on the size of available material and human resources than on the ability of the Arab national movement to complete the path to liberation from imperialism, to bring an end to dependency and to pursue concerted policies aimed at using these resources to serve the interest of the Arab nation as a whole.

In the period following World War II, the national movement scored significant victories in its liberation struggle and, despite the implantation of Israel as an imperialist expansionist body in the heart of the Arab nation, succeeded in achieving the political independence of all the Arab countries, with the exception of Palestine. Most of these countries became independent in the fifties and sixties, while the remainder followed suit in the early seventies. Having attained political independence, the Arab countries set out to achieve economic growth. While the paths of each followed to this end differed as to orientation, all shared a common goal, namely, to bring about fundamental changes in the prevailing economic and social structure. A number embarked on important steps directed at building an independent national economy. The struggle to achieve some sort of Arab unification was stepped up, and measures—albeit limited—were initiated to promote economic and political co-operation among the Arab countries.

Despite the demoralizing effect of the military defeat of 1967 on the Arab national movement, despite the negative effects which the long years of preparing for war had had on the economies of some Arab countries, notably Egypt and Syria, and despite the Zionist occupation of new parts of Arab land, the Arab national movement made substantial headway up to the mid-seventies. The early seventies saw the liberation of the south and east of the Arabian peninsula from occupation. The Palestinian people stepped up their national struggle and, under the leadership of the PLO, realized major political and national gains. Also in the early seventies, the oil-producing countries revised the terms of oil concession contracts in their favour and, during the successful battle waged by the Arab armies against Israel (the October 1973 war) and at the peak of the anti-imperialist struggle, imposed, in co-ordination with the rest of the OPEC members, a more equitable price for their oil. They began to fix oil prices away from the domination of the oil companies and most of the Arab countries regained full control over domestic production of crude oil. This increased the revenues of the oil-producing countries, which embarked on ambitious programmes of urban development and modernization, as a result of which labour mobility between the countries of the Arab nation was greatly activated. Then too the presence of petro-wealth in countries with a limited absorptive capacity stimulated the flow of Arab money between these countries. Arab organizations and institutions were established and proliferated, both on the level of individual states and on the pan-national level, some of which sought to use part of the oil capital in developing the non-oil producing countries, others to take advantage of the opportunities available to make a quick profit in this Arab country or that. With OPEC regaining control over oil, two questions came up for the first time: the need for a North–South dialogue and, within that framework, the need in particular for a dialogue between Western Europe and the Arab nation with a view to establishing stable relations between the producers of oil and its major consumers. Despite these successes, many obstacles and bottlenecks prevented the positive elements in the Arab position from being used to the full. Without going into the reasons for this here, we shall mention some of the main failures and negative phenomena that limited the exploitation of Arab potential. In spite of the relative success realized by the Arab armies in their battle to overcome Israeli aggression in 1973, and of the considerable role which the use of Arab oil in that battle played in redressing the balance of power in favour of the Arab liberation movement, the positive results of the 1973 war were to a great extent wasted.

A number of decision-makers and opinion-leaders believed that the influx of sudden wealth could solve the problem of development and elevate its owners to the ranks of the rich countries of the world, so that their dealings with the industrialized countries, specifically the US, could be conducted on the basis of common interests and the joint protection of these interests. This theory was way off the mark when it came to understanding the realities of development on the one hand and of imperialism on the other. It was the proponents of this theory who helped increase American influence in the Arab nation, most dramatically illustrated in the separate—and unjust peace that the Egyptian government concluded with Israel under the sponsorship of the US.

Along with the positive effects resulting from the Arab countries regaining control of oil resources, and despite the vast potential created by the readjustment of oil prices in favour of the producing countries, a number of adverse effects were produced by oil wealth and by the growing disparity in income levels between Arab countries. Dependence on oil 'rents' often led to a profligate use of resources, to a disregard of the cost–benefit analysis and to the demotion of many productive activities. It also led to the gravitation of a number of activities towards areas where wealth was concentrated rather than where markets were available, as well as to speculation and parasitic activities as one of the means by which to redistribute oil revenues. In addition, it gave rise to a growing trend for conspicuous consumption, especially in the oil countries, which exported this pattern of consumption to other, less wealthy, Arab countries.

As income disparities between the Arab countries grew, so too did a narrow state nationalism, and with it the feeling that prospects of achieving Arab unity, one of the most important goals of the Arab struggle throughout the fifties and the sixties, were unlikely, if not impossible.

This feeling was fuelled by growing feuds among the Arab leaderships, some of which escalated to the point of becoming basic contradictions. One-man rule and the absence of democracy in most Arab countries led these feuds between the leaderships to assume the form of disputes between the Arab countries—in some cases going as far as armed confrontation—and to the spread of repression. Not surprisingly, all these developments had a demoralizing effect on substantial sectors of the Arab national movement, who were increasingly coming to feel the futility of struggle in such a context. There was growing scepticism as to the ability of the Arab countries to draw up a coherent strategy for pan-national development, or even to adopt a common stand towards fundamental Arab issues, let alone to achieve Arab unity.

The ability of the Arabs to make the best possible use of their manpower resources, which are expected to equal those of the US by the year 2000, to exploit all their cultivable land (whether this amounts to 114 million hectares as estimated by Mesarovic and Pestel, or 163 million as per the projection of the MOIRA model), to channel their oil revenues and financial surpluses into developing infrastructures and in building an advanced industrial base in the Arab world capable of meeting the rising expectations and growing needs of the Arab people and to build an independent Arab economy capable of sustained development in future, depends in the main on the ability of the Arab national movement to close ranks and to overcome the obstacles and negative phenomena impeding efforts to liberate the Arab economy from dependency. It also requires coordinated Arab action in the face of challenges, and a pan-national deployment of available material and human resources in the interests of the Arab nation as a whole, in line with the concept of collective self-reliance adopted by the Group of 77, as the group of Third-World countries is called in UN circles, to counter the stiff resistance put up by the industrialized nations to the idea of establishing a new international economic order.

2. Different challenges facing the Arab world

In its bid to realize an overall renaissance, the Arab nation comes up against many challenges, some due to its historical underdevelopment, others to the constraints imposed by material resources on the possibilities of progress—at least within the realm of the possible as we know it today—and others still to current changes on the global and regional levels.

The legacy of underdevelopment and shortcomings in the development effort

The most important of the challenges stemming from the historical underdevelopment of the Arab nation are those linked to low productivity, imbalances in the structure of production, the absence or primitiveness of infrastructures in—or between—many of its states, and to a limited technological capacity. In addition, there is the fragmentation imposed by the colonial powers, which has led to the creation of a number of political entities displaying none of the real attributes of statehood.

A characteristic common to all the Arab countries is that only a limited proportion of the population is engaged in economic activities. Out of a total population of approximately 170 million at the beginning of this decade, the labour force represented only some 45 million, viz., a proportion of participation of not more than 26.5 per cent. This phenomenon is due to the age composition of the population and to the limited contribution by women to organized productive activities outside the home and family. In terms of age structure, Arab countries are young, with approximately 45 per cent of the population falling in the under-fifteen age bracket. As for the occupational distribution of Arab manpower, this is concentrated on the lower rungs of the ladder of professions and crafts, with a relative shortage on the higher rungs which require advanced theoretical and practical formation, as well as by a relatively high incidence of desk and office jobs and a high percentage of unskilled workers in the production, construction and transportation sectors.

The bulk of the Arab labour force is still concentrated in agriculture, despite its declining share of the labour force throughout the sixties and seventies. In the mid-seventies, those working in agriculture accounted for some 52.5 per cent of the total labour force, while the manufacturing industries were represented by only 9.5 per cent and the extracting industries by 0.8 per cent. Despite the low proportion of participation in economic activities, many Arab countries are still plagued by unemployment (especially of the disguised variety), in agriculture and service industries, notably in the areas of government administration and informal or casual services.

Economic performance in the Arab countries is marked by low productivity of labour. For example, a worker's productivity in Egypt and Sudan was estimated in the mid-seventies at approximately 15 and 7 per cent respectively of that of their Japanese counterpart. Productivity is particularly low in agriculture. Many factors contribute to this—the poor qualifications and skills of the workforce, the nature of the technology used, values and customs related to work ethics, the sense of belonging and participation and the level of efficiency at which management of economic activity operates.

To realize just how underdeveloped the Arab workforce is, one has only to look at the illiteracy figures. Although education is accorded a high priority by most Arab countries, as attested to by the fact that nearly 5 per cent of the aggregate Arab GNP was spent on education in the mid-seventies, primary-school enrolment figures fall far short of the actual number of school-age children. In addition, there is a high drop-out rate which means an increase in the real number of illiterates, even if the rate of illiteracy has decreased. In 1975, the illiteracy rate for the over-fifteen age group was 64 per cent of the total Arab population in that group.

Another factor affecting the efficiency of the Arab worker is the state of his health. Although Arab countries have made significant progress in improving the health standards of their populations, increasing life-expectancy at birth during the third quarter of this century, life-expectancy at birth still remains below sixty years for all Arab countries except Kuwait and Lebanon. In Somalia, the Sudan, North and South Yemen, Syria, Tunisia, Algeria, Libya and Iraq, it is only forty-five years. The poor health standard is underlined by the high rate of child mortality in the 1–4 age bracket, which in some Arab countries (Somalia, the Sudan, North and South Yemen and Saudi Arabia) is thirty times greater than that recorded for the same age bracket in the industrialized countries, while in Egypt, Morocco, Jordan, Syria, Tunisia, Iraq and Libya, it is fifteen times greater.

The lopsided economic structure prevailing in the Arab countries is clear from the predominance of the primary sector (agriculture, fishing, extracting industry) and the negligible showing by the manufacturing sector. With the exception of Algeria, the primary sector is by far the largest contributor to the economies of the oil-producing countries and, in this sector, it is the extracting industry which figures most prominently. Its contribution to the aggregate Arab GNP in 1975 amounted to approximately 48.8 per cent, while that of agriculture came to 8.8 per cent. In other words, the primary sector as a whole contributed more than 57.6 per cent to Arab GNP in the mid-seventies. The manufacturing sector, on the other hand, contributed no more than 8.5 per cent. Although the Arab countries recorded relatively high rates of development in both agriculture and industry during the seventies, both sectors are still beset with major problems which have, in many cases, begun to tell adversely on development rates.

The most formidable challenge as far as agriculture is concerned is the low output, both per agricultural worker and per hectare, in most Arab countries. With agricultural production unable, as a result, to keep pace with their food needs, the Arabs have become increasingly dependent on the outside world to meet those needs. Nearly all of the Arab countries, some of which had, until as recently as ten years ago, enjoyed a grain surplus, now find themselves with a shortfall in grain, especially wheat. Indeed, they had to import some 40–50 per cent of their wheat consumption over the last decade. And the food gap continues to widen as the rate of food consumption rises by about 5 per cent annually while grain production rises at an average annual rate of no more than 2 per cent. In addition, such efforts as have been made to develop this sector were channelled for the main into setting up grandiose projects that take years to mature, while all attempts at horizontal or vertical expansion come up against sluggish bureaucracies. At the same time, the attempt to institute social and cultural change in the countryside with a view to achieving integrated rural development was neglected. This has driven many productive elements to migrate from the countryside in search of better job opportunities in the construction and services sectors in the city.

As for the manufacturing sector, its weakness is underlined, first, by its limited contribution to the aggregate Arab GNP, second, by the nature of the consumer goods industries which have proliferated in the Arab world and, third, by its modest contribution to Arab exports (with the exception of hydrocarbon industries). We mentioned earlier that manufacturing industries account for some 8.5 per cent of the Arab GNP. Of these, the most prominent are consumer goods industries—particularly food processing and textiles—followed in importance by oil-based industries of intermediate goods. Then too, most Arab manufacturing industries are peripheral, comprising one stage, two at the most, of the manufacturing chain. Rarely has an integrated industrial chain been established between Arab states—or even inside one Arab state, for that matter. Arab industrial planning is still national rather than pan-national in orientation, with industries set up either to meet the limited needs of the domestic market or to produce exports for world markets, and with no serious attempts to establish an integrated industrial base. Arab industries suffer from duplication and from high industrial costs as a result of low productivity, scarcity of managerial and technical skills and a shortage of skilled labour. In addition, despite the small size of the Arab manufacturing industries, many of their productive units operate below full capacity, idle capacity occasionally reaching proportions of preposterous waste.

Bottlenecks in infrastructures still remain major obstacles to development in the Arab countries, especially in the less developed amongst them and in the confrontation states,* whose infrastructures deteriorated during the period of heavy investment in military spending in preparation for war with Israel. The less-developed Arab states face a real crisis in this domain, suffering as they do from critical shortages in all sectors. The development of their infrastructures is made still more difficult by their wide areas, dispersed communities and the disparate

*Confrontation states are the states confronting Israel mainly, Egypt, Syria and Jordan.

levels of development between one region and another. Indeed, no such development can be envisaged without massive aid from the richer Arab countries. In addition to the negative effects of military spending, another reason for the deterioration of infrastructures in the confrontation states is rapid urbanization and a demographic concentration in the towns.

The Arab nation as a whole also suffers from a certain lack of cohesion between its various component parts, and from a shortage of inexpensive means of transport and communication which can raise the level of interdependence between the Arab states and make for greater cohesion and integration. Like most of their fellow Third-World states, those of the Arab world remain dependent basically on imported technology. For all the differences between their historical circumstances, factors of production and political systems, the Arab countries in their drive for development have, as a rule, all been more interested in acquiring equipment, plants and factories than in technology proper, that is, expertise, skill and the ability to apply scientific and technical principles to production and service units. Although some effort has been made to establish centres for scientific research, these remain attached to academic institutions, completely isolated from the productive base. As a result, and in spite of the vast number of projects which have been established in the Arab region since independence, especially over the last decade, the pool of technological expertise that has been built up is limited. In addition, the development of local technologies related to traditional activities has been totally neglected in favour of external alternatives which are not always appropriate.

The real limits imposed by material resources

Contrary to the once prevalent view that there exist limits to growth which, because of the finite nature of certain natural resources, cannot be overcome, most economists today agree that there are no rigid limits to natural resources, and that the main problem facing the world is, rather, how to acquire access to some of these resources at reasonable cost and effort. Valid though this approach is, it should not cause us to lose sight of the fact that Arab efforts at overall development will—or could—find themselves up against constraints, whether short-, medium- or long-term, which impose limits on the potential to achieve a certain development target or that may affect the shaping of trends and rates of development. On the other hand, this in no way implies that these constraints cannot be modified or their timing postponed by applying alternative development strategies, by using a new, more appropriate technology or by adopting better lifestyles—an issue we shall deal with in some detail later.

To take the question of sources of energy first: although energy is now plentiful in the Arab nation, assuring new energy sources in the long-term ranks as one of the major challenges confronting the Arabs and one which they must start working to overcome. Despite their vast oil and gas reserves, the Arab countries are poor in sources of alternative energy other than solar energy or their limited sources of hydroelectric power. Early in 1978, the Arab world's proven oil reserves were estimated at about 346.7 billion barrels, that is, 46.6 times as much as the production of 1977. If Arab consumption of oil continues to grow at the present rate and Arab exports of oil remain at the 1977 level, then, according to the estimates of a group assessing the future of the Arab development process in a study on the Arab world in the year 2000, sponsored by the Arab Planning Institute of Kuwait in March 1980, the Arab oil reserves remaining at the end of the century will be enough to cover only eighteen and a half years. And, if the export quota rises, the period will be even shorter.[1]

In view of the scarcity of alternative sources of energy in the Arab world—other than solar energy which, if its use is to be economical, requires extensive research and concerted efforts to develop it—the Arab nation must adopt the necessary policies first, to extend the life-span of its oil reserves as a source of energy and as a basic raw material for industry and, second, to develop the sources of alternate energy on which it can rely when its oil reserves have been depleted. Otherwise the Arab countries will become importers of energy from the advanced industrialized countries on which they are already dependent in many other areas. This would increase their dependency and limit the possibilities of growth.[2]

In the light of available knowledge on the Arab world, the industrialization models prevailing and the technology used, it appears that it faces another problem related to a scarcity of minerals in general. Statistics on known global reserves of twenty-one main minerals reveal that no Arab country has a significant share of these minerals and that their production is concentrated essentially in the industrialized countries.[3] As most of this production is consumed domestically, world trade in minerals is largely dependent on Third-World production. While the actual per capita consumption of these minerals in the developing-, including the Arab, countries does not exceed 10 per cent of the per capita consumption in the advanced countries, it can be assumed that, as their economies develop, so too will their consumption of these minerals increase. Although there are no rigid limits which could prevent Third-World countries from raising their production of these minerals in future, resorting to sources with higher costs could lead to an increase in their relative prices. According to a study by Leontieff on the future of the world economy, prices of minerals will rise relative to both agricultural and industrial goods. Although scarcity of minerals—or of any other resource, for that matter—does not constitute an insurmountable limit to Arab growth, the region's entry into the stage of industrialization at a time when the cost of raw materials is increasing and sources of energy—or the relative price of sources of exportable Arab energy—are decreasing, can undermine potential rates of growth and affect the future structure of production.

In addition to the shortage of minerals available for Arab industry, Arab agriculture will in all probability be unable to furnish the primary products required for industrial growth. It has been mentioned earlier that food production in the Arab countries lags behind food needs, and that there is a growing dependence on imports to satisfy these needs. This has left the region's security exposed and has curtailed its ability to make basic decisions, whether on political pan-Arab issues or on economic issues, making the realization of a greater degree of self-sufficiency in food one of the strategic aims of Arab development. According priority to the production of food will inevitably limit the possibility of developing other agricultural products that could be used as primary products in industry.

Although a number of Arab countries can now afford to import all they need in the way of agricultural products, either to meet industrial production or food demands, their situation could well become more critical in future when the relative importance of oil declines or if, as expected, the prices of other primary products rise still further. Ensuring sufficient water for irrigation is an important determinant for the development of Arab agriculture, as can be illustrated by a comparison between the areas of arable, cultivated and cropped land in the Arab world, where the area of arable land is approximately six times greater than that of cultivated land and more than nine times greater than cropped areas. Of an estimated 301 million arable hectares, only 50 million were under cultivation in the mid-seventies while the number of cropped hectares came to no more than 31.5 million. The meagre proportion of cropland is due to the fact that many Arab countries leave substantial areas of land lying fallow every year, either because of a shortage of irrigation water, as in the case of Libya, Saudi Arabia and Jordan, or of agricultural labour, as in Sudan and Iraq.

Inequitable foreign relations

Some of the political and economic developments of the past ten years, on both the global and regional levels, have posed new challenges to the Arab world at the same time as they have offered it new chances for development and growth. As it is difficult to go into all these developments here, we shall deal only with those which have made most impact on Arab issues.

It should be remembered first of all that overall Arab development is not taking place in a vacuum, but within a framework of political and economic relationships, both global and regional. In the final analysis, real pan-Arab development entails a process of emancipation from the shackles of dependency, a righting of the imbalances in the overall Arab economy and the achievement of a high degree of internal integration.[4] To achieve emancipation, the Arabs must struggle, jointly and together with other Third-World countries, against foreign hegemony in its various and multiple forms. This struggle, or at least its results, will be influenced not only by developments in the Third World but also by those in international relations as a whole: relations between industrialized and Third-World states, between them and the European socialist countries and between the latter and Third-World states. The early seventies saw the successful implementation of global *détente* between the community of European socialist states and the community of advanced capitalist states. This led to a thaw in the cold war and to greater economic intercourse between the two camps. As the spectre of an armed confrontation between them receded, the nuclear arms race slowed down and both sides came to accept limitations on the development of strategic arms.

The climate of global *détente* was favourable to many national liberation movements, which were able to score significant victories, notably in Vietnam and Africa. The non-aligned movement acquired greater weight as a large number of Third-World countries joined its ranks. As the Cold War receded, the movement turned its attention to economic issues and concentrated its efforts on changing international economic relations in favour of the developing countries. At several international conferences held within the framework of the United Nations and its specialized agencies, Third-World countries succeeded in pushing through a number of important resolutions calling for the establishment of a new international order, for a reappraisal of the international division of labour and for the initiation of a North–South dialogue for the purpose of effecting these changes.

With the onset of the eighties came a change in the international climate. The industrial states adopted an uncompromising stand towards Third-World demands. The various links in the chain of North–South negotiations came up with no more than a limited number of procedural measures. Most of the negotiation sessions ended without passing any resolutions binding on all the parties, while some ended without passing any resolutions at all. Thus the famous dialogue ground to a virtual halt. At the same time, tensions began to rise again between the western states and the European socialist states threatening a revival of the cold war. The repercussions of these tensions were felt by the non-aligned movement. Its membership, which had greatly increased under *détente*, began to lose its force as some members moved closer to one or other of the two world camps. As a result, the last non-aligned conference got bogged down with internal disputes to the detriment of the movement's role as political leader of the Third World. If the Group of 77—or the trade union of the Third World—is still united in calling for a new international economic order and for a new international division of labour, this is basically due to the fact that the common interests they share still have precedence over any conflict of economic interest. All these developments emerged against the backdrop of the crisis now besetting the western industrial states, with its repercussions on the political and economic attitudes of their governments on the one hand and its effects on Third-World countries on the other. The most important political expression of the growing crisis has been the accession to power by conservative political forces in most of the industrial states. The policy of these governments has been characterized by attempts to liquidate many of the rights acquired by the masses under the pretext of fighting inflation, by an increase in war production justified in terms of escalating global tensions and by completely ignoring Third-World demands while consolidating their grip over it by economic, political and military means.

Arab countries are among the most sensitive to international political events and trends. Conversely, what takes place in the Arab countries has a profound impact on the international situation. The region's strategic location, its vast oil reserves and its role in supplying the advanced capitalist countries with much of their energy needs, place Arab countries in an excellent position to exploit the climate of *détente* to their advantage on the one hand and, on the other, to make them among the most sensitive to global conflicts resulting from the renewal in tension. By virtue of its size, location and resources and, because of its national liberation movement, the Arab nation is a trend-setter, as it were, for the Third World, particularly for the non-aligned countries. That is why, despite the crushing military defeat which some leading Arab states suffered at the hands of Zionism in alliance with world imperialism, the Arab national movement was able to score a number of important victories within the framework of *détente*.

The success of OPEC encouraged Third-World countries to step up their struggle to complete the liberation of their resources and to introduce a new international division of labour. But this same development prompted a number of advanced countries to reconsider the nature of their relations with the developing countries and to devise new mechanisms that could perpetuate relations of dependency under the new economic and social conditions.

Although international conditions favoured a stepped-up Arab drive to solve some of the major problems plaguing the Arab nation, notably the liberation of territories occupied in the 1967 war, the establishment of a Palestinian state and the realization of an independent Arab development, the chance was lost as a result of some of the Arab policies mentioned earlier. The Iranian revolution offered new opportunities for the Arab liberation movement, inasmuch as it brought about the downfall of the Shah's regime. But at the same time, it provoked widespread reverberations throughout the Arab region, particularly in the Gulf area. A chain of new conflicts emerged and tensions rose to a new pitch, especially after the Afghan crisis, the Soviet intervention and the spiral chain reaction this provoked in the Gulf area in particular and the Middle East in general. In a bid to restore or consolidate their political and military influence over the region, certain imperialist quarters played on the fears of conservative Arab regimes that the changes taking place in the Horn of Africa, Iran and Afghanistan threatened Arab 'stability'. The Iraq-Iran war, which destroyed oil fields in both countries, was held up as a confirmation of these fears. In the name of protecting the security of the Gulf, the US was able to obtain military bases and facilities in a number of countries in the region. A regional trend to invest much more heavily in military spending was encouraged by the war industries in the US and Europe—as long as the arms they sold to the Arabs were not used to liberate occupied territory or to liquidate foreign bases. In addition to the heightened global tensions in the Gulf area and to Egypt's political departure from the Arab fold, the Arab nation has to contend with the many (sometimes armed) conflicts, which have erupted between various Arab states—and sometimes even within one state. International forces play a major role in kindling and fanning these conflicts. The most violent and debilitating of these conflicts is the Lebanese civil war, with its devastating effect on the Lebanese economy, not to mention its impact on the very structure of the Lebanese state, which has disintegrated into a number of separate mini-states. Nor is Lebanon the only arena of armed conflict in the Arab nation. The deterioration in the Arab situation and the attempts to contain the region politically, even militarily, must be seen in the context of certain global economic developments, some of which confirm attempts at containment, while others betray a conflict of interests between the major industrial nations, notably the US, and the conservative Arab regimes. We refer, for example, to the state of the world monetary system after the collapse of the system based on the Bretton Woods agreement, which has led to growing dangers due to fluctuations in exchange rates and to the ubiquitous presence of inflation as a permanent feature of the world economy. Having failed to use inflation to cure their ills, the industrialized nations are now trying, through floating exchange-rates and high interest rates, to operate it to their advantage.

Both the fluctuations in exchange rates and inflation have had a major impact on all the Arab countries. The oil producers among them find their financial surpluses depreciating in real terms, while the non-oil producers, for their part, see their balance of payments deficits growing. In the case of the oil producers, inflation decreases the real price of their oil, whatever OPEC may decide in the way of indexing oil prices to the strength of the dollar. Moreover, stagnation in production has enabled the industrialized nations to stockpile oil and so reduce world market-demand at the same time as inflation is eroding the real value of financial assets held by the capital surplus countries. As to countries with balance of payments deficits, their situation has deteriorated as inflation has driven up prices of imports while higher interest rates have made the burden of foreign debts heavier. It is hard to see how these countries will be able to repay the enormous debts they have run up, especially as these debts continue to grow as the disappointing results of their efforts to develop, and the barriers placed by the industrialized nations in the face of Third-World exports, force those Arab countries to secure new loans at conditions which, because of soaring interest rates, are even more stringent.

Arab and other developing countries are also coming to feel the adverse effects of rapid technological development in the advanced industrial countries, a problem that is acquiring serious dimensions with the emergence of a number of new technologies which are very different from the standard forms used and which could revolutionize technology as we know it today, with serious long-term consequences for developing societies. Among the sophisticated technologies now in use are micro-electronics, biological technology in industry and genetic engineering and fusion nuclear energy. Third-World, including Arab, countries, have no choice but to take these new technologies into account and study their implications on their development.

The new technological developments in the advanced countries have been accompanied by a process of global relocation of production, whereby a number of industries (mainly pollution-generating ones) were shifted from the advanced capitalist countries to the developing countries. Some of these industries form the first links in an integrated industrial chain whose subsequent links are located in the advanced industrial countries themselves. This process has, needless to say, created new forms of dependency. The multinational corporations, which monopolize actual and future technologies and which are, with the backing of governments, the biggest investors in the world-wide search for new sources of energy and more developed technologies, are acquiring an increasingly prominent role in restructuring the world economy. They also play a major role in relocating the industrial process with a view to retaining in the industrialized countries the more advanced stages in this process. To this end, the multinationals are going all out to co-opt the political and social systems in the developing countries, including the Arab countries, and to subject them to their conditions. The technological underdevelopment of the Arab countries at a time when other Third-World countries are trying to accelerate their rates of development, not least in the modern sectors, leaves them at the mercy of multinational manipulation.

Notes

1. See Mohamed Mahmoud El-Imam, ed., *Evaluating the Future of the Arab Development Process in the Context of International and Regional Variables*, Arab Planning Institute, Kuwait, 1980, pp. 9-24 (henceforth cited as 'Evaluating the Future of the Arab Development Process . . .').
2. The signs are clear in the trend to import nuclear power stations on a large scale. Over and above their complete control of the manufacture and supply of these stations and of the technology used in operating them, the industrial countries exercise complete control over the uranium without which nuclear power stations cannot operate. They codify their control by insisting on exercising a supervisory function over these stations, despite the fact that they are closely monitored on behalf of the international community by the UN Nuclear Energy Agency.
3. See El-Imam, op. cit., p. 44.

4. See Ismail-Sabri Abdalla, *Alternative Patterns of Development and Life Styles in Western Asia: A Keynote and an Overview*, United Nations, Economic Commission for Western Asia (ECWA); United Nations Environment Programme (UNEP), Beirut, December 1979, p. 108 (henceforth cited as 'Alternative Patterns . . .').

13 DIVERSITY OF DEVELOPMENT PATHS

1. Downfall of the 'development models' fetish

As they stand at the crossroads, the Arabs do not have before them a ready-made model for development which they need only study carefully and apply efficiently, no fail-safe prescription to cure underdevelopment, like the prescriptions found in medical books of old. It has now been established that any society striving for development and cultural progress can follow any one of many possible paths, and that it is difficult to judge, a priori, the validity of a given path before testing its effectiveness in terms of the results it can produce in the long term. Contrary to the belief that prevailed until recently, the question is not one of choosing from among models already tested and proved successful in given historical circumstances. Nor is it a choice of models determined solely by ideological or class considerations as sometimes appeared to be the case.

Each of the various development experiences was the product of specific historical and objective conditions unlikely to recur. In addition to the political choice involved, each experience is linked to the stage of development attained by the state applying the experiment, its relations with the outside world, its material and human resources, the size of that state, the diversity of its resources and, finally, to the nature of the cultural values prevailing, their historical origins and their specific characteristics.

Development theories applied in the Third World during the last thirty years were the product of western thought. All departed essentially from the premise that, to achieve development, the underdeveloped nations had only to follow the same path that the advanced capitalist nations had followed at an earlier stage, the inference being that there was one unique model for development: that prevailing in the more advanced capitalist countries. It followed that the difference between underdeveloped and developed countries was no more than a time-lag on the same growth path towards greater progress. The way of capitalist development is to reshape structures and institutions in line with the requirements of capitalist growth and to replace the culture, customs and values in the developing countries—considered to be among the main impediments to their development—by those prevailing in capitalist societies.[1] In the logic of these theories, development meant nothing more than achieving high rates of economic growth. The analysis they presented departed from the premise that low income levels in developing countries made for small volumes of domestic savings which in turn made for limited new investments that were inadequate to achieve the required rates of growth—and thus kept incomes low. The proponents of these theories maintained that this vicious circle could only be broken in one of two ways:

(1) by encouraging high incomes at the expense of social justice, to finance savings;
(2) by encouraging the inflow of foreign capital to increase the volume of investment at the expense of economic independence.

The development experience of the last three decades and the difficulties which most Third-World countries encountered in their drive to overcome underdevelopment, even though they had assiduously followed the advice of development 'experts' and 'specialists' in the advanced capitalist countries and of international institutions dominated by these countries, cast doubts on the validity of the formulas they prescribed. In their critique of these neo-classical theories, Third-World economists stressed that the historical conditions in which capitalism had originated and flourished in Western Europe, America and Japan would not recur. They noted that the capitalist systems on the periphery differed considerably from those prevailing, or which used to prevail, in the countries of the centre, and that *peripheral capitalism* had failed to provide suitable conditions for real economic and social growth conducive to economic liberation from imperialist domination and to satisfying the needs of the vast majority of the people.[2] Although specific conditions could allow a number of countries on the periphery to achieve rapid economic growth, this growth would remain distorted and dependent. Authoritative studies confirm not only that poverty remains pervasive, but that it is actually becoming more acute in some cases. They point also to the growing problems of unemployment in many developing countries, even those which have recorded relatively high rates of economic growth.

All these factors, in addition to growing balance of payment deficits and the accelerated rate of external debt accumulation, gave rise to a new school of thought, which called for an 'alternative' development, one directed at satisfying basic human needs, at raising living standards, at releasing human potential, developing man's personality and promoting his creative abilities. This would come about through the citizen's democratic participation in the development process, in which he would both set out the goals and become the instrument with which to achieve them.

The failure of formulas for development imposed from above, which ignored the cultural identity of developing countries had held western civilization up as the only model worth emulating, prompted second thoughts about the very meaning and concept of civilization and invalidated the contention that the West alone carried the torch of 'civilization' and that it was only in western civilization that the values and trends necessary for economic and social progress could be found. Modern trends in development literature stress the importance of preserving the cultural identity of different peoples in order to assure their active particpation in the required processes of change and emancipation. They point out that there are positive elements in most cultures that can be preserved and developed in conformity with changing conditions, reconciling authenticity and renewal so that a society's distinctive personality is not destroyed but, on the contrary, asserted.

Just as capitalist theoreticians were wont to 'deify' the capitalist model of growth as the only valid solution to problems of underdevelopment, so too did socialist, and particularly Marxist, literature tend at one stage to hold up the *Soviet model of development*, industrialization and the building of socialism as the only possible model to be followed if rapid growth and the building of a socialist society were to be achieved. Two factors helped foster this tendency. One was admiration at the speed with which the first socialist state had managed to overcome the economic ravages of World War I, the

Revolution, the civil war and the war of intervention; at its successful assault on economic and social underdevelopment; at its ability to build an independent and advanced industry and to institute agrarian reform and development which enabled it to defeat the superior military might of Nazi Germany; and finally, at the Soviet Union's rapid recovery from the massive destruction of World War II without any outside help. The other factor can be ascribed to the dogmatism which characterized Marxist thought during the Stalinist personality-cult period, and to an inability to differentiate between the particular and the general in the Soviet experience to build socialism and achieve economic progress.

The duplication of the Soviet experience in the East European states, with their smaller size and different historical conditions, provoked a number of political and economic crises which raised the need to question just how 'sacrosanct' the Soviet model was and how far it could be generalized, whether in respect of development or the building of socialism. At thc same time, the rejection of capitalism by many national forces in the Third World, some of whom opted for socialism and others for a path to development inspired by socialist experiences, raised many issues for which there were no ready answers in socialist developmental literature, which had been more concerned with studying the origins of underdevelopment than the ways and means of development. Among the main issues which came in for discussion was the fact that underdeveloped countries were not part of European civilization and that the productive forces in these countries were weak. What made a reappraisal of such issues possible was the return of vitality to Marxist thought after the 20th Congress of the Soviet Communist Party. Orthodox Marxism has since come to adopt the thesis that there are many paths to economic and social development and for the building of socialism. Marxist methodology became acceptable to many thinkers who did not belong to communist parties or who did not accept the philosophical aspects of Marxism. At the same time, however, the ideological differences between the Soviet Union and China came to the fore. China projected itself as being a part of the Third World, which had suffered from imperialist domination and which continued to suffer from the 'collusion' between world imperialism and the new 'social imperialism'. This, coupled with China's success in building a different model of development in conditions of high population density and limited resources—especially agricultural—relative to the number of inhabitants, its raising of the slogan of 'self-reliance', its drive to achieve technological development in traditional sectors of production while stressing the importance of retaining the cultural identity of the Chinese people, captured the imagination of many revolutionary elements in different parts of the world. These tended to 'deify' the Chinese experience and advocated following the same path to development, despite the fact that conditions in their countries were different from those in China, whose experience was the product of an historical evolution specific to it and which reflected historical and objective conditions intrinsic to Chinese society. In the event, the recent changes on the Chinese stage, the post-Mao opening onto the capitalist West, the violent criticism of the Cultural Revolution and of some aspects of China's development experience, further confirmed that neither of the two world-models for development was as sacrosanct as their respective proponents or partisans had supposed.

The downfall of the present development model 'fetish' is a positive phenomenon in that it has opened the field to creative thought and objective research into existing conditions, to find the most appropriate means by which the Arab nation can achieve development without foregoing its cultural identity. This entails testing the viability of different ways and means to this end, essentially through undertaking futures studies which examine the future in the light of alternative and diverse options and try to assess the possible impact of decisions taken today on the future shape of Arab society.

Finally, the downfall of the models fetish allows for more in-depth and detailed discussions of the components of development and for an uninhibited and constant search for different approaches to these components. It has also brought to the fore the need for, and possibility of, alternative approaches to the various issues facing underdeveloped societies, within the framework of the ideological choice of these societies for the socialist or capitalist pattern of development. We cite below two important examples that graphically illustrate the concept of alternative paths to development.

2. Alternative approaches to some issues of development: technology[3]

Not surprisingly, a number of Arab scholars consider planning in the technological field to be 'perhaps more important for national development than investment planning'.[4] The reasons for technology's importance in development are many. To cite but a few:[5]

> technology can be regarded as one of the factors of production, being both a resource and the development of new resources;
>
> it has become an instrument of social liberalization (or repression), which can be used either to improve the quality of decision-making in the direction of achieving social goals for the masses or to tighten control over them;
>
> it has become the factor to which can be attributed the integration of the labour force and work values into the production milieu or, conversely, their alienation from this milieu, as well as an area in which human values can be prompted or a tool that can render human existence meaningless.

The debate over technology is also a debate over the heterogeneity of cultures, over living in harmony with the environment, over striving towards high rates of human performance, over developing human potential and over a proper understanding of the realities of development. To talk of technology is thus necessarily to touch on aspects of social and political science, even of political psychology.

In addressing themselves to the question of adapting technology to a given society, some writers found themselves dealing with 'a problem having many variables, only a few of a purely technological character, most belonging to the fields of economics, sociology or social psychology. These variables together constitute the set of assumptions which represent a frame of reference for the system of research and development (R. & D.).'[6]

Much of what we regard as a western cultural pattern in consumption, production and production techniques implicit in global models is couched in the structural assumptions of these models, essentially in their estimates of cost and limits of resources, constants and technical coefficients, which are usually taken for granted. To illustrate, let us explain here what is meant by structural assumptions in estimating future resources. We find, for example, that estimates of world reserves of resources do not differ greatly from one global model to the next.[7] This betrays the implicit projection of the same technologies into the future. Reserves are usually divided into 'proven', 'potential' or 'likely', proven reserves being those which can be exploited within the scope of prevailing technologies and economics, and potential reserves being those which can be exploited only through using technologies which, though available, are not yet economically viable. To assume, as does this classification, that the technological and economic conditions prevailing today will continue to hold in future is indefensible. For example, the introduction of a genuine indigenous effort in oil-prospecting activities and in increasing output from present oil-fields could transform a substantial portion of potential reserves into proven reserves,[8] as successfully demonstrated by the Mexican, Chinese and other experiences.[9]

To take another example: the Arab world now flares a substantial amount of natural gas, because economic and technological constraints are placed in the way of exporting it by the multinational corporations.[10] But these economic mechanisms could change radically if the Arabs were to exploit the gas themselves in petrochemical industries or as fuel. In an integrated Arab world, or at least one that co-ordinates its activities, the question of technological problems standing in the way of transporting natural gas would not come up whenever the question of Arab resources is discussed. The same point can be made with respect to land resources for agriculture. Estimates of future availability of these resources assume, a priori, specific technologies and economic structures for the horizontal expansion of uncultivated land as well as for vertical expansion to increase yield per hectare. But estimates of agricultural land resources can vary greatly according to whether they depart from the assumption that present socio-economic structures will continue to prevail in the Arab world or that diferent concepts of development, comprising different economic criteria and different forms of technology, which can define for us what we mean by 'cultivable land', will come to prevail. Global studies and models were naturally not concerned with discussing how costs could be reduced if small local tractors, more in keeping with land tenure patterns in some areas of the Arab world, were developed as they have been in China, Japan and India. Nor did they think to include part of the areas given over to grazing in Somalia among the land designated as suitable for cultivation. Moreover, they did not bother to compare the difficulties of cultivating non-arable land in the Arab region with the difficulties encountered in other regions, such as China, where new land was developed at moderate costs and showed reasonable productivity. At the same time, cultivable land as designated in the data base (on which global models and future studies are based) is subject to availability of water.[11] Water is also a resource to which the above arguments could be applied, whether as regards rationalizing its use or choosing from among the alternative uses to which it can be put. The question of setting up projects to increase the Arab world's share of water must be discussed in terms of integration and co-ordination between Third-World countries in the field of water resources.

This line of reasoning could be developed still further. For example, how can Arab human resources interact dynamically so as to become an integrated whole that can change the concept of resources and potential, affect productivity and the limits of economic absorption, rather than their simple algebraic summation into figures representing total population, the total availability of a given resource, etc.? How can one measure, for instance, available Arab phosphates? The figure would obviously differ according to whether the bulk will be exported or whether the intention is to maximize the domestic use of this mineral together with its thorium content, for present and future generations.

We are also entitled to explore such possibilities as developing new sources of renewable energy, at no great capital cost, from rivers, the sun's rays, waste matter, etc, or acquiring resources of copper, lead and zinc from mining the geyser regions in the Red Sea bed.

A number of studies have demonstrated how the interaction of research and development efforts in the Arab nation can markedly affect some coefficients and constraints of technological change in the construction of any model to study the future. In the oil and natural gas sector, for example, we would find that the interaction rather than the simple algebraic summation of Arab scientific efforts could enable them to realize the following accomplishments which are closely related to 'technology assessment' projections in any model.

Search for economic and social criteria more representative of Arab interests than the economic interests of the foreign partner, to govern the exploitation of already discovered deposits of oil and gas.[12]

Co-ordinate in the domain of technology transfer, to avoid importing energy-intensive machines that the West wishes to dump in the present conditions.

Exchange experience in the area of linking oil concessions to industrialization contracts.[13] Algeria has concluded many such 'package deals' that are worthy of study and analysis.

Co-operate in solving technical and administrative problems and in providing fuel for nuclear energy, should it become apparent that the nuclear alternative is a long-term imperative.[14]

Develop scientific resources and capacities needed for research and development of oil-processing industries. The Arab nation, or groups of Arab countries, can achieve a great deal of research and development in manufacturing hydrocarbon products.[15] Directly linked to fundamental science which is accessible to all, the technology required in this domain is mature in that it is close to applied science from the start, and advanced in the western sense of the word, whether in terms of means of production or manufactured products. It is also a technology in which no one expects sudden, dramatic leaps. That is why there are good chances for creative local contributions in developing countries.[16] Technological development is central to this industry if it is to respond to strong demand and because of the high rates of return expected from technological advances in the area of hydrocarbon industries.[17]

At this point it is necessary to discuss the concept of 'technological forecasting'. This concept has been greatly abused by global models, whose predictions in the area of technology are accepted without question. Moreover, there is a prevalent misconception that technological development is a variable which is independent from the rest of the socio-economic structure, much as though it were some kind of wild plant impossible to control. We would like here to develop the discussion we began in Part I of this book, around the correct understanding of probing the future as an integral and consistent whole, by adding some points which are directly linked to the question of technological forecasting as such.

Some of the approaches used by global models to predict trends of technological changes in the future in fact reflect the failure of economic theory to grasp the essence of mutual interrelationship between technological change and economic phenomena. For many years, Keynesians and neo-classicists dealt with technical changes as though they were outside the economic system. They addressed themselves to the effects arising from technological progress, but did not usually analyse the factors, even the economic ones, governing such progress. Because of this historical legacy, technical change has received little attention in studies of long-term growth. Some of those who have written on the subject of technical—or technological—predictions in futures studies, agree that 'our ability to predict the rate and nature of technical change in general has not improved much since Malthus and Marx'.[18] A strange admission, in view of the importance that traditional Marxism gives to the technological factor, of the previous works of J. D. Bernal and of the intensive work that has been carried out over the last twenty years in "R. & D.", its effects, and the factors governing its spread'.[19]

Because of this crisis, which limited the accuracy of predictions of the overall technological effects on the economic structure, we find many global models using statistical trends of technological change exhibited by advanced industrial countries in the past to predict future trends of technological change in developing countries. This methodological approach, which was adopted without any theoretical discussion was used, for example, in respect of the technical coefficients applied to the sectors of agriculture and environmental pollution by *The Limits to Growth*,[20] as well as in the capital/production coefficients contained in the same study.[21] It was also used by Leontief in the technical coefficients he includes in his analysis of inputs and outputs and in the sector of pollution in various regions of the world. The basic defect of this approach is that coefficients borrowed from the advanced industrialized countries cannot be extrapolated onto the future structures of developing countries. Obviously the historical experiences and conditions in which these trends for change in the technical field and economic structure accumulated will not be repeated. On the one hand, the developing countries will not be able to obtain the cheap natural resources in future in the way imperialism did from the developing countries in the past; on the other hand, the future technology of the West—in terms of its impact on structure, in the light of world crises in energy, food and pollution and of accelerating rates of technological innovation—will not be a simple reproduction of old technologies.

It is clear from the above that if we are to avoid the illusions, fallacies and pitfalls of technological forecasting, we must elaborate a theory of development which gives reciprocal relations and effects (between technological change on the one hand and the political-economic-social order in its entirety on the other) their due. We must also investigate trends in the accomplishments of basic science and create suitable conditions and structures to benefit from these accomplishments. Contrary to what some people think, recognizing the need to choose the appropriate technology is not an admission of inability on the part of Third-World countries to assimilate scientific and technological progress, so that they have no choice but to settle for whatever technologies that the developed West sees fit to throw their way. Rather, it denotes a concern to emphasize the interaction between technology and the economic, political, social and cultural structures from a developmental perspective. Thus any vision of the Arab future should take into account the expected accomplishments in science and technology in order to select the appropriate ones among them. To probe the trends of accomplishments in basic science, therefore, we shall begin by determining the likely framework in which these accomplishments and their technological implementation will take place. What is likely is that the present concentration of scientific and technological research, or what is called 'Big Science', will continue in future, with all this implies in the way of directing research and financing to resolving present problems.[22] This will involve a growing role for the State together with the multinationals.[23] Thus the applications of scientific research in the field of basic science will be governed by both the type and source of demand for technological development.[24] The demand for technological development in the multinational corporations comes from the developed industrial countries and, accordingly, new technological solutions will not be the best and most appropriate possible for the whole of mankind.[25] From the industrial revolution onwards, technological development has proceeded under the influence of two factors: first, the manufacturer's desire to maximize profits and, second, the demand of military requirements. Neither of these factors offers a sufficient guarantee for a rational choice. Moreover, a feature of our time is the growing interpenetration between states and multinational corporations in the field of research and development.

If we try to classify the likely accomplishments and applications of basic science under general headings, these would be: the revolution in biological sciences, the revolution in the field of communications and computers, uses of renewable sources of energy, the search for new sources of food, the search for new or alternative sources of minerals, developing new horizons for the use of nuclear energy. In all these fields, except nuclear energy applications, groups of developing countries could, if they combined their resources and scientific abilities, achieve a great deal. The basic science for these expected accomplishments is accessible, and technological solutions, suited to the environment and to prevailing conditions, could be found by local scientific efforts.

If we take the revolution in biological sciences, which is represented in making use of biological energy and, thanks to biological fertilizers, in developing new sources of food, in biological industries and genetic engineering[26] we would find that the necessary knowledge is available[27] and that Arab scientific research could score technological accomplishments in all these fields of applications. Indeed, the first steps have been taken in this direction, especially in Saudi Arabia and Egypt, which are producing proteins from unicellular organisms derived from oil, although these accomplishments are still linked to western scientific research.

As to the revolution in communications and computers, basic science is readily available for all applications other than microprocessors. In fact, the industries based on technological development in this area were nominated by some Arab specialists to become a leading sector in future Arab industry.[28]

The Arab world, an example of a grouping of developing countries where the sun shines every day, is relatively privileged in the field of renewable sources of energy and their applications in agriculture and food.[29] The abundance of both natural gas and sunlight in the Arab nation can, in conjunction with basic science actually available, achieve much in the area of developing crops, drying and preserving harvests, cultivating non-irrigated land, manufacturing food from natural gas and developing mineral substitutes.[30]

When we try to probe the future of technological variables included in the overall economic structures, by devising comprehensive alternatives for the whole socio-economic order, we can draw on many other comparable experiences for measures of trends of change in techniques and the like, in addition to some partial measures from developing countries which we discuss further in this section. There are some global measures from pre- and post-revolutionary China, when the economic structure was re-oriented in light of satisfying basic needs and achieving self-reliance.[31] There are many global measures from the Japanese economy, which has been characterized—in comparison with the industrial West—by a conscious intervention to rationalize the long-term use pattern of resources, to benefit from local advantages and to avoid dependency on the outside world as much as possible.[32] In addition, a comparison between technological development in Japan and the corresponding development in the West shows the difference in technical coefficients between them.

3. Eco-development

Most global models are concerned with two environmental issues, namely, the finite nature of natural resources and the phenomenon of pollution.[33] One possible reason why environmental issues and their relationship to development are limited to these two issues is that both can be measured and, consequently, subjected to mathematical treatment. However, neglecting other aspects is unforgivable. The model on which the famous report by the Club of Rome, *Limits to Growth* was based, is characterized, first, by its strong emphasis on, and, second, by its pessimistic outlook to, these two issues.[34] The conclusion reached by the report is that the earth's resources will be depleted within a relatively short time-span and that pollution will eventually attain intolerable levels. Both factors impose material limits to economic growth, and the report warns that an overshoot of these limits would have cataclysmic consquences for the human race. Accordingly, it makes an urgent appeal for a reduction of world demographic and economic growth.

The call to curb population growth is nothing new. Ever since the fifties, the West has been loud in its condemnation of the 'population explosion', which it considers responsible for all the misery of the Third World and the harbinger of ruin and devastation for the whole planet. What was new in the report, however, was the theme it developed of limits to economic growth and it is this which explains why it came in for so much attention, not only from specialists, but also from millions of ordinary people who either read the report or a summary of its conclusions.[35] A school of economists emerged to advocate an immediate 'zero growth rate'.[36] There is no need to expound at length here on what the implications of such a trend would be for Third-World countries. Very briefly, then, while it may be theoretically possible, even desirable, in many cases to reduce growth rates of material production in industrialized countries which have attained a high degree of affluence, to call for such a reduction in Third-World countries is to ask them to abandon development, and resign themselves to living in misery.

Not all models, however, adopt the same line as the Club of Rome. As we saw in Part I, the Fundacion Bariloche model set out to prove that the earth's resources are sufficient to meet the whole of humanity's basic needs, provided only that certain alterations are brought to the existing economic, social and political structures.[37] The MOIRA model, which was concerned mainly with food resources, proved for its part that a thirty-fold increase could be brought to present world availability of food if man rationalized all the elements of the situation under his control. The problem, according to this model, is not one of natural potentials but lies rather in the socio-economic factors which affect the performance of production factors. Leontieff's approach to the problems of resources and pollution is also one of cautious optimism. He sees the determinants of growth—at least until the end of the century—as being political, social and institutional in character, rather than material limits to natural resources. The exhaustion of resources is not envisaged for the end of the century according to Leontief, but the relative prices of some of them will increase substantially. As for pollution, he believes it can be kept under control and calculates the cost of pollution abatement in his model. Without going back to all the global models and futures studies to determine the attitude of each of the issues of finite resources and pollution, we can say that on the one hand OPEC's adjustment of oil prices—or what was termed in the West, 'oil shock'—and the possibility of this phenomenon spreading to other primary products which had hitherto been easily—and cheaply—accessible to the West, posed a serious economic problem for the industrialized world which it had to overcome by all possible means. On the other hand, public opinion in the West has become so sensitive to the issue of pollution and to the necessity of protecting the environment and improving the quality of life, that the economic and social policies followed by western governments must take this factor into account.

Apart from an active—and not unimportant—minority which calls for a reappraisal of lifestyles and, consequently, of modes of production, to protect the natural environment and raise the quality of life,[38] and the organized consumers' movements which expose dishonest advertising or the adverse side-effects of certain products,[39] the predominant trends in leading government and multinational circles can be summed up as follows.

Pollution Efforts are directed in the short term at evolving pollution abatement devices, at laying down standard specifications for some products (e.g. cars) designed to reduce pollution, and at banning the use of certain chemicals with dangerous side-effects in the manufacture of drugs and insecticides. In the longer term, the trend will probably be to stop expansion of the more environmental-polluting industries and to build new plants for these industries in Third-World countries, under the auspices of the multinationals. This solution will at the same time appear to respond to the desire of Third-World countries for rapid industrialization, all the more so in that some of the industries earmarked for relocation to the Third World are considered to be essential components of industrialization.

In a study published by the United Nations Conference on Trade and Development (UNCTAD), we find a list of the following industries: oil refining, iron and steel, primary processing of non-ferrous metals, paper and paper products, some chemical industries, etc.[40] This trend is not contradictory to the interests of the industrialized countries and the multinational corporations. In fact, the latter have been calling for the industrialized countries to focus their efforts on developing technology—intensive industries which, by their nature, control many economic activities, wherever they happen to be located. This then is the answer they are preparing to the Third World's demand for a reappraisal of the international division of labour.

Mineral resources Recycling programmes will probably be stepped up, together with a search for cheaper substitutes for some of these minerals. At the same time, the grip of the multinationals on the markets for mineral resources will be asserted in new ways, including that of allowing primary processing of minerals to take place where the mines are located, as well as the manufacture of some intermediary products in Third-World countries. The important thing as far as the multinationals are concerned, is that the terms of trade remain in their favour. They control world industrialization at the source and at the outlet, that is, when they supply machinery, equipment and expertise at the prices they determine, when they market Third-World products in world markets and when they undertake related operations of transportation, insurance, financing, advertising, etc. Space does not permit a detailed explanation of the methods and mechanisms by which the multinationals maximize their profits and tighten their grip.[41]

Energy Two trends have emerged simultaneously. The first seeks to conserve energy by limiting forms of wasteful consumption and by taking high energy prices into account in new technological development. The second aims at reducing dependence on oil as far as possible. This is represented first in a return to coal after long years of neglect and, second, in the development of new energy sources, from expanding in the field of nuclear energy and of transforming it from a fission to a fusion technology, to using solar, geo-thermal, tidal or wind energy etc. It might be useful here to refer to the dual-price policy applied by the industrialized countries in respect of oil. Through taxes and other means, oil and oil products are sold to the consumer at much higher prices than those reflected in OPEC's prices, to limit their use on the one hand and, on the other, to make the use of alternative energy sources economically viable despite their high costs.

In fact, the crisis of natural resources and the problem of pollution are both very closely linked to the pattern of capitalist development in the West. Industrial growth in the West occurred in conditions where western countries exercised full control over all the earth's resources. Economic thought at the time accepted that these resources were available in unlimited quantities. Some, being a gift of nature, cost nothing and therefore had no price. Economic textbooks spoke of natural resources either as a production factor whose price was governed by market forces of supply and demand, or as free goods, like water and air, which had no place in economic theory since this was concerned only with scarce commodities, that is, those having a cost of production. On the philosophical level, progress was epitomized in man's domination of nature and in his ability to partake of its riches at will, as though man was not himself a part of nature. This intellectual climate and the ready and cheap availability of resources were not conducive to self-restraint, and technological development did not take into account that some natural resources, being stocks that had built up over millions of years, would inevitably dry up one day. Indeed, man's interference in nature can disrupt even the continuous and regular flow of renewable resources. A case in point is wood. Deforestation, either to use the land for agricultural purposes or as a site for man's cities, airports, factories, roads, etc., has so reduced forest areas that wood, a renewable resource in forests, is now in critically short supply, with the result that we now have a crisis of wood and of the paper produced from its pulp. As to the squandering of stocks of natural resources, the most telling example is how a cheap and plentiful availability of oil at a certain stage gave rise to the heavily oil-dependent consumer society in which the use of private cars is so widespread that in the industrialized countries there is today on the average one car for each two people. Needless to say, this situation has raised enormous problems in these countries.[42]

To each technique of production prevailing in a given society at a specific moment in its history corresponds a given technological product which evolves according to the scientific knowledge available at the time, the natural resources controlled by that society, the cultural philosophy it embraces and the economic interests by which it is governed. Capitalist growth departed from the assumption that the general good of society could be realized spontaneously through the striving of individuals to maximize profits (in the case of producers) or utility (in the case of consumers). It would be out of place here to dicuss the validity of this assumption. What need concern us is that it gave rise to defective economic calculus by implying that each individual, whether a producer or a consumer, makes his decisions according to his own personal calculations.

In fact, the decisions which shaped the economies of the industrialized countries were those taken by the producers. For utility is a subjective notion that is impossible to measure, while consumption habits are imposed by the prevailing social pattern more than by the individual decisions of millions of consumers who are in any case influenced to a great extent by advertising and other marketing techniques. Profit, on the other hand, is an objective phenomenon that can be measured in monetary terms. Moreover, the producer is no longer an individual but is now a company or a conglomerate of companies with the means to undertake precise economic calculations. In a market economy, maximization of profits for any product is a function of three factors: production cost, size of the market and sales price. In the early stages of capitalist development, producers did not have complete control over prices. Thus their efforts were directed essentially at reducing production costs. One of the most important ways of doing this was to externalize some elements of cost, that is, to have society or the environment pay these costs, for example, dumping waste in rivers, disposing of it through municipal waste-disposal facilities, or benefiting from the proximity of a port, a railway network, a city constituting a big market, etc. Another way of reducing the production cost of one item of a given commodity is to increase the volume of production and sales, or what is known as economies of scale, even if this should entail concentrating industrial production in huge units and raising environmental pollution to a critical threshold. In order to increase sales, producers had to spur consumers into buying more, through advertisements, diversification of commodities and filling the market with totally useless commodities, never mind the resources squandered to feed such feverish consumption.

In other words, the producer was required only to maximize his own profits, without taking into account the cost to society. Economic feasibility studies of projects are still based essentially on micro-calculation, with no systematic attempt at macro-calculation going beyond the simple summation of micro-calculations to try and assess the elements of cost which will be borne by society. This approach is all the more dangerous in that the individual producer—even a company—is concerned mainly with short- or medium-term calculations, being uninterested in calculating what can happen in the long or very long term, which is anyway beyond his control, while by their very nature environmental phenomena, notably pollution and depletion of resources, only make themselves felt in the long or very long term. For these reasons, the means of production and the patterns of consumption linked to them in the West led to the development of technologies which are highly wasteful of resources and pollute the environment in a way likely to seriously jeopardize human existence. The fault does not lie in industrialization or in the development of agriculture, health, housing or means of transportation as such, but in the economic, political, social and ideological framework in which this development historically took place.

The authors of *Limits to Growth* failed to analyse the nature, historical roots and aims of development, and the strong links between socio-economic structures on the one hand and political, cultural, technological and ecological conditions on the other, leading some western writers to comment that the world is not divided into developed and underdeveloped countries, but suffers from maldevelopment in both developed and Third-World countries.[43]

Going back to the Third World, of which our Arab nation is a part, let us begin by refuting a number of fallacies. As we have previously stated, underdevelopment is in fact distorted, extroverted and dependent development which, because of world capitalism's control of the world economy, is a by-product of that system's historical evolution. While this statement does not negate the manifestations of underdevelopment in the Arab world that we have already cited, it does refute the contention that the historical responsibility for underdevelopment is ours alone, either because of inferior genes (the racist interpretation of underdevelopment), or because Islam, by preaching resignation, is not conducive to enterprise and hard work (the explanation of those subscribing to the view that western civilization is superior to all others).

Moving on to the contention that population growth is the real obstacle in the way of development, it might be useful to point out here that, while population density may be increasing in certain parts of the Arab nation, the ratio of population to the overall area in the Arab world gives one of the lowest population densities in the world. It is also useful to remember that people are the makers of development, and not, as a great many economists tend to regard them, only a 'resource'. We reject this narrow, not to say demeaning, view of man, and point to the simple fact that each individual is a producer who has, ever since the simplest stages of technological development, been producing more than he consumes. From this perspective, then, the issue of development becomes one of providing productive work for every individual able to perform it.

We would like to take this argument even further by discussing here the essence of what is termed the 'population explosion'. From a reading of demographic history, we find that the population in all societies has two stable equilibrium positions and one situation of disequilibrium. The first case of equilibrium is one in which the human species has lived for thousands of years. It is characterized by high birth- and death-rates, which lead to a low rate of natural growth in population. This is the case of societies with low income levels, or which suffer from poverty to this day.[44] The second position of equilibrium occurs at a high income level, and is characterized by a sharp drop in both birth- and death-rates. By equilibrium here is meant that, barring any unforeseen eventualities, the situation in either of the two cases can remain stable for many years.

As to the case of disequilibrium, this occurs when incomes begin to rise (by incomes is meant what the individual receives in the way of monetary income and services in kind), enough to bring about an immediate drop in death-rates (in the modern age, this was helped by the discovery of medicines effective in curing the epidemics that used to periodically wipe out whole segments of the population), but not enough to reduce birth-rates (through generalizing education, including education of women, thus raising age at marriage; women's entry into the labour market; the parents' desire that their children's living standards should be at least as good, if not better, than their own, etc.). In this case, the birth-rate does not increase but remains more or less stable, while the death-rate drops, making for a marked increase in rates of natural population growth. We have described this situation as one of disequilibrium in the sense that it cannot continue for long. Either development achieves a sustained growth, in which case birth-rates decline and society moves closer to a position of stable equilibrium at the high income level, or development efforts are unsuccessful, in which case poverty increases and the death-rate rises once again. This is not just conjecture: famine has reared its ugly head in recent years, causing a great number of deaths in a number of Third-World countries, including those lying on the African belt that extends from Ethiopia to Senegal. It is clear therefore from what has been said that the most effective method of birth-control is successful development.[45] Accordingly, there is no danger of a global population explosion where, because of the depletion of resources, people will be reduced to cannibalism.

Numerous studies have proved that the number of people on earth relative to the resources available now or until the end of the century do not constitute an intolerable strain on the environment and that the real issue is to evolve economic, social, political and cultural structures that would link people to resources, so that unemployment would be considerably reduced or disappear completely. There remains one population problem that is found in some and not all Third-World countries (and some, not all, Arab countries), namely, the dependency ratio. Because man does not work the moment he is born society spends money to raise and train him to perform a productive activity for a period commonly accepted as fifteen years. Given that life-expectancy at birth is still modest in most of our countries, the proportion of the labour force (the members of the population of working-age) in the total population is lower than it is in the industrialized countries. Finally, international organizations have recently revised their projections of population size at the end of the century, lowering their estimates in the light of a trend that has emerged in a number of Third-World countries towards lower rates of population growth.

Having said all this, it is only fair here to give due credit to global models and futures studies. By no means can all their efforts be dismissed as exercises in futility, nor all the conclusions they reached be rejected out of hand. On the contrary, some of these can be adapted to conform to Third-World conditions. Thus the first thing we can deduce from the debate that arose over the depletion of resources is the impossibility of imposing the American pattern of consumption on the whole world, because this would make the depletion of resources a very real and imminent danger. A few examples can be cited here to illustrate this point. If the average energy consumption in the US (nearly 12 million tons coal-equivalent a year) were to be generalized, this would entail a twenty-fold increase in annual world energy production. If the pattern of food production, transportation and consumption prevailing in the US were to become universal, 30 per cent of all available energy would have to be allocated to the production of food alone.[46] The third example relates to private cars. The rate of car-ownership in the US stands at slightly more than one car for each two members of the population, including children and old people. In 1976, as much as 41 per cent of the total number of private cars in the world were found in that country.[47] If this pattern were to be generalized, the cars now in use world-wide would increase twenty-five times over. The mind reels at the sheer quantity of metals and other raw materials that would go into their production, the amount of energy required to fuel them, the volume of investments necessary to build the roads and highways to accommodate them, etc.—not to mention the level of pollution which would result from the use of so many cars.

The examples would fill many pages. But we should not deduce from this that the earth's resources are barely enough to maintain life at the subsistence level, and that material living standards in the industrialized countries would have to be lowered if there is to be any kind of equality between the peoples of the world. The fact is that production and consumption patterns in the US display an appalling degree of extravagance and waste that was made possible by that country's control over natural resources, both in its own territory and in many other parts of the world. This is clear if we look at some figures from other industrialized countries which are comparable to the US in terms of level of industrialization and average income. We find, for example, that the average per capita consumption of energy in West Germany is only slightly over 6 million tons coal-equivalent, while in Japan it is only about 4 million.[48] The ratio of cars to people in Western Europe is 1:4, while in Japan it is 1:6. All this highlights the need for Third-World countries to search for other development paths based on energy-efficient technologies that will neither deplete non-renewable resources nor overdraw on renewable resources.

Another deduction we can make is that western production and consumption patterns threaten to pollute the natural environment and human life. As we have already mentioned, the industrialized nations are trying to limit pollution by various means, the most important being pollution-abatement devices. At the same time, these nations have passed bills banning the manufacture of products that pollute the environment or affect human health. Research and development trends are directed at limiting pollution in the new technologies and abandoning environment-polluting industries. These anti-pollution measures are very costly. The limited efforts furnished so far have removed sizeable chunks from the GNP of industrialized states. In the period 1971–1980, Japan spent between 3 and 5.5 per cent of its GNP on fighting pollution. Anti-pollution programmes in the US, Holland and Italy 1976–1980 cost between 1.3 and 1.7 per cent of the GNP of these countries.[49] But, costly as they were, these efforts were concentrated essentially on alleviating the immediate effects of pollution, and did not come to grips with such long-term effects as the increase of CO_2 content in the atmosphere, the change in climate, etc. The UN has set up an entire apparatus, the United Nations Programme for Environmental Affairs, to monitor the deterioration of the environment world-wide, study its reasons and effects and propose counter measures. However, the continued recession in the western countries has driven many of their governments to reduce allocations for the protection of the environment. For all these reasons, simple logic dictates that Third-World countries, still at the early stages of development, must resist any attempts on the part of the industrialized countries to export environmental polluting activities to their territories, and to constantly search for 'clean' technological solutions.

As it is, the Arab environment is already threatened by the dangers raised in global models and world futures studies. In terms of resources, the Arab nation exhibits two contradictory phenomena simultaneously: overdrawing on non-renewable resources, such as oil and thus threatening stocks in some Arab countries with rapid depletion, while at the same time neglecting renewable resources, such as forests and pastures, of which vast areas have already been lost while the few remaining areas in North Africa are on their way to disappearing. To this should be added the inroads made by industry in urban areas, and the non-agricultural use to which vast tracts of farmland are put, despite the fact that cultivable land is known to be limited. Still on the question of resources, although some raw materials (e.g. phosphates) can be processed locally, their exploitation is neglected because they have a limited competitive edge in the export market. As to pollution, its effects have appeared in the high rates of desertification, in the pollution in the areas of oil production and refining and in areas of industrial concentration, such as Helwan in Egypt. There is also the pollution arising from heavy urban congestion and the disposal of urban waste in rivers, lakes and seas, the adverse side-effects of pesticides which have begun to affect the health of the 'fellah', etc.

But do alternative paths to development actually exist? The question has in fact now gone beyond the stage of academic debate. In agriculture, for instance, specialists have been wont to hold up the American pattern of agriculture as the ideal towards which all development efforts in this sphere should strive—despite the fact that it is based on enormous industrial inputs of equipment, fertilizers and pesticides, with associated storage, transportation and distribution processes also based on mechanization, so that each American worker in agriculture is supported by ten in industry. Moreover, it is extremely costly in terms of energy consumption, and has led to environmental damage to both man and the land. In contrast, other countries poor in both workers and land have succeeded in achieving notable increases in agricultural production through means which are less costly in terms of investment and less damaging to the environment. One can point here to China, India and

Mexico, all densely populated countries with acute food shortages which succeeded in solving this problem to varying degrees,[50] while Japan's experience has proved, for its part, that agriculture can be greatly developed within the framework of small land-holdings.[51] This is particularly relevant for the Arab countries which combine density of population with limited land area. In this connection, it is useful to point out that the Arabs can produce the fertilizers they need thanks to their oil and natural gas resources.

However, the question is, what type of fertilizer is needed for the different types of soil and the crops which can be grown in them? What are the quantities of fertilizer which can be used without causing any side-effects, such as earth or water pollution, from harmful chemicals? The Arabs can also produce what they need in the way of pesticides and herbicides, although these should be used with extreme caution because of their harmful effect on useful living organisms such as birds and plants and on the human consumers of agricultural products. Chemical fertilizers usually contain toxic substances such as lead, mercury and cadmium compounds, which go through a complete cycle, sometimes lasting as long as twenty years, passing from plants to animals to humans through the earth's rivers, seas and air. Thus every effort should be made to develop life-sustaining biological means to combat plant pests to expand their use and limit that of chemical fertilizers.

As to mechanization, obviously such factors as the quality of the oil, the type of crop, the pattern of land tenure and the size of the labour force must be taken into account when designing and generalizing equipment. But even more important is to focus on the human factor in agriculture. As we have seen, there is a continuing exodus of the educated, young and active rural elements to the cities, with only those unable to leave staying behind. Needless to say, the latter develop feeling of frustration, which are reflect in the peasants' lack of motivation and in their indifference to agricultre and its development. Thus the question of modernizing agriculture is that of overall rural development which provides the required number of educated peasants, creates non-agricultural job opportunities in the countryside and raises the standard of the village in terms of social and cultural services, to retain in the agricultural sector a productive and enthusiastic workforce capable of assimilating technological development.[52] All this shows that modernizing agriculture in the Arab nation requires changing the economic, social, political, managerial and cultural structures, as well as espousing the appropriate technology. Otherwise there can be no question of achieving an overall sustained agricultural growth capable of solving the food problem and of furnishing industry with its raw material requirements, without having to rely on an imported technology that developed in conditions very different from our own.

While it is true that industrialization is a prerequisite for development, it is also true that industrialization can take different patterns. In the final analysis, the basic factors governing industry are natural and human resources on the one hand and markets on the other. What is missing is a global vision of how industrial growth should proceed in the Arab world. The choice of industry must take into account the availability of raw materials, of trained manpower at different levels and of Arab markets capable of absorbing the bulk of the chosen industry's output. This in turn entails keeping links between the various industries in mind, so that, wherever possible, an integrated productive chain covering entire sectors, from the manufacture of machinery and equipment to intermediary products to consumer goods, can be set up on a pan-Arab level. Meanwhile, the availability of markets in the Arab countries entails raising the income levels of the broad masses to provide the required purchasing power that can enable the citizens to satisfy their basic needs from integrated Arab industries. The choice of sites for these industries cannot be left to chance if we want to avoid congestion and pollution. Rigorous standards must be set to safeguard the interests of society as a whole and to ensure continuous progress for coming generations.

Thus it is essential to achieve a balanced industrial development between different regions and countries. Similarly, the choice of technique must be made with a view to satisfying the environmental imperative, to reducing the discrepancies between town and countryside and to curbing the cancerous growth of big cities. Just as technological development in western societies responded to the needs and potentials of these societies, so too must we take the needs and potentials of the Arab nation into account and avoid the adverse effects that accompanied industrial growth in the West. Probably we would need to strengthen and develop traditional, labour-intensive industries as well as to depend on a large number of small and medium industrial units disseminated throughout the Arab region side by side with the huge industrial units whose size is a decisive factor in reducing costs of production. All this requires tireless efforts in research, study and analysis, as well as giving rein to creative and innovative abilities in the Arab world. We can point here to the important role still played by cottage industries in Japan, small industry in China and handicrafts in India.

To conclude this review of examples of alternative paths, we would just like to mention here that there are also alternative paths in the field of services which can raise the standard of human forces and the efficiency of their performance by solving problems of education, health and nutrition in a reasonable span of time and at much lower costs than those required to apply the western model of providing such services in rich and advanced societies.[53]

Notes

1. This theory is most clearly and blatantly expressed in W. W. Rostow, *The Stages of Economic Growth*, Cambridge, Cambridge University Press, 1960. Translated into many languages, this book was for a long time the bible of development planners and decision-makers in most Third-World countries.
2. For the most important analysis of peripheral capitalism and its shortcomings, see Raul Prebisch, 'A Critique of Peripheral Capitalism', *CEPAL Review* (Etats Unis, Commission Economique pour L'Amerique Latine), **1**, First Semester 1976, and 'Socio-Economic Structure and the Crisis of Peripheral Capitalism', *CEPAL Review*, **2**, Second Semester 1978.
3. This section relied mainly on scientific material prepared by Dr Aly Nassar. (Translator's note.)
4. Organization for Economic Co-operation and Development (OECD), Interfutures, *The Problem of Technology Transfer between Advanced and Developing Countries*, Paris, OECD, 1978, Interim Reports, Chapter 3: Ismail-Sabri Abdalla, 'Appropriate Techniques and Technological Capacity in Third World Countries'. (Translator's note.)
5. Compare p. 41 of Introduction of A. J. Dolman, ed., *Global Planning and Resource Management: Towards Decision-Making in a Divided World*, London, Pergamon Press, 1980. (Translator's note.).

6. Amiclar O. Herrera, 'An Approach to the Generation of Technologies Appropriate for Rural Development', in A. B. Zahlan, ed., *Technology Transfer and Change in the Arab World*, Oxford, Pergamon, 1978, p. 138.
7. H. S. D. Cole, *Global Models and the International Economic Order*, London, Pergamon Press, 1977, Chapter 3.
8. There is a real chance of raising the percentage of oil extracted in the Arab world by about 30–45 per cent through the use of technical means which, though available, would require Arab co-operation in the domain of research and development. See K. Balasino and G. Faffer, 'Future Evolution of Technical Research in the Domain of Oil', *Oil and Arab Cooperation,* **4**, 3, 1978.
9. A. A. Meyerhaff, 'Best Chances on Shore Are in China and Russia', *Oil and Gas Journal*, August 1977, special issue.
10. The Arab world flared 15 per cent of the natural gas released worldwide in the early seventies. See Mustapha Borhan, 'Projects to Exploit Natural Gases in the Arab Countries and The Needs to Process Them Domestically, *Oil and Arab Cooperation,* **3**, 1, 1977.
11. The Mesarovic study based its assessment of the maximum limits of vertical expansion in the Arab region on data from Revelle's study, whose assessment was linked to the present availability of river water. See R. Revelle, 'Will the Earth's Land and Water Resources be Sufficient for Future Population', in: United Nations Conference on the Human Environment, Stockholm, 1972.
12. Compare Adnan El-Jenaby, 'Different Formulas for Criteria of Optimum Exploitation of Arab Oil Resources, *Oil and Arab Cooperation,* **3**, 1, 1977. Although technically speaking much has been achieved in the way of increasing the degree to which oil wells can be exploited, putting these achievements to use comes up against economic constraints. But the question that poses itself here is: economic from whose point of view? See a number of articles reviewing achievements in this field in: *Oil and Gas Journal: Petroleum 2000* (August 1977), pp. 229–75 (special issue).
13. Compare Ahmed El-Qosheiry, 'Stability and Development in the Legal Methods Employed by Industrializing Countries', *Oil and Arab Cooperation*, **2**, 3, 1976.
14. Compare Youssef Rasheed and Adnan Shehab El-Dine, 'Future Oil-Nuclear Energy Balance in the OAPEC Countries', *Oil and Arab Cooperation,* **2**, 2, 1976, p. 41.
15. Abdel-Aziz El-Watary, 'Research and Development in the Oil Processing Industries', *Oil and Arab Cooperation,* **3**, 1, 1977.
16. A case in point is Mexico, where some 70 per cent of the technological requirements of the Mexican oil industry were developed from Mexican scientific sources, abilities and labour. The activities of the Mexican institute responsible for this creativity are expanding at an

annual rate of 20 per cent, and the institute is now transferring technology outside Mexico. See Organization of Arab Petroleum Exporting Countries (OAPEC), 'OAPEC Field Report on Mexico', pp. 43-9.

17. Standard Oil recouped what it had spent on a four-year research and development programme in petrochemicals within only thirteen years. See El-Watary op. cit.
18. Christopher Freeman *et al.*, 'Policies for Technical Change', in: Christopher Freeman and Marie Jahoda, eds., *World Futures: The Great Debate*, Falmer, Brighton, University of Sussex, 1979, p. 207.
19. For studies over the last twenty years compare: ibid., pp. 207 and 213; pp. 223 and 227.
20. The many criticisms levelled at these assumptions can be found in C. Julien and C. Freeman in: H. S. D. Cole *et al.*, eds., *Thinking about the Future: A Critique of the Limits to Growth*, London, Chatto and Windus, 1973.
21. See a review of these criticisms of Leontief's assumptions in Cole, *Global Models and the International Economic Order*, Chapter 3, (ii) and Freeman *et al.*, 'Policies for Technical Change', pp. 207–13.
22. This expression is used to denote the highly concentrated nature of modern science, much the same way as the term 'big business' is used in a different context.
23. Compare National Institute for Research Advancement, 'Japan Toward the 21st Century', Tokyo, August 1978.
24. Technology transactions between developing and advanced countries do not exceed 10 per cent of the technology market.
25. Compare F. R. Sagisti, 'Knowledge is Power', *Mazingira,* **8**, 1977. In addition to addressing the issue of developed countries' demand for technological development, Sagasti shows that more than 50 per cent of investments and technology world-wide is directed at producing advanced weapons, while about two-thirds of the balance goes in producing non-essential commodities.
26. Compare Edgard Di Silva *et al.*, 'An Integrated Microbiology Technology for Developing Countries: Point of Departure Towards Economic Progress', *Science and Society*, (UNESCO paper), September-November 1978.
27. Compare basic documents presented to the Conference organized by United Nations Industrial Development Organization (UNIDO), Exchange of Views with Experts on the Implications of Advances in Genctic Engineering for Developing Countries, Vienna, February 1981, Draft Report.
28. Ossama Amin El-Kholi, *Long-Term Projection of Science and Technology in Egypt Until the Year 2000*, 'Egypt in the Year 2000' Series, Cairo, National Planning Institute, 1977.
29. Compare Abdel-Aziz Amin, 'With the March of Science Towards the Future', *'Alam El-Fikr,* **10**, 4, January–March 1980, pp. 176–7, and

Mahfouz Ghanem, 'New Sources of Food', *'Alam El-Fikr,* **3**, 1, April–June 1973, pp. 145-65.

30. See Sellwyn Enzer *et al.*, 'World Food Potentials Over the Next Twenty Years', *Al-Magal*, September 1979, translation of an article published in *Futurist* in 1978.
31. Some of these global measures for technical change in the Chinese economic structure are available in Edward L. Wheelwright and Bruce McFarlane, *The Chinese Road to Socialism: Economics of the Cultural Revolution* (foreword by Joan Robinson), New York, Monthly Review Press, 1970; Akio Hosono, 'Industrial Development and Employment: The Experience of Asian and Latin American Development Strategy', *CEPAL Review*, 2, Second Semester 1976; S. Swamg, 'Economic Growth in China and India', *Economic Development and Cultural Change,* **21**, 4, (July 1973), and T. G. Rawski, 'Economic Growth and Employment in China', *World Development*, 8/9 (1979).
32. See Industrial Research Institute, 'The Role of Technology in the Change of Industrial Structure', Tokyo, April 1978.
33. Abdalla, 'Alternative Patterns . . .'
34. See Part I.
35. *The Limits to Growth* was translated into eighteen languages and reprinted in several of these.
36. This came to be known as the 'Zero Growth School'.
37. See Part I.
38. This refers to the ecological movement, which drew attention for its vigorous resistance to expansion in nuclear energy, as well as for the votes it won in the elections for the European Parliament (4 per cent of the total votes cast).
39. The Consumers' Movement, which first became active in the United States some years ago, is now equally alive in Western Europe, where it constitutes a pressure group.
40. See Charles Pearson, Implications for Trade and Investment of Developing Countries of the United States Environmental Control', United Nations Conference on Trade and Development (UNCTAD), (E-H-11 D.5).
41. See Ismail-Sabri Abdalla, *Towards a New International Economic Order: A Study on Issues of Economic Development, Independence and International Relations,* Cairo, 1976, the references quoted therein, and Hossam Issa, *The Multinational Corporations*, Beirut, Arab Organization for Studies and Publishing, 1980.
42. See L. R. Brown, C. Flavin and C. Norman, 'The Future of the Automobile in an Oil-Short World', *Worldwatch Paper*, No. 32, September 1979.
43. See the many writings by Ignacy Sachs on this theme, most recently Ignacy Sachs, *Stratégies de l'écodéveloppement,* Paris, Editions Economie et Humanisme; Editions Ouvrières, 1980.

44. Despite the inaccuracy of statistical data available and the tendency to exaggerate demographic growth rates, the World Bank classifies among the poorest countries in the world a number in which the population grows at less than 2 per cent per annum, namely, Haiti at 1.7, Laos at 1.3 per cent and Upper Volta at 1.6 per cent. See World Bank, *World Development Report, 1980*, Baltimore and London, Johns Hopkins University Press for the World Bank, 1980.
45. See *Proceedings of the United Nations Conference on Population*, Bucharest, 1974.
46. See Albert Sassoon (an American expert on plant biology) in *Science and Society* (UNESCO paper), June–August 1980.
47. See Brown, Flavin and Norman, 'The Future of the Automobile in an Oil-Short World.
48. World Bank, *World Development Report, 1980*.
49. G. Royston, *International Programme for Environment Management Education*, Geneva, Coastal Environment Inc., 1977.
50. See Sartaj Aziz, *Rural Development: Learning from China,* London, Macmillan, 1978; Cynthia Hewitt de Al-Cantra, *Modernizing Mexican Agriculture*, Geneva, United Nations Research Institute for Social Development (UNRISD) 1976, and Keith Griffin, *The Green Revolution: An Economic Analysis,* Geneva, UNRISD, 1972.
51. See T. Okura, *Agricultural Development in Modern Japan*, Tokyo, 1963.
52. See Ismail-Sabri Abdalla, 'Depaysanisation ou développement rural? un choix lourd de conséquence', *IFDA Dossier* (International Foundation for Development Alternatives), No. 9 (July 1979).
53. See V. Djukanovic and E. P. Mach, *Alternative Approaches to Meeting Basic Health Needs in Developing Countries*, Geneva, United Nations International Children's Fund (UNICEF); World Health Organization (WHO), 1975; United Nations Educational, Social and Cultural Organization (UNESCO), *Thinking Ahead: UNESCO and the Challenge of Today and Tomorrow*, Paris, UNESCO, 1977, and Rajni Kothari, *An Alternative Framework for Rural Development, Report to the Government of India,* New York, Dag Hammarskjold Foundation, 1977.

14 THE NEED FOR ARAB FUTURES STUDIES

1. Shortcomings in available studies

In Part I of this book, we reviewed the different images of the Arab future projected by the most important global models and world futures studies while in Part II, we reviewed key Arab strategy documents, and identified the main lines of the future images they project.

The review of global models and world futures studies shows that the models were developed in an attempt to find answers to a given set of questions of particular concern to the parties sponsoring and supervising the models. It also showed that most of the models and studies departed from a basic assumption concerning the development model which Third World—including Arab—countries were likely to follow, viz, that they would try to emulate the western model, using the same technical means, albeit with a time lag, and that they aspired to the consumption of the same commodities and services prevailing in western consumption patterns. Hence the preoccupation of these models with the economic factor and their neglect of social and cultural aspects. They were also governed to a great extent by the neo-classical economic theory prevalent in the West.

It is not surprising that, within this framework, these models looked to the Arab nation simply as one of the main sources of oil in the world.[1] Nor that the emphasis in many of the models and studies was on ensuring a constant flow of oil to the main industrial countries and to other oil-consuming countries at prices suitable from the consumer's point of view. This preoccupation with oil led most studies to divide the Arab nation into groups which, though not always containing the same countries in all the studies, in most cases classified the oil-producing and exporting countries in a separate group from that containing the non-oil Arab countries. In many cases, non-Arab countries were included in one or the other of two groups.

None of the models and studies took the trouble to analyse the results that could come about from greater regional co-operation and integration in the Arab world as a whole, although one study did mention that if the prospects of regional co-operation ever materialized in the Arab world, it would become a basic element in its future.[2]

We shall not repeat here our methodological critique of the global models and world futures studies, nor our criticism of their approach to the Arab nation, which was the subject of analysis in Part I. We do wish to reiterate, however, that the shortcomings of these models and studies are the logical result of their orientation, the type of questions they put forward and the assumptions on which they are based. There is, of course, no reason to expect any global model or world futures study to address itself to questions which are of specific concern to the Arab world: particularly those relating to studying the impact which Arab co-operation and integration is likely to have on the future of the region, or those concerned with studying the effects of cultural and historical factors on likely patterns of Arab development, or those seeking to identify the nature of present Arab realities and problems, the different courses these can take and the impact they can have on the Arab future, or, finally, those relating to studying the effects of alternative strategies and different policies on Arab development and, consequently, on the future image of the Arab nation.

Only studies of the Arab future undertaken by Arabs can be expected to broach such issues. For enterprises of this kind require long and arduous efforts to evolve special research methodologies, and to study, painstakingly and in-depth, a great many issues, structures and processes which have a bearing on the Arab future. Obviously an innovative approach is necessary here: they would have to do more than simply follow in the same footsteps as global models and world futures studies. Inter-disciplinary efforts and co-operation between research and study institutions in the Arab nation must go into Arab futures studies. For there can be no question of importing a ready-made technology with which to study the Arab future.

There are those who might wonder why new efforts in this domain are necessary, especially since many areas of Arab concern and problems of development have already been the object of study and research by a large number of Arab and foreign researchers and scholars and have been discussed in numerous Arab conferences and symposia. Moreover, a number of Arab organizations have participated over the last few years in proposing Arab development strategies covering various activities and sectors, and have attempted to formulate a strategy for joint Arab action and to define the framework of a pan-national plan in this domain.

While in no way wishing to detract from the importance of previous Arab studies or of the efforts that have gone into formulating Arab strategies for development or for joint action, we must point out that these efforts share the following characteristics.

(1) Many of the major issues in the Arab world were studied independently of one another. It was rare when a study emphasized the interaction between these issues and problems and how the development of one could affect the other or impact on the future of comprehensive Arab development. Looking back, for example, to the most important of the studies and conferences which dealt with issues such as the evolution of Arab civilization and its present crisis, the Arab–Israeli conflict, Arab economic co-operation and integration and the effect of oil wealth on Arab development, we find that, although each of these issues interacts with the others, they were usually treated separately without regard for the dialectical relationship between them.

(2) Because of this piecemeal approach to such vital issues, development problems were dealt with essentially as economic issues. Arab scholars were primarily concerned with economic problems, and only rarely addressed themselves to such issues as the effect of social structures and relations, of processes of cultural change in society, and of political changes on development in the Arab nation. Even when they did, it was either partially or in terms of established theoretical propositions.

(3) As we saw in Part II, most of the strategies for Arab development adopted a sectoral and partial approach to issues of development. Not only that, but these sectoral and partial strategies were not always consistent with one another. They concentrated essentially on setting a number of

'desirable' targets, without any real attempt to study the means and mechanisms by which they would be achieved. Even the document which came closest to a global approach —the strategy for joint Arab economic action—did not depart from an overall outlook to the alternative options open to the Arab nation, but concentrated essentially on the economic aspects of joint action. Accordingly, it does not present alternative images of Arab futures.

(4) The main point of weakness in most of the available Arab studies is that they did not come to grips with the inconsistency between ends and means, in other words, with the divergence between the avowed Arab aim of integration and comprehensive development on the one hand, and the steps actually being taken by the Arab countries on the development front on the other. The latter represent deepening fragmentation and increasing links to the present world order and its mechanisms of which we spoke earlier.

Because of political considerations and certain ideological trends there is a reluctance to admit the existence of a contradiction between Arab integration and the increasing links pulling the Arab countries towards the centre of the world order.

The failure of both global and Arab studies to date to provide likely images of the future Arab nation, that take into consideration the special circumstances of that nation, its present realities, historical and cultural development and the nature of the issues particular to it, might not in itself have been sufficient incentive to undertake efforts in this direction, were it not for the fact that there is an objective justification to do so and that the returns on these efforts will exceed the costs, both financial and human, which will have to go into them.

To justify such efforts, it is not enough to point to the proliferation of futures studies throughout the world and the elaboration of global or regional models, either by international organizations or by private research groups and institutes, although the proliferation and elaboration of these studies and models could be indicative of the importance and feasibility of undertaking similar Arab studies. On the one hand, some of the reasons why this phenomena has become so widespread on the global level could be the very same reasons why similar Arab efforts should be made. On the other hand, global models and futures studies are among the tools now used by the advanced industrialized countries in planning the future of the world—which, naturally, includes planning the future of the Arab region. If planning is conducted on a world scale then, *a fortiori*, the Arabs should undertake the planning of their region themselves, within the global context. To do so, they must have their own viewpoint regarding the likely developments and changes on the global level and the different possibilities for the development of their own future within that framework. Finally, the elaboration of global models and futures studies can contribute to the development of methods and tools of futures studies in general, and, consequently, help Arab researchers and scholars develop their own methods and tools.

But the real need for Arab futures studies stems from the fact that the Arab nation at this stage in its history harbours vast potential for development and an overall cultural renaissance while at the same time it faces formidable challenges on both the internal and external fronts. There are many paths it can follow to reach its objectives and to overcome the difficulties and challenges facing it. It is difficult, a priori and without in-depth study, research and investigation, to choose the optimum and safest path, especially after the downfall of the fetish of present development models as far as the Arab and other Third-World countries are concerned. This applies as much to the western capitalist development model as to the Soviet or Chinese development models.

A sound and conscious choice of the steps to be taken now, and of the best paths to development and progress, can only be made on the basis of knowing what effects these choices are likely to have on the future. At the same time, the effects of any given choice cannot be correctly gauged in isolation from other choices and without studying the way in which they interact within the framework of the socio-economic-cultural system of the society in which the choice, planning and implementation is made and, finally, without assessing the likely repercussions on both the regional and global levels.

All the above reasons underline the pressing need for Arab futures studies based on a thorough knowledge of the present and its problems, of the historical and cultural evolution of the Arab nation, of the prevailing socio-economic pattern of relations, of the economic, social and cultural structure, of the processes of change, both conscious and unconscious and of their mutual effects and interrelations within the framework of the dynamics of the Arab socio-economic-cultural order and its links with the various components of the outside world.

Moreover, as we saw in the Introduction, to try and discern alternative traits of the future is an exercise related not only to the future but also to the present. Since the different shapes that tomorrow can take are largely determined by decisions taken today, assessing the cumulative effects of these decisions in the long term can help us rationalize them in the present and thus move closer to the best of the alternative futures open before us. Making the right decisions early enough can secure enormous savings for society and increase its ability to speed-up the process of overall growth and development. Conversely, delaying necessary decisions could exacerbate problems and make them more intractable in future as a result of cumulative effects and the difficulties they create.

For example, because of fluctuations in rates of exchange, Arab financial assets are exposed to serious risks. By the same token, it will become more difficult for the Arab countries to transform their huge surpluses into real investments in future, either in the advanced countries or in Third-World countries, as the advanced countries themselves will become more inclined to limit the degree of liquidity available to the Arabs in their markets in future, especially when oil loses its quasi-monopolistic position. Some of the problems arising from the formation of Arab financial surpluses can be solved today, while it may be impossible to solve some of the difficulties related to this phenomenon in future.

Another example that can be cited is that of the trend towards conspicuous consumption which, if it is allowed to proceed unchecked, will produce cumulative effects in the form of new patterns of consumption that will become so entrenched and widespread that trying to get rid of them in future will be virtually impossible. Yet another example is the danger arising from the growing indebtedness of Arab deficit countries, whose situation will deteriorate as the size of their debts grow. Nor can they solve their problem by contracting new loans, since they will soon reach a point where what they have to pay annually just to meet interest and instalment payments will be greater than any loan they can hope to obtain.

Similarly, the greater the Arab economy's integration into the world economy and the longer it continues to succumb to the domination of the multinational corporations, the more difficult it will be to end this domination without exorbitant social cost and the more remote will be the chance for Arab integration and unity. On another hand, it will take a relatively long time to raise the quality of education and to build up a technical capability in the Arab world. Even if the drive to develop the educational system in the direction of meeting the requirements of progress and development can be launched immediately, the products of the present educational system will continue for a period of between ten and fifteen years.

All this points to the urgency of rationalizing decisions today and, consequently, of undertaking futures studies which could help in this direction. We say 'could', and not 'will', advisedly, because undertaking futures studies, or even ascertaining the best solutions for actual or future problems, will not necessarily lead to the most rational decisions from a national or pan-national standpoint. The choices of the decision-makers are influenced by their economic and social interests and ideological attitudes, as well as by pressure groups and by the struggles between various contending forces in society. Futures studies are therefore one of the tools by which decisions can, but are not a guarantee that they will, be rationalized. This does not mean to say that they are not important as guidelines for the decision-making process.

Finally, undertaking futures studies is highly remunerative in that it provides the opportunity to test opinions, policies and strategies propounded by various schools of thought and disseminated among large numbers of intellectuals and professionals. Thinking ahead in all these cases can contribute to settling many profound debates and can help form a national and pan-national consensus concerning acceptable images of the future and the indispensable means by which to achieve them. The efforts furnished in research, study, comparing results and fixing means will govern what Arab experts formulate in the way of practical proposals in most fields. In addition, the debates that are bound to accompany these scientific efforts have an informational, indeed, an educational role, which will affect Arab public opinion as some world futures studies have affected public opinion in the industrialized countries. The formation of a popular public opinion on development issues is in itself important, while the impact it would have on decision-makers cannot be ignored.

2. Availability of Arab skills

Given that studies of the Arab future are indispensable, and that, as we have seen, imported technologies are not the answer, these studies must be the product of Arab minds that are fully cognizant of our situation, that are steeped in our culture and that have a personal stake in our future. The expertise required to undertake such studies is available in the Arab world. But what is required first is an awareness of the need to probe the future, then a commitment to exert every effort in this direction and, finally, a pooling of the multi-disciplinary talents required to undertake such an exercise.

Most Arab countries have gone beyond the stage of development based on a piecemeal approach to projects and have established planning bodies and ministries. As governments became aware of the need to speed up development and of the state's responsibility in this, and in view of mistakes which arose from a number of partial or short-sighted decisions, twelve member states in the Arab League resorted to medium-term planning. In eight of these, a not inconsiderable measure of state intervention is exercised through the application of plans. The approximations required for planning prompted an increased interest in compiling statistical data. Arab and international organizations helped gather and standardize these data.[3]

Moreover, a number of Arab countries and organizations focused their attention on sectoral studies with a more distant time horizon than medium-term planning. In fact, this long-term approach is one of the main characteristics of the various strategy documents prepared by Arab organizations which were reviewed in Part II. At the same time, universities and scientific research centres addressed many issues and problems of development, both country-specific and on the pan-Arab level. However, their efforts were for the main part marked by a high degree of technical specialization. Through such diverse activities, generations of Arab experts were formed who are well-versed in many of the skills on which futures studies are based.

Since the mid-seventies, there has been an awareness of the need to gather partial analyses and trends into an integral whole through the use of quantitative models, in order to raise the efficiency of medium-range planning by providing long-term background material which could show the links between the different variables, serve as a basis for projections and forecasts and pave the way to long-term planning.[4] On the pan-Arab level, concern with laying down sectoral strategies was accompanied by the first endeavours to devise quantitative models encompassing the whole Arab nation. To do so, it was necessary to become familiar with global models and study their techniques and classifications with a view to selecting what could be useful for Arab futures studies. Efforts in this direction were made by the Long-term Planning Group for the Arab countries,[5] otherwise known as 'the Cairo Group', which was established in Cairo's Institute of National Planning as an independent entity. This group collaborated in the scientific field with the Arab Fund for Economic and Social Development, as well as with UNIDO, from which it obtained financial assistance.

It also made contact with a number of international institutes interested in futures studies, as well as with the authors of some global models. For example, members of the group visited the Fundacion Bariloche, the University of Cleveland, and the International Institute for Applied Systems Analysis. They also held discussions with the team working on the construction of the UNIDO model, etc. Among the Cairo group's most important contributions was its assessment of the major global models and various Arab sectoral studies. It published papers reflecting this experience and containing preliminary proposals to build an Arab model, which unfortunately never got off the ground.[6] Economists at the Arab Fund for Social Development were also interested in global models. Quantitative methods were used to study the future of various sectors, with the encouragement of OAPEC, as can be seen from some of the papers presented to the First Arab Energy Conference (February 1980).

Similar activities have already been undertaken in this domain by a number of research centres in the Arab world, while others are still at the planning stage. An important fact worth mentioning here is that the Arab nation owns computers of the size required to deal with intricate models which have many variables, which it is not currently using at full capacity. It is very difficult to see how a global Arab model to investigate the future can be constructed by a group drawn from any one Arab country, no matter how experienced and skilled they may be. Rather, the best Arab talents should be brought together for this purpose and given complete access to any of the computers in the Arab world to use as they see fit.

Perhaps the major stumbling-block in the way of futures studies is the weakness of the data base, which reflects the concerns of decision-makers and of planners, both short- and medium-term. As these went by the implicit assumption that production technologies—and consumption patterns—would come from abroad, there did not seem to be a need to collect data on the future of technological development and consumption behaviour. Nor did the prevailing view of development, as simply a matter of catching up with the West, provide an incentive to gather data on variables such as the pattern of income distribution, the cost of importing technology or the long-term effects of this technology, data that had to be available for counter assumptions to be made and their results tested through models.

3. Methodology of futures studies

Our intention in pointing to the availability of Arab skills is not to minimize the efforts required in this domain. Futures studies are a recent scientific endeavour and their methodology is still the subject of debate, but it appears to us from our critique of global models and world futures studies that, to be undertaken in a satisfactory manner, an Arab futures study must meet four conditions:

(i) a thorough grasp of Arab reality;
(ii) constant follow-up of developments in basic sciences and their technological applications;
(iii) a receptive attitude to modern developmental thought which embraces all the social sciences;
(iv) the use of quantitative means to test different paths of development.

For futures studies are an attempt to envision features of alternative futures to which we may be headed because of the decision-maker's choice of options or of the course events might take. These features are formed by the mutual interaction between the set of options selected and courses followed and between them and various aspects of the socio-economic-cultural order of society.

The ability to envision these alternative features is linked to our understanding of the socio-economic-cultural order and its sub-structures and relations, as well as of how events interact within the framework of the overall order. Furthermore, the greater our scientific knowlege of present realities, of the historical development which bred these realities and of how the present emanates from the past and the future from the present, the greater our ability to envision accurately the future.

Accordingly, any serious futures study must begin by scientifically studying present reality, its origins and historical development, with special emphasis on sub-structures and systems and the relations and processes through which change and development occur within the framework of the overall order of society. Unfortunately, however, this proposition is not taken for granted in the Arab world. We find, for example, that the main sources quoted in the books used in our universities on Arab history are foreign sources. We also find many intellectuals and decision-makers to be insufficiently aware of the roots of Arab civilization, of its impressive contribution to mankind's scientific and philosophical heritage, or of the factors which contributed to the deterioration of our present situation. Indeed, foreign writings on various aspects of current Arab realities are probably more numerous than Arab writings.

Further, there are many aspects of these realities which have not been subjected to serious and exhaustive study. Just as the present has grown out of the past, so too will the shape of the future be moulded to a greater or lesser extent by the present from which it emanates. There are constraints, however, on the options open to any society at each historical stage; these are imposed by objective conditions such as the basic structures and set-ups of which the society is formed, the resources of which it disposes, the scientific knowledge available on the laws governing the relationship between various phenomena, how they operate and how they can be used to serve man.

However, these constraints are themselves subject to change and development. Many of the processes which produce change are effected by man and are the outcome of conscious choice on his part. Even the structures and systems prevailing in society, though among the acknowledged facts in any decision-making process, are themselves the product of past developments which man contributed to bringing about. As such, they are subject to further changes and developments which can either occur gradually or, in some cases, take the form of radical or revolutionary changes. Similarly, the resources of which a given society disposes cannot be regarded as constants for, through scientific development, new uses can be discovered for hitherto unexploited resources or, conversely, resources now in high demand can be discarded. Moreover, through social re-organization and the mobilization of human forces, elements which were considered social and economic burdens on society can be transformed into participants in production and the development of society. Thus, our scientific knowledge is constantly increasing, enabling us to reassess more accurately our potentials. This means that the choices we make today on the basis of the knowledge now available are also subject to change in the light of the new knowledge we acquire of our present reality and of its possible impact on our future. To benefit from this constantly growing fund of knowledge, futures studies must become an ongoing process that seeks to depict new images of the future in the light of the events and trends unfolding in the present.

But while remaining true to our cultural identity and seeking to know our reality within its own historical dynamics, we must not close in on ourselves. Advances are being made in all branches of science, constantly and at an accelerating pace, and knowledge is power. Thus, while we can rightfully be proud of the achievements of the Islamic Arab civilization in its Golden Age, we must also remember that our ancestors translated the works of Greek, Indian and other civilizations into Arabic and carefully studied them before transcending them with original creative thinking and making the Arab land a mecca for Europe's seekers of knowledge in the Middle Ages. Stressing the need to build an independent Arab technological base in no way implies turning our backs completely on technological development in any other part of the world.

On the contrary, building such a base entails an exhaustive study of all the technologies available with a view to selecting those best suited to Arab conditions. It also entails adapting imported technologies to these conditions as well as studying what is known as 'traditional technology', in order to develop and increase its use wherever possible, in view of this technology's low-capital profile and its high capacity to absorb manpower. All this will enable Arab technological capabilities to grow and enhance creative thinking in this field. Scientific and technological progress is an essential variable that must figure prominently in any picture we draw of the Arab future. Thus while the contribution of historians, sociologists and anthropologists is indispensable to any attempt to probe the future, contributions by prominent figures in natural and mathematical sciences and their technological applications are equally important.

The question is more complex when we talk of social sciences, whose subject is society and man who only lives in society. Social sciences came to their present shape, defined methods and tools of research and formulated theories through studying western industrial societies. But social phenomena are not as durable as natural phenomena and vary from one place or time to another. Accordingly, it goes without saying that these sciences in their actual form are valid for studying Arab society, but applying them is a necessary but not sufficient condition. Faced with the task of studying given societies which are very different from the western industrial societies, researchers in Third-World societies have no choice then but to direct their efforts at trying to understand and analyse the mechanisms and processes governing the course of their societies. It should also be noted that social sciences have tended towards overspecialization, forking out into many branches, even though the subject matter of all the social sciences is man in society or society composed of people. These constitute an integral whole, despite the different manifestations of their activities. Among the results of this lack of a global societal and humanistic vision was that development came to be equated with economic growth, usually measured in terms of GNP, whose validity as an index for measuring development is now being called into question. The seventies saw the evolution of developmental thought, which was coming to accept that development was more global in content, covering economics, sociology, culture, politics, health, education, lifestyles and value systems.

Any future study should therefore adopt a multi-disciplinary approach, drawing on social scientists from every discipline who are in close contact with the latest developments in their field and capable of evolving its tools in line with the distinctive conditions of Arab reality. They should subject its theories to critical analysis, reveal their limitations and elaborate new theoretical assumptions in analysing Arab reality. This does not imply that we should wait for new theories to be elaborated before embarking on futures studies, but only that present theoretical formulas should not be taken for granted—rather, they should be open to investigation and new assumptions added to them. The research activities of Arab future study projects will no doubt in themselves help develop our understanding of social sciences.

Finally, futures studies must resort to quantitative means, not only because the numerical representation of any phenomenon is more accurate than its descriptive representation, but, first and foremost, because mathematics offer the tools with which to deal with quantitative variables in order to identify the possible long-term results of different policies. Once again, we should stress that using mathematical models in no way implies the neutrality of these models. We are not dealing with the field of pure mathematics, which is based on abstract assumptions, but with social realities towards which the researcher is bound to have attitudes, whether conscious or unconscious, overt or repressed. All the models used to date can be classified under four headings: intuitive, exploratory, normative or total systems models. The first kind is based on attempting to identify the interactions and interlinkages leading to a predetermined scenario of the future, which the model builder does not attempt to verify. This underlines the importance of subjective factors in this type of model—for intuition is not an inspiration from on high, but simply an assessment made by some people who are imbued with the values of the society to which they belong. Even the scientific theories to which they subscribe could, in their turn, express specific interests. From the theoretical point of view, exploratory models are perhaps more objective. However, they are not completely devoid of the subjective factor, being employed to explore the long-term effects of certain, and not all, assumptions. The choice of assumptions to be tested plays a role in the design of the model, as none exists capable of testing *all* assumptions. This means that the assumptions selected by the builder of an exploratory model are inevitably affected by his subjective attitudes, since selection is, by definition, a subjective process involving a value judgement. The subjective factor is even more pronounced in the normative model, which fixes specific goals in advance and then elaborates the models in such a manner as to allow the behaviour of the variables in the model to determine policies conducive to achieving such goals. Finally, we have the total systems model, which is concerned with the interwoven effects of phenomena in their totality and the reactions between their various components and variables. None the less, the model is necessarily based on specific assumptions, inasmuch as it designates which variables are to be considered exogenous and which endogenous, defines parameters and coefficients, etc.

The question is not one of favouring one type of model over another, since futures studies would need to resort to each type at different phases, but, rather, not to let mathematical models replace theoretical debate whether in the economic, political, social or cultural fields, or to act as a screen concealing implicit choices in these fields. The use by Arab futures studies of models to try and determine the long-term effects of any development path that researchers consider appropriate for the Arab nation is a necessary condition for their success, provided, however, that their choices are explicit. The model remains a means of testing different paths of development, in order to choose the most appropriate among them, but is not in itself a solution to problems of development, nor a new fetish inspiring awe by its technical complexity. Of course, the easiest way in which models can be put to use is on the basis of the assumptions prevailing in the traditional theory of development. However, the question becomes a stimulating intellectual challenge when they are used to choose development theories and paths other than those spoon-fed to use by the West. The mathematical model can be no more than a tool to help us identify possible images of the future and to rationalize our decisions accordingly. It is not an alternative to testing development theories but a means to measure their effects and results.[7] Efforts in this area should not stop at denouncing the fetishism of models. As their use in investigating the interlinkages between economic, social, political and behavioural phenomena is a relatively recent scientific endeavour, at least in so far as looking to the future is concerned, the mathematical approximations that go into constructing a model are still open to discussion. Research methodology is still an open field, and modelling specialists in the Arab world must follow-up, indeed contribute to, efforts furnished in this direction. Often the best theoretical contribution is simply the product of insisting on dealing with tangible reality.[8]

4. A step along the path

The preceding considerations show the importance of, and need for, futures studies of the Arab region being undertaken by citizens of that region who are familiar with the cultural components of the Arab people, aware of the nature of current problems facing them of how these can affect their future and of the role of historical, social, political and cultural studies in identifying the factors that can influence the shape of likely futures for the Arab nation. On the basis of this premiss the 'Arab Alternative Futures' project, of which the present book is the first product, was launched to contribute, however modestly, in the field of futures studies of the Arab nation.

Without going into the details of the project, which are contained in the AAF project document put out in both English and Arabic, we should mention here one project—that designed by a team of Arab intellectuals and approved by the United Nations University in December 1980 to run for four years and begun in January 1981 by focusing on a number of research areas which, though highly relevant to the identification of likely futures of the Arab nation, have not been sufficiently investigated to date. Though falling within the framework of futures studies which try to anticipate possible and likely scenarios for the Arab region, the project does not aspire to build quantitative models of possible developments in the Arab world as a whole, despite the importance of such an undertaking in exploring the future as we have previously shown.

The aims of the Arab Alternative Futures project are more modest, if no less important than building quantitative models.

The project aims at arousing Arab awareness of the importance of futures studies, at showing that there is more than one possible future and, finally, that any alternative future will be a product of the social, political and cultural choices we make today. Finally, by showing how decisions taken today will affect the shape of the future, the project hopes that the identification of possible images of the future can help rationalize decisions in the present.

The project departs from an awareness that the evolution and development of the Arab nation will not be a function of its economic growth alone, nor will it be measured in terms of the possible increase in some indicators of production, distribution or consumption, but that real Arab development can only come about in the context of an overall cultural evolution. Accordingly, the research areas to which it addresses itself consist of many studies on the various elements of Arab cultural development.

Given that a project of this scope cannot possibly be undertaken by an individual institute and in view of the need for the collective efforts of many social and natural scientists and of constant co-ordination and dialogue between them, the project aims from the outset at building up a multi-disciplinary network of research institutes, centres and units throughout the Arab world, which will remain in contact for the duration of the project and even beyond. This network will focus on unexplored areas that can help probe the future. Although these areas cannot be completely identified beforehand, since many will be discovered as work progresses, the AAF project has begun with a list of topics partly elaborated in the course of planning the project. The precise designation of research projects will be made during discussions and consultations with the network of Arab institutes. They include the following:

(i) *Relationship between socio-political structures and development.* The study and analysis of class stratification in the Arab countries and the relationships among various social forces. The focus has to be on the impact of social structures on national power structures, development patterns, inter-Arab relations, and integration into the existing world order.

(ii) *The decision-making process.* This is an attempt to

comprehend how decisions are actually made at country level. It includes the analysis of the respective roles of institutions and individuals, the assessment of arbitration between conflicting interests, the relative weight of internal and external factors, the relative shares of experience, research and preparation, and expediency, etc., as factors influencing decision-making.

(iii) *Democracy, mass communication and popular participation.* Since development is supposed to be geared to the benefit of the people, no conflict should arise between development and democracy. Yet the most common practice in the Third World has been to sacrifice democracy in the name of development. A different approach should not only challenge this practice in principle but also try to find practical and effective conditions for popular participation in development to take place. This goes farther than the issue of human rights. It requires investigation into how public opinion is led or manipulated by the powerful modern communications media (e.g. satellite-transmitted television, video systems, and cassette tapes) and how citizens' awareness and knowledge can be improved so that their participation in the decision-making process becomes both operational and effective.

(iv) *Socio-political and cultural attitudes.* The current processes of change are not viewed in the same way by the people as a whole. If the élites are in favour of the present development patterns, Arab societies show many signs of dissent expressed in various political trends: moderate nationalists worry about national independence, cultural identity, and Arab unity, while revolutionary ideologies advocate socialism and unity. Last, but not least, the region is in the centre of the new wave of *Islamic revival.* These trends must be submitted to analysis with a view to their bearing on the Arab future.

(v) *Mechanisms of dependency.* A survey and analysis of the mechanisms that shape Arab development in such a way as to enhance the integration of the region into the centre of the present world order, to the detriment of endogenous development and Arab integration. Special attention must be given to the actions of transnational corporations and in particular foreign consulting firms. Thus, the concept of dependency can be analysed in concrete terms and its processes revealed.

(vi) *The Arab region and the changing world order*. Whatever might be the outcome of the so-called *North–South Dialogue*, the world order as it used to be up to the sixties is undergoing a process of change. The relative weights of major powers have changed. There have been shifts in alliances. Several centres are disputing the management of the system. The Third-World—or at least a large number of its countries—is becoming more and more aware of the iniquities of the present state of the world order and keen to obtain more leverage in international affairs. Such developments will affect the Arab future. Consequently, planning for the future necessitates a clear vision of the role of the region in the emergence of the new world order.

(vii) *The unexplored effects of oil wealth*. Beyond the discussion about oil reserves, prices, and surpluses, the sudden oil wealth gave birth to important new phenomena in the region that call for investigation and assessment. To mention a few: Arab labour movements across borders, contradictions between rich and poor countries, shifts in the relative weights of individual countries in Arab politics, and emergence of *rentier* societies and associated values, societal organization, and patterns of consumption.

(viii) *Human resources*. A key factor in development, human resources must be studied both quantitatively and qualitatively. This includes processes of formal and informal learning and skills acquisition. The issues of motivation of the labour force should be addressed, given the important 'brain drain' from the region.

(ix) *Resources and uses of science and technology*. Assessment of the Arab potential in science and technology and analysis of factors that impede its full use and further growth. The focus of the study will be the feasibility of building up local and regional scientific and technological capabilities.

(x) *Arts and literature*. Traditional means of expression of culture must be surveyed. The objective of the study includes uncovering the roles of arts and literature as factors of unity and diversity in the Arab region. This leads to the evaluation of the impact of traditions on the one hand

and external influence on the other and to what extent creativity can reconcile modernity and cultural authenticity.

(xi) *The institutional framework for Arab integration.* Since the creation of the League of Arab States in 1945, a web of inter-Arab organizations has been established with the declared purpose of promoting Arab integration and establishing Arab unity. Yet the traditional indicators of integration (share of inter-Arab trade, movement of labour, and capital flows) remain far below expectation. An assessment of this institutional framework should be geared to uncover means to render it more effective.

(xii) *Arab unification and the issues of minorities.* The Arab region contains various minority groups. Any serious approach to integration and to the establishment of a kind of political unification must deal adequately with this central issue.

In the aim of stimulating an open, continuing and wide-ranging dialogue between all those interested in studying the Arab future, whether research centres, researchers, opinion-leaders or decision-makers, the project issues the 'AAF Dossier', which will reproduce scientific papers and reports issued in the course of regular seminars held within the framework of the project, as well as the preliminary findings of various research projects. The Dossier will also provide a forum for discussion and debate, thus offering a stimulus to the interaction of ideas and the co-ordination of efforts in the direction of identifying an image of the future which can upgrade the Arab nation and the Arab citizen.

It is our heartfelt hope that these studies and debates will help shed more light on the factors governing the shaping of the Arab future and, consequently, help determine the assumptions on which we can safely count and the nature of the constraints of which we must be aware when attempting to draw a comprehensive picture of possible Arab developments, whether these attempts take a quantitative or contemplative form.

Notes

1. The importance of OPEC countries derives from their share in the export, not the production, of oil, since it is a well-known fact that all

the OPEC countries together produce no more than 25 per cent of total world production.

2. See Organization for Economic Co-operation and Development (OECD), Interfutures, 'Research Project on the Future Development of Advanced Industrial Societies in Harmony with that of Developing Countries', Draft Final Report, Paris, January 1979.
3. Eight Arab countries have input–output tables where the number of sectors ranges between 13 and 70.
4. Efforts in this direction were initiated by Egypt's National Planning Institute since the mid-sixties and by Iraq's Ministry of Planning in the early seventies.
5. The founder of this group and the co-ordinator of its activities was Dr Ibrahim Helmy Abdel-Rahman.
6. The Group remained active for more than two years, in the course of which it issued fifty-eight memoranda which can be obtained from the National Planning Institute in Cairo. See Mohamed Mahmoud El-Imam, 'World Models', in *Annual Scientific Conference for Egyptian Economists*, Cairo, 4 May 1979 and Ismail-Sabri Abdalla *et al.*, eds., *Economic Development and Social Justice in Contemporary Developmental Thought with Applied Reference to Egypt*, Cairo, Egyptian Society for Political Economy, Statistics and Legislation, 1981.
7. See Aly Nassar, *A Critical Study of Egypt's Experience of Applying Models in National Planning*, Cairo, National Planning Institute, 1973.
8. See the important study issued by the United Nations: C. Mihai Botez and Mariana Celac, 'Global Modelling . . . Without Models?' in United Nations University, *Project Goals, Processors and Indicators of Development,* New York, GPID, 1981.

SELECTED BIBLIOGRAPHY

Books

Abdalla, Ismail-Sabri, *et al.*, eds, *Economic Development and Social Justice in Contemporary Developmental Thought with Special Reference to the Case of Egypt*, Cairo, Egyptian Society for Political Economy, Statistics and Legislation, 1981.

Abdel-Fadil, M., ed., *Papers on the Economics of Oil*, New York, Oxford University Press, 1979.

Abdel-Fadil, M., *Oil and Arab Unity*, Beirut, Centre for Arab Unity Studies, 1979.

De Al-Cantra, Cynthia Hewitt, *Modernizing Mexican Agriculture*, Geneva, United Nations Research Institute for Social Development (UNRISD), 1976.

Al-Sayigh, Yusif, *The Determinants of Arab Economic Development*, London, Croom Helm, 1978.

Aziz, Sartaj, *Rural Development: Learning from China*, London, Macmillan, 1978.

Barney, Gerald O., (Study Director), *The Global 2000 Report to the President of the United States: Entering the Twenty-First Century*, Washington D.C., Government Printing Office, 1980, 3 vols.

Brandt, Willy and Anthony Sampson, *North–South: A Programme for Survival on International Development*, London, Pan Books, 1980.

Bronwell, Arthur B., ed., *Science and Technology in the World of the Future*, New York, Wiley, Krieger, 1970.

Bruckmann, G., ed., *Global Modelling Review*, Laxenburg, Austria, International Institute for Applied Systems Analysis (IIASA), 1980.

Chase, Stuart, *The Most Probable World*, New York, Harper and Row, 1968.

Cole, H. S. D., *Global Models and the International Economic Order*, Oxford, Pergamon, 1977.

Cole, H. S. D., *et al.*, eds, *Thinking about the Future: A Critique of the Limits to Growth*, London, Chatto and Windus, 1973.

Djukanovic, V. and E. P. March, *Alternative Approaches to Meeting Basic Health Needs in Developing Countries*, Geneva, United Nations International Children's Fund (UNICEF), World Health Organization (WHO), 1975.

Dolman, A. J., ed., *Global Planning and Resource Management: Towards Decision Making in a Divided World*, Oxford, Pergamon, 1980.

Dumont, René, *Utopia or Else?* (trans. Vivienne Menkes) London, Deutsch, 1974.

Ehrlich, Paul R. and Anne H. Ehrlich, *Population, Resources, Environment—Issues in Human Ecology*, San Francisco, Freeman, 1970.

El-Bendary, Aziz, 'The Industrial Future of Arab Countries up to the year 2000', in *Research Project on Industrial Development*, Cairo, National Planning Institute, 1979.

Fargany, Nader, *Wasted Potential: A Study of How Far the Arab People Have Progressed Towards Their Aspirations*, Beirut, Centre for Studies on Arab Unity, 1980.

Feinberg, Gerald, *The Prometheus Project: Mankind's Search for Long Range Goals*, New York, Doubleday, 1969.

Ferkiss, Victor C., *Technological Man, the Myth and the Reality*, New York, Braziller, 1969.

Food and Agriculture Organization (FAO), *Production Yearbook, 1977,* Rome, FAO, 1978.

Forrester, J. W., *World Dynamics*, Cambridge, Mass., Wright Allen, 1971.

Freeman, Christopher and Marie Jahoda, eds, *World Futures: The Great Debate*, Falmer, Brighton, University of Sussex, 1979.

Garcia, John David, *The Moral Society: A Rational Alternative to Death*, New York, Julian Press, 1971.

Griffin, Keith, *The Green Revolution: An Economic Analysis*, Geneva, United Nations Research Institute for Social Development, 1972.

Haq, Mabulul, *The Poverty Curtain: Choices for the Third World*, New York, Columbia University Press, 1976.

Heilbroner, Robert L., *Business Civilisation in Decline*, New York, Norton, 1976; London, Boyars, 1974.

Heilbroner, Robert L., *An Inquiry into the Human Prospect*, New York, Norton, 1974.

Herrera, Amilcar, O., *et al.*, *Catastrophe or a New Society? A Latin American World Model*, Ottawa, International Development Research Centre, 1976.

Illich, Ivan, *Medical Nemesis: The Exploration of Health*, New York, Bantam, 1977.

Kahn, Herman and Anthony J. Wiener, *The Year 2000, a Framework for Speculation on the Next Thirty-Three Years*, New York, Hudson Institute, 1967; London, Macmillan, 1967.

Kahn, Herman, W. Brown and L. Martel, *The Next Two Hundred Years: A Scenario for America and the World*, New York, Morrow, 1976.

Kosolopov, V., *Mankind and the Year 2000*, Moscow, Progress, 1976.

Kothari, Rajni, *An Alternative Framework for Rural Development, Report to the Government of India*, New York, Dag Hammarskjold Foundation, 1977.

Laszlo, G., *et al.*, *Goals for Mankind: A Report to the Club of Rome on the New Horizon of Global Community*, New York, Dutton, 1977.

Leontief, Wassily, *et al.*, *The Future of the World Economy, Preliminary Report*, New York, United Nations Department of Economic and Social Affairs, 1976.

Linnemann, H., *et al.*, eds, *MOIRA: Model of International Relations in Agriculture*, Amsterdam, North Holland-Elsevier, 1979.

Maddox, John, *The Doomsday Syndrome: An Attack on Pessimism*, New York, McGraw-Hill, 1972.

Martin, James T. and Adrian R. D. Norman, *The Computerized Society, an Appraisal of the Impact of Computers on Society over the Next Fifteen Years*, Automatic Computation Series, Englewood Cliffs, N.J., Prentice-Hall, 1970.

Massé, Pierre, *Le Plan ou l'anti-hasard*, Paris, Gallimard, 1965.

Meadows, Donella H., *et al.*, *The Limits to Growth*, New York, Universe, 1979.

Mesarovic, Mihajlo D. and Edward C. Pestel, *Mankind at the Turning Point, the Second Report to the Club of Rome*, New York, Dutton, Readers' Digest Press, 1974.

Modrzhinskaya, Elena D. and C. A. Stephanyan, *The Future of Society: A Critique of Modern Bourgeois Philosophical and Socio-Political Conceptions*, Moscow, Progress, 1973.

Nassar, A., *A Critical Study of Egypt's Experience of Applying Models in National Planning*, Cairo, Institute for National Planning, 1973.

Organization for Economic Co-operation and Development (OECD), Interfutures, *Facing the Future: Mastering the Probable and Managing the Unpredictable*, Paris, OECD, 1979.

Organization for Economic Co-operation and Development (OECD), Interfutures, *The Problem of Technology Transfer between Advanced and Developing Countries*, Paris, OECD, 1978.

Okura, T., *Agricultural Development in Modern Japan*, Tokyo, 1963.

Petroleum Economist, *OPEC Oil Report*, 2nd edn, New York, Nichols, 1979.

Romanian Academy of Science, *The Revolution in Science and Technology and the Contemporary Social Development*, The Romanian Academy, 1977.

Rostow, W. W., *The Stages of Economic Growth*, 2nd edn, New York, Cambridge University Press, 1971.

Royston, G., *International Programme for Environment Management Education*, Geneva, Coastal Environment Inc., 1977.

Sachs, Ignacy, *Stratégies de l'ecodéveloppement*, Paris, Editions Economie et Humanisme, Editions Ouvrières, 1980.

Scholnik, H. D., *On a Methodological Criticism of Meadows' World 3 Model*, Bariloche, Buenos Aires, Fundacion Bariloche, 1972.

Schumacher, E. F., *Small is Beautiful. A Study of Economics as if People Mattered*, New York, Harper and Row, 1973; London, Blond and Briggs, 1973.

Spengler, Joseph J., *The Economist and the Population Question*, Princeton, N.J., 1966.
Taylor, Gordon R., *The Doomsday Book*, London, Thames and Hudson, 1970.
Tinbergen, Jan T., (Co-ordinator), *Reshaping the International Order*, London, Hutchinson, 1977.
United Nations Educational, Social and Cultural Organization (UNESCO), *Thinking Ahead: UNESCO and the Challenge of Today and Tomorrow*, Paris, UNESCO, 1977.
United Nations University, *Project Goals, Processes and Indicators of Development,* New York, GPID, 1981.
Vacca, Roberto, *Il Medievo Prossimo Ventura*, Rome, 1971; *The Coming Dark Age*, New York, Doubleday, Anchor Books, 1973.
Warshofsky, Fred, ed., *The Twenty-First Century: The New Age of Exploration*, Twenty-first Century Series, New York, Viking, 1969.
Wheelwright, Edward L. and Bruce McFarlane, *The Chinese Road to Socialism: Economics of the Cultural Revolution* (Foreword by Joan Robinson), New York, Monthly Review Press, 1970.
World Bank, *World Development Report, 1980*, Baltimore and London, Johns Hopkins University Press for the World Bank, 1980.
World Population Trends and Policies, New York, 1979, Vol. 1.
Zahlan, A. B., ed., *Technology Transfer and Change in the Arab World*, Oxford, Pergamon, 1978.

Periodicals

Abdalla, Ismail-Sabri, 'Depaysanisation ou devéloppement rural? un choix lourd de consequence', *IFDA- Dossier* (International Foundation for Development Alternatives), **9**, July 1979.
Brown, L. R., C. Flavin and C. Norman, 'The Future of the Automobile in an Oil-Short World', *World Watch Paper,* **32**, September, 1979.
Galtung, J., 'Limits to Growth and Class Politics', *Journal of Peace Research*, 1973.
Hosono, Akio, 'Industrial Development and Employment: The Experience of Asian and Latin American Development Strategy', *CEPAL Review* (Etats Unis, Commission Economique pour L'Amerique Latine), **2**, Second Semester 1976.
Kaya, Yoichi, *et al.*, 'Global Constraints and a New Vision for Development', *Technological Forecasting and Social Change,* **6**, 3 and 4, 1974.
Meyerhaff, A. A., 'Best Chances on Shore are in China and Russia', *Oil and Gas Journal*, August, 1977, special issue.
Oil and Gas Journal: Petroleum 2000, August 1977, special issue.
Prebisch, Raul, 'A Critique of Peripheral Capitalism', *CEPAL Review* (Etats Unis, Commission pour L'Amerique Latin), **1**, First Semester 1976.

Prebisch, Raul, 'Socio-Economic Structure and the Crisis of Peripheral Capitalism', *CEPAL Review,* **2**, Second Semester 1978.

Rawski, T. G., 'Economic Growth and Employment in China', *World Development*, 8/9, 1979.

Richardson, J. M., 'Global Modelling (1): The Models', *Futures,* **12**, 5, October 1978.

Richardson, J. M., 'Global Modelling (2): Where to Now?' *Futures*, **12**, 6, December 1978.

Sagasti, F. R., 'Knowledge is Power', *Mazingira,* **8**, 1977.

Swamg, S., 'Economic Growth in China and India', *Economic Development and Cultural Change,* **21**, 4, July 1973.

Papers and Documents

Abdalla, Ismail-Sabri, 'Alternative Patterns of Development and Life Styles in Western Asia: A Keynote and an Overview', United Nations, Economic Commission for Western Asia (ECWA), United Nations Environment Programme (UNEP), Beirut, December 1979.

Abdel-Rahman, I. H., 'Concepts and Practice of Future Studies Using Models in the Arab Region', Regional Office for Education in the Arab Countries, Beirut, 1980.

Industrial Research Institute, 'The Role of Technology in the Change of Industrial Structure', Tokyo, April 1978.

Mesarovic, Mihajlo D. and Edward C. Pestel (directors), 'Present State in the Development of the Multilevel Tregionalized World System Models'. Systems Analysis Inc. (SAI), Cleveland, 1977.

National Institute for Research Advancement, 'Japan Toward the 21st Century', Tokyo, August 1978.

Organization of Arab Petroleum Exporting Countries (OAPEC), 'OAPEC Field Report on Mexico'.

Organization for Economic Co-operation and Development (OECD), Interfutures, 'Intermediate Results: Review Phases A and B, Comparative Evaluation of World Models', April 1977.

Organization for Economic Co-operation and Development, 'Research Project on the Future Development of Advanced Industrial Societies in Harmony with that of Developing Countries', January 1979 (Draft Final Report).

Organization for Economic Co-operation and Development, 'Summary of Global Models, Intermediate Paper: FUT/DW/SI/A Current Research and World Models', November 1976.

Pearson, Charles, 'Implication for Trade and Investment of Developing Countries of the United States Environment Control', paper presented to the United Nations Conference on Trade and Development, UNCTAD (E-H-11 D.5).

Systems Analysis Inc. (SAI), 'Cost/Benefit of Human Resources Mobility: Example of Scenario Analysis', Cleveland, 15 December 1976.

United Nations Industrial Developmental Organization (UNIDO), 'The Implications of Global Models for Developing Countries'.

Conferences, Seminars, Symposiums

International Institute for Applied Systems Analysis (IIASA), Symposium on Global Modelling, 2nd and 3rd, Laxenburg, 1976, *MOIRA: Food and Agriculture Model*, ed. Gerhard Bruckman, Laxenburg, Austria, IIASA, 1977.

International Institute for Applied Systems Analysis (IIASA), Symposium on Global Modelling, 4th, Laxenburg, 20–3 September 1976, *SARUM and MRI: Description and Comparison of a World Model and a National Model*, ed. Gerhart Bruckman, Oxford, New York, Pergamon, 1978.

Proceedings of the Wisconsin Seminar on Natural Resource Policies, Madison, Wisconsin, Wisconsin University, Institute for Environmental Studies, 1978.

INDEX

*Adjoining a page number indicates a reference to a Table.